K
P

ΤΝΕ WEF̄   ΤΝ

Knowledge and the Probation Service

Raising Standards for Trainees, Assessors and Practitioners

Philip Whitehead

National Probation Service, Teesside, UK

and

Jamie Thompson

Northumbria University, Newcastle upon Tyne, UK

John Wiley & Sons, Ltd

This publication is designed to provide accurate and authoritative information in regard to the
subject matter covered. It is sold on the understanding that the Publisher is not engaged in
rendering professional services. If professional advice or other expert assistance is required, the
services of a competent professional should be sought.

Other Wiley Editorial Offices

John Wiley & Sons Inc., 111 River Street, Hoboken, NJ 07030, USA

Jossey-Bass, 989 Market Street, San Francisco, CA 94103-1741, USA

Wiley-VCH Verlag GmbH, Boschstr. 12, D-69469 Weinheim, Germany

John Wiley & Sons Australia Ltd, 33 Park Road, Milton, Queensland 4064, Australia

John Wiley & Sons (Asia) Pte Ltd, 2 Clementi Loop #02-01, Jin Xing Distripark, Singapore
129809

John Wiley & Sons Canada Ltd, 22 Worcester Road, Etobicoke, Ontario, Canada M9W 1L1

Wiley also publishes its books in a variety of electronic formats. Some content that appears in
print may not be available in electronic books.

Library of Congress Cataloging-in-Publication Data
Whitehead, Philip, 1952–
    Knowledge and the probation service : raising standards for trainees, assessors and
practitioners / Philip Whitehead and Jamie Thompson.
        p.   cm.
    Includes bibliographical references and index.
    ISBN 0-470-09203-3 (cloth : alk. paper) – ISBN 0-470-09204-1 (pbk. : alk. paper)
    1. Probation.   2. Probation officers – Training of.   I. Thompson, Jamie, 1952–
II. Title.
    HV9278.W53 2004
    364.6′3′0683–dc22

                                                                                2004003686

British Library Cataloguing in Publication Data
A catalogue record for this book is available from the British Library

ISBN 0-470-09203-3 (hbk)
ISBN 0-470-09204-1 (pbk)

Typeset in 10.5/12pt Times and Stone Sans by SNP Best-set Typesetter Ltd., Hong Kong
Printed and bound in Great Britain by TJ International Ltd, Padstow, Cornwall
This book is printed on acid-free paper responsibly manufactured from sustainable forestry
in which at least two trees are planted for each one used for paper production.

Love and thanks to our respective families for their patience, help and encouragement: Carolyn, Alex, Tim and Jenny; Di, Alison, Joe, Lucy, Sam and Eddie. It gives us pleasure to dedicate this book to them.

Contents

About the authors

Philip Whitehead has worked for the Teesside Probation Service since 1981. He has published several books and articles in relation to probation, community supervision of offenders, temporary release schemes and reconviction, and managing the probation service. Since 2001 he has been working as Senior Practice Development Assessor, which involves teaching and coaching trainees undertaking the Diploma in Probation Studies to prepare them to work as probation officers.

Jamie Thompson worked for Northumbria Probation Service for 19 years. He has been involved in the training of probation officers as a practice teacher, training manager and joint appointment. He was course leader for the probation degree and coordinating Internal Verifier for the Community Justice NVQ Assessment Centre at Northumbria University. He is currently Principal Lecturer and Learning and Teaching Coordinator and a joint manager of the Community Safety Research Unit. He is an active researcher and has published in relation to probation, community safety, and teaching and learning issues.

Preface

This book appears at another signal moment in the history of what is still known as the probation service. In 2004 we will see the developing impact of the 2003 Criminal Justice Act. However, perhaps more significant in the long term: the Correctional Services Review by Patrick Carter has just been published (Carter, 2003); the Home Office response to that review has appeared (Home Office, 2004); and the National Probation Service's Annual Plan for 2004/5 has been circulated (National Probation Directorate, 2004).

It appears that the nature, structure and priorities of probation practice will continue to change. All three documents are characterised by a kind of managerial thinking, primarily focused on efficiency and value for money, which has been a theme of probation service strategy since the Statement of National Objectives and Priorities in 1984. It is a theme that predominates in a national service directly answerable to ministers, who are inevitably sensitive to the costs of criminal justice and to the presentation of criminal justice practice.

This book is particularly timely. There will be much debate about the planned changes (e.g. in relation to the changed use and status of Pre-Sentence Reports and the impact of closer relations with the prison service) and the impact of those changes on the nature of the probation officer role. Some in the probation service will welcome the changes, some will not and many will be anxious, uncertain about or alienated from their professional identity that may have been nurtured over many years. In this book we argue that in preparing people to become probation officers it is not enough to be driven by a managerial agenda preoccupied with consistency, minimum standards and measurable performance. As much as it is important for probation officers to learn for consistency, it is also important to learn for individuality. The probation service, as part of the criminal justice system, must of course strive to be consistent but also to be responsive to the individuality of offenders. Equally, those who deliver the probation service need not only to know that their own individuality is valued but they also need to learn that it is the engine of their own motivation and is central to successful working relations with colleagues and offenders. In this book we analyse and explain the knowledge requirements of the Occupational Standards for probation officers and set that analysis and explanation in the broader context of values, emotions, learning, and the sometimes ineffable that constitute the real experience of probation practice.

It is difficult to predict what the National Probation Service, or more accurately the National Offender Management Service, will look like in even the medium-term future. One thing that seems certain is that it will grow. Community correction seems to be a thriving, growth industry. It will be interesting to see if those who enter this industry in future will continue to think of themselves as probation officers or will share the same values, vocation and animation as today's officers and trainees. Will we still be able to make a clear connection to the heritage and traditions of the early probation service? To what extent and in what ways will it contribute to and impact on criminal justice and social policy? What kinds of knowledge will be, and importantly *should* be, required in future? We have our own views on knowledge that are linked to the notion of vocational excellence that we will explore in what follows.

Acknowledgements

This book could not have been written without the help of certain people who have consciously and unwittingly contributed. Therefore we want to express our thanks to Mike Waddington, Richard Watson, Deborah Heath, Martyn Shakespeare, David Nicholson, Virginia Davey, Tracey Brittain and Pauline Wilkinson, who have been importuned on numerous occasions. We are grateful to Angus McIntosh and members of staff who comprise the TPO Managers' Group within the North-East Consortium for taking an interest. Innumerable trainees during the previous three years, and PDA colleagues within the consortium, have also played their part in the genesis of the book.

Chapter 1

Training and knowledge in probation: A historical overview

The importance of the probation officer as an official of the Court who is also a social worker dealing directly with the vital problem of turning asocial and anti-social persons into good citizens of the State, can hardly be overrated. His calling is not easy, and the qualifications needed for success are many and varied.

LE MESURIER, 1935, p. 52

Introduction

Since 1998 the knowledge base of the probation service has been provided by and delivered to trainee probation officers through the component parts of the Diploma in Probation Studies (Dip.PS). This is a two-year training course comprised substantially of theoretical and practice-based elements that the trainee must negotiate successfully before being endowed with the status of probation officer and receiving a licence to work with offenders. Even though all trainee probation officers must achieve the Dip.PS in order to qualify, it should be acknowledged that from the autumn of 2003 the routes to qualification will be different, particularly in relation to the academic component. For example, while some trainees will attend university for two days each week for face-to-face contact with academic staff, others will receive their academic inputs by distance learning methods (Portsmouth University has been awarded the academic contract for four separate regions: South-East and South-West; North-East and North-West). Consequently questions have been posed in certain areas of the country about the implications of these new arrangements that could result in a diminution in the quality of academic inputs and hidden financial costs within consortia; alternatively, greater flexibility, afforded by distance learning, could result in positive benefits for local area services without any reduction in quality. We will return to consider important aspects of current training arrangements, particularly the delivery of knowledge, in more detail at the end of this chapter and in Chapter 3.

Even though it is appropriate to allude to the Dip.PS at the beginning of this book in order to set the scene for what will follow, it should be acknowledged that the substance of this first chapter is to provide an overview of training arrangements, and the delivery of knowledge to probation staff, throughout the history of the probation service. As we attempt to do this it should be said that it is impossible to trace the origins and development of training and the knowledge base of probation without alluding to the wider history of the probation service itself. By focusing on training and knowledge within a broad context, and by alluding to a variety of interrelated themes, it is our intention to adopt a discursive and therefore flexible approach to the history of probation. However, at this point it should be stated that we are conscious that the history of the probation service can be recounted from a variety of perspectives as the following discussion elucidates.

The first approach is the type of history articulated by Le Mesurier (1935), King (1964), Bochel (1976) and, to some extent, Haxby (1978). This may be described as the Kings and Queens approach because it traces and plots significant events in a chronological, ordered and sequential manner. This type of history can, of course, be interesting and informative (and trainee probation officers should be encouraged to familiarise themselves with this material), but it has its limitations primarily because it focuses on description rather than analysis; it talks about what happened and when, but says little about the manner in which certain events happened.

The second approach focuses on identifying different underpinning and sustaining ideologies within the probation service from 1876 to the 1930s, the 1930s–1970s, the 1980s and the 1990s to the present day. This approach is primarily represented by the stimulating quartet of essays produced by William McWilliams (1983, 1985, 1986 and 1987). It should be clarified that McWilliams incorporates the first type of history in his approach, but it is fair to say that he adds an entirely new dimension that captures the imagination of those who want a more rounded understanding of the history of the probation service (and these essays are essential reading for probation staff). Importantly, he alludes to the origin and development of training in the second of his essays in 1985.

The third type of history is waiting to be written where the probation service is concerned. This is the approach adumbrated by David Garland in *Punishment and Welfare* (1985) where he analyses the history of penal policy, specifically the transition that occurred in penal arrangements between mid-Victorian society and the early twentieth century. Garland analyses this transition in terms of a complex historical process that involved the influence of the new criminological science (positivism); eugenics; social insurance introduced by a reforming Liberal government; social workers; charity organisations; penal administrators; in addition to wider political, social, economic and ideological changes. In Marxist terms it is the transition from liberal to monopoly capitalism that accounts for penal change; but Garland is at pains to avoid crude economic determinism in his analysis. Therefore, if Garland's approach was applied to the probation service then we would have to begin by recognising that it is an organisation with its own unique history and internal dynamics; it has its own way of doing things, making decisions, and thinking about offenders. However, it should also be understood that the probation service does not exist in an organisational vacuum or in isolation from wider political, economic and social realities. In other words, it is a state-directed practice and the state, in the form of the Home Office (and

since 2001 the National Probation Directorate), has been increasingly intervening, directing and centrally controlling the service since the Statement of
National Objectives and Priorities (Home Office, 1984). It is interesting to
observe that the transition from Victorian penal arrangements to the twen-
tieth-century penal-welfare complex that is analysed by Garland is coterminous with the beginning of the probation system within Victorian society
with religiously minded missionaries.

Given the nature of this book – that it is intended to make a contribution
to the training of trainee probation officers (TPOs) and therefore the acquisition of important items of knowledge – the authors must state at this point
that our historical excavations in this chapter do not claim to reach
the exalted analytical heights scaled by the Garland trilogy (1985, 1990,
2001). This would require detailed empirical research. Nevertheless, we do
acknowledge that the history of training and knowledge within the context
of the probation service as a whole can be understood in different ways and
that it is multifaceted in nature. We hope that this chapter will capture some
of the complexities and contingencies involved, albeit briefly. Therefore, with
these preliminary thoughts in mind we need to clarify for the reader that
what follows throughout this chapter will be unapologetically discursive, in
the sense that we will dip in and out of the themes of training and knowledge as we come into contact with a number of related areas of concern that
appear to be unavoidable. Before we return to the Dip.PS, the authors consider that it would be instructive to step back in time to explore the history
of training, which is a subject of interest in its own right.

Emergence of probation

The probation system in Europe emerged against a background of dissatis-
faction with the principles and limited explanation of crime within the paradigm of classical criminology. But as time passed classicism evolved into
neo-classicism and then positivism (see Taylor et al., 1973, for detailed exposition); furthermore, it is important to refer to the practices of judicial
reprieve, bail and the recognisance as the precursors of probation. While
there is some additional evidence to indicate that the origins of probation
can be traced to the Police Courts of Boston in 1841, as well as certain
enlightened Magistrates in England during the nineteenth century, it is to
1876 that we must turn and the suggestion made by Frederick Rainer to the
Church of England Temperance Society that it should extend its work to
the Police Courts. Therefore, after 1876 the Magistrates' Courts, initially in
London, began to use Police Court Missionaries on an informal basis to
supervise offenders released on a recognisance which had been made possible by the 1879 Summary Jurisdiction Act. During the last quarter of the

nineteenth century it was the task of the missionary, when drunkenness was an acute problem, to reclaim inebriates appearing before the courts (for a fuller discussion, see Whitehead, 1990, and specifically Chapter 1; Heasman, 1962; McWilliams, 1983). The missionaries were engaged in the theological enterprise of saving offenders' souls by divine grace. They were involved in work that was motivated by a profound religious conviction and it may be suggested that they wanted to bring about metanoia in the lives of offenders. (*Metanoia* is a Greek word, with theological undertones, which means a complete change of heart and mind.) However, it may be observed that it is difficult to uncover any evidence of a specific training course at this inchoate stage of the probation system to equip missionaries for their evangelical oriented tasks, primarily during the last quarter of the nineteenth century. It may be suggested that their knowledge and understanding of offenders, and the job they were beginning to undertake, were rooted in faith and theology.

Training in the early years

It is instructive to refer to the research of Dorothy Bochel who says that Miss E.P. Hughes, a former Principal of a Cambridge Training College for Women Teachers, visited the United States in 1900–1901 to investigate the probation system on behalf of the Howard Association. Miss Hughes discovered that probation officers were being trained in the USA (but Bochel does not expand upon precisely what or tell us how they were being trained) and that she wanted to see a similar system developed in England (1976, pp. 17–18). If it is the case that Police Court Missionaries during the period 1876 to the early years of the twentieth century were not being trained in the sense of attending a specific training course to work with offenders, this is an intriguing situation to consider as the following indicates. During the last decades of the nineteenth century it could be suggested that the new science of criminology (positivism) was beginning to make its influence felt. The new criminology was concerned with aetiology (the causes of crime), observation and measurement; therefore it may be described as interventionist in nature, compared to the tenets of classical criminology. It is interesting to speculate on the degree to which the early missionaries were aware of this new thinking about the criminal, and if anyone considered that training was necessary in what amounted to a new offender knowledge base, beyond theology, with far-reaching implications. However, and this is important for our discussion, Garland argues that the new criminology was kept at arm's length by the British penal establishment which carries the implication that the Police Court Missionaries would not have been expected during the period under discussion to have received training in this new approach

(Garland, 2002, p. 29f). Furthermore, it is interesting to speculate on how many, if any, missionaries had even heard of positivism.

Alternatively, other possible knowledge influences during the early twentieth century, going beyond the spheres of theology and criminology, were psychiatry, psychoanalysis and psychology, thus indicating the potential for a growing knowledge base within the fledgling service prior to 1907. Clive Hollin reminds us that psychology was established as an academic discipline within British universities by the early 1900s (2002), but there appears to be no sign of a specific probation training course covering these academic disciplines at this time. Garland reminds us that, prior to the 1930s, criminology did not exist as a university-based academic discipline. Moreover the 'scientific criminology that developed in Britain between the 1890s and the Second World War was heavily dominated by a medico-psychology approach, focused upon the individual offender and tied to a correctionalist penal-welfare policy' (2002, p. 38). Nevertheless it should be acknowledged that in the period after the 1907 Probation of Offenders Act it was being recognised that there was a need for training. Cecil Leeson (1914), for example, said that training could develop along the lines of the Social Studies Courses in the newer universities.

The position reached at this stage in the historical overview is that even though it appears that a specific training course did not exist during the early years of the probation system, as we move into the twentieth century there is a growing recognition that there was the need for such an initiative. In fact Bochel reminds us that social work training in general was in its infancy when the probation system was put on a legislative footing in 1907. Interest in social work training

> *was centred mainly in the university settlements and the Charity Organisation Society and its offshoots such as the Council of Almoners. The largest group of probation officers, the missionaries, were not of this stable. Where training touched them, if at all, was through schemes run by religious bodies for parochial workers.*
>
> BOCHEL, 1976, p. 86

Not even the Departmental Committee of 1909, established in the aftermath of the 1907 Act in order to discuss its implementation, discussed the issue of training.

Prior to leaving this early period it is possible to introduce another line of enquiry by entertaining the notion that there was little justification for training because of the theological framework within which the missionaries operated, specifically before 1907. These were people of religious vocation and conviction who were characterised by sympathy, tact, common sense and firmness (King, 1964, p. 15), and whose ontological approach to offenders in its purest form was based upon the evangelical notion of saving offenders' souls by divine grace (rather than human intervention). If this was the case (see McWilliams, 1983, for a full discussion) it may be cogently argued that the system did not require a trained workforce on the grounds that character and religious conviction were sufficient when working with offenders, in addition to divine intervention. Concomitantly it may also be argued that the early years of the probation system are coterminous with the period of reform from 1876 to the early twentieth century (as opposed to rehabilitation and the influence of positivism) which would be accepted by Bottoms and Preston (1980) yet challenged by Hudson (1987; see Hudson's first chapter for a full discussion of the differences between reform and rehabilitation).

However, if we accept the analysis and chronology of Bottoms and Preston, which state that reform became rehabilitation only after the Second World War, indicating that those initial religious and moral impulses eventually became 'secularised, psychologised, scientised' (1980, pp. 1–2), then it may be suggested that there is the possibility of an ideological fit between reform and the probation period of saving souls. This is because the concept of reform is characterised by the free will of the offender, individualism, repentance, and a responsibility for his own future that comes about by reflection, prayer and discipline. If only the offender would prayerfully reflect upon his situation, then he would realise that reform was possible through faith in God's grace rather than by human intervention (we will contrast reform with rehabilitation later in this overview, in addition to the accompanying ontological shift that occurred). What, therefore, was the point of training the missionaries during the immediate aftermath of 1876 if the system was premised upon reform that had religious connotations fundamentally dependent upon God's grace? In what subjects and approaches would they be trained? In addition to theology, what else was required?

It seems important to differentiate the 1876–1907 period and the years after the 1907 Act in our excavation of training and knowledge. It should be recalled that despite the introduction of the Probation of First Offenders Act in 1887, the system had to wait until the 1907 Act for the creation of statutory supervision for offenders. After 1907 the missionaries were established as social workers of the court who were involved in the following tasks (see Le Mesurier, 1935, pp. 57–58):

- Applications for summonses under the Married Women's Acts

- Parents who want advice about out of control children

- Advice to unmarried mothers

- Persons requesting advice about adoption

- Destitute persons seeking help

- People seeking work

- Discharged prisoners

- Friends or relatives of attempted suicides.

Moreover, the probation officer could be called upon to undertake investigations to determine the suitability of an offender for probation supervision (see Chapter 5 for further information on these investigations).

Importantly, in addition to the personal qualities of tact and patience, Le Mesurier (p. 58) says that the probation officer required two types of knowledge:

(1)   a sound knowledge of the law;

(2)   a working knowledge of charitable organisations in order to provide the probationer with practical assistance (latter-day partnership arrangements).

Le Mesurier also refers to Sir William Clarke Hall who apparently said that probation officers needed more than a religious vocation or a humanitarian disposition. In other words, they required knowledge of the origins of crime and how to deal with it according to three principles:

> (1) *The great majority of criminals are normal (i.e. born with normal mental equipment; this is opposite to the positivist standpoint that believes that criminals are fundamentally different to law abiding people).*
> (2) *That normal persons may become criminal through ascertainable and preventable causes.*
> (3) *The treatment of crime should, with possibly a few exceptions, be remedial.*
>
> LE MESURIER, 1935, pp. 59–60

Consequently, it may be argued that these comments by Clarke Hall, particularly that offenders are normal, add weight to the earlier evidence that during the early decades of the probation system the tenets of criminological positivism did not have a dominant intellectual influence within the probation service, with obvious implications for training and knowledge requirements. By contrast, Le Mesurier refers to the growing influence of psychology and the need for probation officers to be aware of conscious and unconscious motives when investigating criminal behaviour (p. 62). It needs to be emphasised, however, that there was a greater awareness of the need for training and knowledge after 1907 than before.

The need for training gathers pace

Dorothy Bochel proceeds to explain that at a meeting of probation officers in 1919 one of them, who had worked as a missionary for 27 years, called for the introduction of training centres for probation officers. 'He claimed that many of his mistakes could have been avoided if he had had more guidance when he first took up the work' (1976, p. 86). In the same year Cecil Chapman, the Metropolitan Magistrate, who was to give evidence to the Departmental Committee that reported in 1922, recommended that probation officers should undertake the training in social work provided by the London School of Economics. It is reported that Chapman stated that

> The work of supervision involves a great deal more than tact and sympathy; visiting and the writing of adequate reports require strength of body and mind, and amateurishness of performance is a mere waste of time and money.
>
> BOCHEL, 1976, p. 86

Moreover, the courts were not places where untrained probation staff should operate. Nevertheless, by the time the Departmental Committee reported in 1922, which had been established in November 1920 by the Home Secretary, Edward Short, to enquire into existing methods of training, appointing and paying probation officers, it is interesting that Bochel should comment that the Committee was weak in its discussion of training issues. However, and what is of interest for this chapter, is the way in which Bochel proceeds to state that, at this time, the Church Army and the Police Court Mission were involved in the training of the missionaries. Unfortunately she does not proceed to discuss the content of this training, which leaves us to speculate about the subjects being covered and, therefore, the precise knowledge base within the service at this specific period (p. 87).

It is clear that the need for training was on the agenda by the early 1920s, despite Bochel's comments about the deficiencies of the 1922 Departmental Committee Report. The stage had been reached when it was being acknowledged that the probation system needs to progress beyond the qualities of sympathy, tact, common sense and, of course, religious conviction. In other words, a case was being made for higher educational attainments through university training. Joan King, reflecting upon the decade after 1926, says that as other social services began to develop, as social conditions began to improve following the economic depression in the 1930s when there were more opportunities to find work for offenders, and as less emphasis was placed upon drunkenness and poverty, there was a general move away from material factors towards medical and psychological features. In other words, greater emphasis was placed upon the personal, mental and psychological factors in criminality as opposed to the environmental and social issues (King, 1964, p. 19f). Consequently, during this period the probation system moved beyond saving offenders' souls and slowly entered the age of diagnosis and the medical-treatment model with its connotations of rehabilitation achieved through the medium of casework. However, before unpacking some of these interesting concepts in relation to training and the developing knowledge base within probation, it is necessary to comment on training arrangements as the system began to enter the 1930s.

The first Home Office Training Scheme

In March 1928 an Advisory Committee on Probation and Aftercare was appointed, and by 1930 was concerned about an official training scheme for those wanting to enter the probation service. Le Mesurier takes up the story by saying that a Home Office Training Scheme was established in 1930. This scheme had two objectives: (1) to provide practical training in court work; and (2) to provide facilities for those candidates in order to develop their education in circumstances in which it was impoverished. According to Le Mesurier, during the summer of each year a handful of people were selected for training consisting of both men and women between the ages of 24 and 30 (p. 66f). Those selected who had a university education, or had obtained a university diploma in social science, received training in practical probation work under the direction of a senior probation officer for not more than 12 months. Those without the benefit of an academic background divided their time between practical probation work and university studies, leading to a diploma in social science. These candidates were expected to achieve the diploma by the end of their training, normally a period of two years, and at the time Le Mesurier was writing her book in the mid-1930s, candidates had been trained at the London School of Economics, and at Essex, Liverpool, Birmingham, Manchester and Sheffield universities. (It is of interest to note that practical probation work consisted of training in the preparation of court reports; supervising probationers; and visits to Prisons, Borstals, Approved Schools and Hostels).

Importantly, it should be noted that in addition to the creation of the first Home Office Training Scheme in 1930, Le Mesurier alludes to the Police Court Mission Training Scheme. The main difference with Home Office training appears to be that the missionary scheme enabled candidates to qualify as probation officers while continuing their existing occupation. In other words, it involved attending classes for one evening each week, during term time, over a four-year period. This scheme was conducted by the London University Extension and Tutorial Classes Council and successful candidates received a Diploma in Economics and Social Science from the University of London, in addition to the Police Court Mission Diploma. The course was designed to improve the candidates' qualifications, but it apparently did not include training in the practical aspects of probation practice. What is of interest is the insight Le Mesurier provides into the content of this training course: social economics, problems of poverty, the psychology of criminal tendencies, criminal law and administration (p. 68). Bochel expands the discussion by saying that this scheme, which began in 1926, remained in existence for a number of years and by 1930 extended its work beyond London to Ruskin College, Oxford, which was based on a cor- respondence course (p. 113, which is an interesting allusion to an early form of distance learning).

As we proceed with this historical excavation of training and knowledge within the probation service, with the occasional detour into related areas of concern, let us remain with the 1930s as there was a growing recognition of the need to establish new standards of qualifications, selection, training and conditions of service. This was the decade that saw a major review of the service in the form of the 1936 Departmental Committee Report, the third report into probation work since 1907 (after 1909 and 1922). The 1936 Committee recommended that probation training should embrace a broad study of social work principles, through a university social science course, in addition to specialised training in probation practice covering practical and theoretical components. From 1937 the Police Court Mission provided a Hostel at Rainer House where probation students took their theoretical course, and Joan King explains that from 1937 to 1939, 117 men and 40 women were trained.

At this point it is important to broaden the discussion by reflecting upon the changing ideological context within which training developments were occurring, which had implications for the knowledge base and modus operandi of probation practice. If the early decades of the probation system were replete with (a) the theological notions of saving souls by divine grace, (b) a sense of a religious vocation and (c) the concept of mercy within the court setting, then by the 1930s the underpinning ideology within the pro- bation service experienced a profound ontological shift in the direction of diagnosis, the medical model, treatment and rehabilitation. This ontological shift may be further elucidated as the shift from sinner to patient, from metaphysics to science, from a plea for mercy in court to professional appraisal and diagnosis, and from evangelical faith and grace to the medium of casework by which change within the lives of offenders would be realised (see the analysis contained within the McWilliams' quartet of essays that theorises upon this significant transition). Therefore if such changes were proceeding during the 1930s, it can be argued that there was an understandable demand for training. Furthermore, McWilliams says that 'towards the end of the 1920s the scene was being set for the gradual emergence of a professionalized probation service' (p. 262). If the probation service aspired to professionalism, it had to have a trained body of staff with a solid knowledge base that justified its growing claim to professional status. Faith and theology were no longer sufficient in this changing ideological and intellectual context.

By this stage we have tried to piece together the emergence of training within the probation service from 1876 to the 1930s, when the service experienced a major review. While undertaking this historical excursion we have attempted to contextualise the subject under discussion by alluding to a significant ideological and ontological shift which occurred during the 1930s, exemplified by a shift from theology and the accompanying notion of reform to the new science of criminology with its diagnostic, interventionist, rehabilitative and correctionalist implications. Along the way we have called at key staging posts in the form of the 1909, 1922 and 1936 Departmental Committee Reports, and differentiated between the training courses for missionaries and subsequently the Home Office scheme in 1930 during a period characterised by dual control. With Le Mesurier we have been able to provide an insight, albeit limited, into the subjects being covered during training thus establishing the knowledge base of developing practice as the service begins to enter a different era. However, prior to continuing to piece together the history of training and knowledge it is important to provide some information on the method of working with offenders that had significant implications for the subject under discussion. In other words, we need to pause to reflect upon the casework method that dominated probation practice for several decades during the twentieth century.

Casework in probation

Casework, a term not *de rigueur* within contemporary probation practice which is more tuned to the language of cognitive-behavioural approaches, had its origins in the scientific charity of the Charity Organisation Society that was founded in 1869. Its methods were subsequently exported to America at the end of the nineteenth century from where they were eventually re-imported to Britain (McWilliams, 1983, 1985). However, it was in the post-1945 period that casework became the medium through which the assessment, diagnosis, treatment and cure of offenders was attempted in probation, and by the late 1950s it may accurately be claimed that it was the dominant method in probation practice. A book written in 1961 argued that probation casework was offering a professional type of friendship (St John, 1961, p. 57). The author claimed that the identity of the probation officer at this time was understood to be a caseworker who displayed similarities to the approach of psychiatric social workers, hospital almoners and child welfare officers. To St John the purpose of casework was to facilitate the reformation and growth of the offender to enable that person to be nourished and made stronger. St John accepted that probation officers were not psychotherapists or psychoanalysts but understood that casework employed certain psychological concepts and applied mild psychotherapeutic techniques (p. 231).

In 1958, when the statutory probation system was 50 years old, Dawtry, in 'Whither probation', expressed surprise that there had been no impartial assessment of the probation service for 22 years, when the first 28 years after 1907 had witnessed three enquiries: 1909, 1922 and 1936. This was rectified in May 1959 when a Committee of Enquiry was appointed under the chairmanship of R.P. Morison. When the Committee reported in 1962 it was clearly understood that the probation officer was a professional caseworker (Home Office, 1962, p. 23), subsequently endorsed during the same decade by Parsloe (1967, p. 8). By using the term 'casework', the Morison Committee understood that the probation officer was involved in establishing a personal relationship with the offender that would help the offender to lead a crime-free life and exist in harmony with society. Even though the term 'casework' is extremely difficult to define with precision – and that McWilliams (1986) has expressed concerns about its morality (for example, probation officers imposing 'meanings' onto clients that may not be justified) – the Morison Committee nevertheless made the following statement:

> Casework, as we understand it, is the creation and utilisation, for the benefit of an individual who needs help with personal problems, of a relationship between himself and a trained social worker. . . . It is a basic assumption of all casework that each person is a unique individual whose difficulties are the product of complex and interacting factors. The caseworker thus needs the fullest possible insight into the individual's personality, capacities, attitudes and feelings and he must also understand the influences in the individual's history, relationships and present environment which have helped to form them.
>
> HOME OFFICE, 1962, p. 24

Over recent years it should be acknowledged that the probation service has moved beyond the casework approach because it has trained its staff in numerous methods of working with offenders and the literature is replete with references to group work, community work, contracts, family therapy, task-centred casework, and behaviour modification, to name but a few (see Coulshed, 1988, and Payne, 1997, for an overview of these methods). It is, however, interesting to recall that empirical research during the late 1980s discovered that the social work method of casework was very much alive in probation practice (Whitehead, 1990, p. 141f).

Prior to leaving this approach it should be further clarified that casework was theoretically grounded in the psychosocial or psychodynamic method that was influenced by Freudian personality theory, with it emphasis on the id, ego and superego (for further information on the psychosocial–psychodynamic approach, see the work of Richmond, 1922; Hollis, 1972; Coulshed, 1988; and Payne, 1997). Basically the aim was to assess, diagnose and treat the person within the totality of his situation – the psychosocial whole. Nevertheless, one of the problems with this approach was the temptation to focus too much on – with a view to changing – the so-called faulty individual rather than on the wider social system (Walker & Beaumont, 1981). On reviewing the casework system at that time, it may be concluded that the vast majority of probation officers were involved in an enterprise that was much more modest than assessing the client's ego strengths – focusing upon defence mechanisms, denial, displacement and projection as the mechanisms that help people to cope with conscious and unconscious anxiety. We certainly cannot recall this language being used in day-to-day encounters with offenders in our offices. Perhaps the most realistic appraisal of the type of casework practised by probation officers is provided by Peter Raynor who says that it should be understood as 'a process of therapeutic work in which the offender's needs and motivations, characteristically hidden behind a "presenting problem", could be revealed through a process of insight facilitated by a relationship with a probation officer' (2002, p. 1173).

Therefore, after this necessary detour into 'casework' that dominated the probation service for many years, with its implications for probation training and knowledge, let us retrace our steps and refocus the discussion.

The 1940s and beyond

Joan King (1964, p. 32) says that by 1947 only a proportion of probation officers had taken the Home Office Training Course established in 1930. In fact Bochel (1976, p. 162) says that between 1940 and 1944, 172 trained as probation officers. In 1944 the Home Secretary appointed a new body, the

Table 1.1 Personnel entering the service after training and without training

Year	After training			Without training		
	M	F	Total	M	F	Total
1960	58	33	91	98	16	114
1965	186	74	260	36	21	57
1970	189	109	298	64	39	103
1974	229	226	455	34	19	53

Advisory Council on the Treatment of Offenders, and the first subject they considered was 'What more can be done to develop the probation service as a highly skilled profession requiring not only a missionary spirit but training and expert knowledge?' (Bochel, 1976, p. 164). Then in 1949 the Probation Advisory Committee and Probation Training Board were replaced by a Probation Advisory and Training Board. During the period 1946–61 approximately 1 in 4 probation officers were untrained, which means that provisions for training were not keeping pace with expansion and demand, particularly during the 1950s. In fact King states that during the 1950s and 1960s a number of new entrants to the service, particularly in the North-East of England, had no specialised training, yet they were appointed by Probation Committees (these officers were known as Direct Entrants). Reference has already been made to the Morison Committee Report of 1962 that aspired to work towards a situation where only fully trained practitioners entered the service, but during the 1960s and 1970s a number of officers entered the service without training. On this issue the supporting data produced by David Haxby (1978, p. 59), which we have summarised in Table 1.1, are interesting to peruse.

In the mid-1960s Haxby says that the vast majority of students completing an approved training course came from courses of one year's duration that were specifically and exclusively designed for the training of probation officers. Prior to this, in 1954, the London School of Economics introduced the first 'generic' course and the Probation Advisory and Training Board sponsored the students. Similar courses were also established at other universities. By 1968 pressure was building for a generic course and a shift away from a central Home Office to provincial courses. Moreover, it was considered that the interaction between aspiring probation officers and those training for other branches of social work would be stimulating. By 1970 the Government announced its intentions to create a single independent statutory training council for social work in the United Kingdom: and the Central Council for the Education and Training in Social Work (CCETSW) was established on 1 October 1971. The statutory responsibilities of the CCETSW were to include training in social work for local authority personal social services: the health service; education; and also the probation service. Therefore the common award was the Certificate of Qualification in Social Work (CQSW).

It should be acknowledged that this development came at the end of the welfare-oriented 1960s, particularly in relation to young offenders. Moreover, the Seebohm Report of 1968 was established to ensure an effective family service, but it also had serious implications for the future of the probation service, including future training arrangements and knowledge base. The debates of these years are no longer topics of conversation but it is interesting to recall that several years before Seebohm reported, the existence of a separate probation service in Scotland came to an end and its functions were transferred to the new social work departments. Subsequently there was the possibility that something similar could happen in England and Wales, but it was eventually decided that a separate system should be maintained because even though the probation service was providing a social work service to the courts, it should also be seen as an integral part of the criminal justice system which endows it with a unique status (see Sainsbury, 1977, p. 73f, and Haxby, 1978, ch. 4, for the arguments during this period). Not only has probation remained a separate service but the 1990s have witnessed a return to a specialised course for TPOs, detached from generic social work training, which has had implications for training and knowledge, but more of this later.

The implications of empirical research

As the probation service moved into the 1970s it began to enter a different ideological phase, a consequence of empirical and academic developments. In fact it may be suggested that this process began with Leslie Wilkins in 1958 and subsequently proceeded through a number of probation research projects which included Simon (1971; methods of predicting reconviction), Davies (1969; stresses in the lives of probationers), Barr (1966; group work) and Sinclair (1971; probation hostels). The combined result was that the efficacy of probation in terms of preventing re-offending by casework and other methods was being questioned. Additionally the work of Hammond (1969) and later the IMPACT research project (Intensive Matched Probation and After-Care Treatment; Folkard et al., 1974 and 1976), which stated that 'Many of the negative findings might seem to suggest that treatment has no effect or even that it makes offenders worse rather than better', was of deep concern to the probation service. In fact it was the IMPACT study that brought to an end the Probation Research Project that had started in 1961. Into this potent mixture we can also throw, for good measure, the work of Martinson (1974) and Brody (1976). In fact it was Brody who, in his analysis of nearly 70 studies from different countries, cast doubt on the rehabilitative efficacy of different treatment programmes, particularly if probation is used for first offenders and confirmed recidivists (see Whitehead, 1990, ch. 1, for a more detailed summary of these research studies). So where does the service go from here in terms of rationale, underpinning ideology, training and knowledge?

It is important to refer, albeit allusively, to these significant research studies because of their implications for probation training and the shifting knowledge base of practice (in addition to the changing rationale of the probation service beyond the phase of diagnosis). In other words, if the probation service no longer understood its role in terms of saving souls (1876–1930s), and if a growing body of research was beginning to call into question the phase of treatment and rehabilitation (1930s–1970s), then what is the rationale and underpinning ideology of probation practice? This is an interesting question to consider within the context of this chapter, which is attempting to provide a historical overview of training and knowledge. We say this because, despite numerous empirical research studies, the main ones of which have been cited above, other research by one of the authors of this book undertaken in the North-East during the mid-1980s (again referred to earlier) suggests that there was a degree of dissonance between the weight of research findings into the efficacy of rehabilitation, and the actual methods of working being applied by a number of probation officers when engaging with offenders. Reference has already been made to the method of casework being employed. When turning to the sustaining ideologies of a number of probation officers' underpinning practice, the language of reducing criminal behaviour, preventing crime and rehabilitation (among others) is being used even as late as the end of the 1980s (Whitehead, 1990, ch. 7). Therefore, it is possible to suggest that the training and knowledge base of many practitioners had not been revised in relation to the new knowledge that was beginning to emerge on the back of empirical research. One of the reasons for engaging in this discursive evaluation in this chapter, where training is being considered against a diverse background of change and development during different periods of time, is to acknowledge that, to some degree, it is at the mercy of numerous factors: political, social and economic influences; ideological shifts; the findings of empirical research which eventually make an impact; the latest academic thinking; and the latest fashion. The business of probation does not exist in a vacuum but is affected by diverse influences that have implications for training and the teaching of knowledge to probation trainees and other practitioners.

Prior to bringing this chapter into the present, it is helpful, for the sake of completeness, to understand that the so-called collapse of the rehabilitative ideal within the probation service was responded to in various ways. For example, the 1980s emphasised the rationale of 'alternatives to custody' and within this framework three schools of thought can be identified. The Personalist understands probation work in moral terms as the process of helping people as an end in itself, thus detaching probation practice from the rationale of instrumentality. Next is the Radical school that seeks to pursue a policy of social change within a Marxist framework. Finally, the Managerial school emphasises accountability, economy, efficiency, effectiveness, the offender within a framework of policy, objectives and targets. It can be argued that, in diverse and complex ways, the three schools interact with each other within a managerial framework that is currently dominated by the language of punishment in the community, risk assessment and public protection (for a more detailed discussion, see McWilliams, 1987).

Towards the present

By 1974 Jarvis was articulating the view that the

> *quality looked for in potential probation officers, in addition to a wish to work with people, is above all else a resilient personality. Good intelligence, a good general education, some varied life experience, some experience of other forms of social work; all these are valuable too, together with flexibility of mind and a capacity for listening to and understanding others. People with these attributes are well suited to go forward to acquire in training the specific knowledge and skills required of a probation officer.*
>
> JARVIS, 1974, p. 268

Jarvis proceeds to explain that training during the 1970s and 1980s took various forms, depending upon the age and educational qualifications of the candidate. For candidates with a degree or other qualifications, numerous universities provided courses in applied social studies. Other universities provided a four-year degree course, including professional training. For those candidates who were at least 23 and without a university qualification, some universities offered a two-year social work training course for the probation service. Moreover, during the 1970s people of 27 years of age and over were considered for courses in London, organised directly by the Home Office, and at various Polytechnics. Jarvis reminds us that the course in London, which is where the probation system began in 1876, 'is based on the Probation and After-Care Training Centre at 114 Cromwell Road, Kensington. The Rainer Foundation managed on behalf of the Home Office residential accommodation for students during their time spent at the Training Centre' (1974, p. 269). Importantly, these training courses culminated in the CQSW, which was the professional social work qualification awarded by the CCETSW. (Chapter 10 of Jarvis, 1974, provides a useful insight into training arrangements within the probation service during the 1970s. His fourth edition, published in 1987, adds little to his previous overview.)

From generic to specialised training in the 1990s

The route to qualify as a probation officer from the 1970s and during the next quarter century was the generic CQSW. However, as we progress into the last decade of the twentieth century it can be discerned that the criminal justice system, within which the probation service is located, became a harsher and tougher environment not only for offenders but also for those who work with them. This is because punishment was emphasised rather more than welfare, particularly after the Jamie Bulger murder in 1993; the good intentions of the Criminal Justice Act 1991, with its just deserts philosophy, were watered down in the Criminal Justice Act 1993, and 1997 witnessed the introduction of mandatory minimum sentences in the Crime (Sentences) Act (see Garland, 2001, for a detailed analysis of this period; also Downes & Morgan, 2002, trace penal policy since 1945). In fact, during October 1993 Michael Howard, the Conservative Home Secretary, announced his 27-point plan for refocusing law and order and the accompanying philosophy that prison works. Consequently, it was against this background of a changing criminal justice climate during the 1990s – influenced by a Conservative Government pursuing a more populist law and order initiative that was ideologically rather than empirically driven – that Jack Straw, the Home Secretary in the elected Labour Government, announced his plans for probation service training on 29 July 1997. It is worth quoting in full what was said at that time:

> I hope to proceed quickly to develop a Diploma in Probation Studies, located in higher education and combined with a National Vocational Qualification, which will become the qualification for new probation officers. I intend that the new arrangements should be employment-led and delivered by consortia of probation services which will manage the recruitment and selection of trainee probation officers.
>
> The combined diploma and NVQ will offer a mixture of academic teaching and work-based supervised practice, all based on the occupational standards that will be developed for probation officers. The new qualification should be delivered through flexible teaching methods which take account of trainees' previous work, academic qualifications and experience so that a wide range of recruits can be attracted to the probation service.

I have decided that training for new probation officers should no longer be linked to social work education. I will be supporting the development of a new and separate Diploma in Probation Studies which will equip the probation officers of the future to play their full part in this Government's plans for an integrated approach to working with offenders. It will focus on Probation's top priority role of protecting the public and reducing crime through effective work with offenders. These arrangements will be developed in partnership with probation service organisations and higher education institutions to provide high quality training for high quality recruits.

HOME OFFICE, 1999: Regulatory Framework

During the 1997–98 period, 12 Probation Circulars were published by the Home Office, focusing on the new training arrangements. It is not necessary to analyse these in any detail in this book but Circular 53/1997 – *Probation Officer Recruitment and Training: Implementation of New Arrangements* – spelt out that the new qualification will be an award comprising academic and practice elements. It will be employer led and the new arrangements will be managed by nine consortia. Additionally the thrust of the new award, as it was emerging at this time, was that it would be based upon specific Occupational Standards that, in 1997, were in the process of being developed. At this stage a great deal of work needed to be done to develop the core curriculum with a view to the first trainees commencing the new course during the autumn of 1998 (Cohort 1).

As the Regulatory Framework emerged it was made clear that the core curriculum would be bifurcated into Phases 1 and 2. Phase 1 should be perceived as corresponding in academic level to year 1 of a degree and to include Foundation Studies. Phase 2 should be perceived as corresponding in academic level to years 2 and 3 of a degree, in addition to the achievement of National Vocational Qualification (NVQ) level 4 in Community Justice (contains 12 separate yet overlapping units). The core curriculum delineates the knowledge requirements that must be met by a TPO in order to qualify at the end of the two-year period of training. It is therefore designed to meet certain Occupational Standards in respect of knowledge and understanding, in addition to developing the notion of lifelong learning and continuous professional development. Therefore, the Dip.PS comprises the following:

- Academic studies that will culminate in a Community Justice degree. This requires the trainee to acquire detailed knowledge of relevant probation-oriented disciplines (Chapter 3 will look at these subjects in more detail).

- Practice studies that focus on the requirements of the NVQ in Community Justice. This means that the trainee will be provided with a range of practice opportunities based upon working with offenders in a variety of situations.

These experiences will enable the trainee to generate and collect practice and knowledge evidence in order to demonstrate confidence in working with offenders and that appropriate tasks can be performed in a competent manner. Moreover, these practice opportunities provide the trainee with the evidence for the NVQ to demonstrate that certain Occupational Standards are being met. Therefore, from the first Home Office Training Scheme in 1930, to the latest arrangements in the form of the Dip.PS that began in 1998, this chapter has attempted to survey the history of training in the probation service.

Conclusion

This book is fundamentally about training and knowledge within the probation service. Both of the authors have a responsibility for training TPOs, which involves teaching them about the diverse knowledge base of the contemporary probation service, in addition to making crucial links between theory and practice. Consequently, this opening chapter has reflected upon these two related themes within a discursive historical context in order to set the scene for the remainder of the book.

At this stage let us try to pin down the notion of training with more precision. Training can be understood in terms of coaching a TPO in a particular mode of behaviour and/or performance. It is about ensuring that trainees are proficient and competent in all areas of probation practice. As an athlete trains for six days each week to function at the optimum level of performance under the tutelage of a specialist coach, the TPO must also be trained and coached by those who have knowledge and understanding of the requirements of best practice. Furthermore, training is linked to knowledge in the sense that trainees must acquire certain items of knowledge to perform effectively and undertake tasks competently. Therefore, let us begin to unpack the notion of knowledge in more detail. Knowledge (and here we are conscious of stating the obvious) can be understood as the state of knowing. It involves insight, awareness and understanding and it should be recognised that knowledge can be acquired within a probation context in different ways: it can be taught and therefore imparted by someone who already possesses a body of knowledge; it can be accessed by reading books, by observing someone perform a task and repeating what has been modelled, or by engaging in a piece of practice and reflecting upon what happened; it can be taught by receiving feedback from a teacher, by seminar work and discussions, and by assessors creating the opportunities and right environment in which to learn.

Knowledge can be understood in terms of acquiring information about something. For example, we would cogently argue that trainees need to know something about the history of the probation service because this knowledge helps to contextualise their own understanding of the organisation within which they have chosen to earn their living and pursue their vocation. This history just happens to be fascinating and of interest as an end in itself, as illustrated by this chapter. Additionally, trainees need to know how to perform certain tasks that characterise the probation profession (procedural knowledge), for example: interviewing; assessment; how to construct a Pre-Sentence Report (PSR) for the court; selecting effective methods of intervention; and utilising partnership resources. The perceptive reader will grasp that these examples demonstrate two different types of knowledge as knowledge of probation history is a different type of knowledge from that required to perform a specific task when working with offenders (a distinction between knowledge 'of' and knowledge 'for', and the notion of constructing a typology of knowledge within the probation service is an interesting concept). As we begin to reflect upon the nature and function of knowledge it is interesting that we tend to shy away from the 'know-all', a term often used pejoratively because of its connotations with a supercilious attitude. By contrast we are drawn to what may be described as 'know-how' as this is linked to skill, understanding and ingenuity, and is calmly and confidently expressed. Knowledge is quintessentially about being well informed and it is important that trainees, in addition to all probation practitioners regardless of the length of service, are in possession of the knowledge base that underpins probation practice in a rapidly changing knowledge environment. This is the essential goal of training.

This preliminary discussion on knowledge within a probation context begins to suggest that it is a potentially complex area of enquiry. As, for example, the concept of punishment can be understood from different standpoints (such as the views of Durkheim, Marxist perspective, Foucault and Elias; see Garland, 1990, for a detailed exposition), the nature, acquisition, meaning and function of knowledge can also be explored in various ways. Furthermore, the knowledge base of a profession, such as probation, is not static, as demonstrated by this historical overview. Knowledge has been shown to change over time as a consequence of:

- an ontological shift from saving souls to diagnosis and curing by casework;

- research that questioned the efficacy of probation to achieve rehabilitation, particularly during the 1970s;

- the latest method of working that shows promise (cognitive-behavioural approaches rather than Freudian casework);

- political change – impacting upon the criminal justice system – that occurred after 1993 when punitive populism gained a foothold that helped to detach probation training from social work education;

- the shift from probation training alongside social workers, education welfare officers and psychiatric social workers, during the period of the CQSW, to the more specialised Dip.PS course from 1998 that has put greater emphasis on criminal justice, penal policy, criminology and punishment in the community, as opposed to social work.

Probation knowledge is also affected by changing values that have implications for how offenders are perceived and understood.

To prepare the ground for a discussion on knowledge within vocational education, which is pertinent within the context of this book, our next task is to continue, in the first part of Chapter 2, the historical tone we have established in this chapter. Consequently, the next chapter begins to narrow the focus of our enquiry.

Summary

This chapter reviews the history of the probation service from a number of perspectives. The early history and the missionary movement are examined and early thinking and knowledge are speculated upon. The notion of reform is distinguished from rehabilitation.

The gathering momentum for training in the 1920s reflects the recognition that probation officers needed more than tact, sympathy and common sense and the developing influence of medical and psychological ways of thinking about the probation task. A culture of diagnosis appeared. The Home Office Training Scheme of 1930 involved practice learning and university teaching. Curricula included social economics, problems of poverty, the psychology of criminal tendencies, criminal law and administration.

The move towards social work was recommended in a service review in 1936. Training was part of a process of professionalising probation.

The history of casework is described, as is the long-lasting impact of the casework model on probation practice since 1945. By the 1960s a model of professional casework based around the particular relationship between officer and offender has emerged and survived in a pragmatic form until the present day.

In the 1950s and 1960s many direct entry (untrained) probation officers were still being recruited. However, the demand for a generic training programme, available regionally, was growing and, following the Seebohm Report of 1968, the CQSW emerged in 1971 as such a course of study. The CQSW would also be the qualifying award for probation officers.

There is a review of the empirical research of the 1970s in which the efficacy of probation practice is questioned, but the impact on practice was slow. By the 1980s a movement of alternatives to custody was a response to a waning of faith in the notion of rehabilitation.

The movement from a welfare orientation in the punitive climate in criminal justice in the 1990s is described. In 1997 the new Labour Government described plans for new and separate arrangements for probation training that would involve academic content, practice and be employer led. A year later the new Dip.PS programmes were recruiting their first trainees.

The prescribed framework for the Dip.PS is described.

The chapter examines the historic connections between theory and practice and, in the conclusion, connections are made between the historical analysis in the chapter and the aims of this book. Questions are raised about the nature of training. The notion of knowledge for practice is a complex one and, as we see in the history of the probation service, it changes over time and is affected by research, values, developments in other disciplines and areas of knowledge, and by political expedience.

Further reading

Additional information on the history of the probation service, divided into five main phases, can be found in Appendix 1. Other useful references are:

Bochel, D. (1976) *Probation and After-Care: Its Development in England and Wales*. Edinburgh and London: Scottish Academic Press.

Garland, D. (1985) *Punishment and Welfare: A History of Penal Strategies*. Aldershot: Gower.

Garland, D. (2001) *The Culture of Control: Crime and Social Order in Contemporary Society.* Chicago: University of Chicago Press.

Haxby, D. (1978) *Probation: A Changing Service.* London: Constable.

King, J.F.S. (1964) *The Probation Service* (2nd edn). London: Butterworths.

Le Mesurier, L. (1935) *A Handbook of Probation.* London: National Association of Probation Officers.

Raynor, P. & Vanstone, M. (2002) *Understanding Community Penalties Probation, Policy and Social Change.* Philadelphia, PA: Open University Press.

The following quartet of essays is important and can be found in the *Howard Journal*:

McWilliams, W. (1983) The mission to the English police courts 1876–1936. *The Howard Journal of Criminal Justice,* **22**.

McWilliams, W. (1985) The mission transformed: Professionalisation of probation between the wars. *The Howard Journal of Criminal Justice,* **24**(4).

McWilliams, W. (1986) The English probation system and the diagnostic ideal. *The Howard Journal of Criminal Justice,* **25**(4).

McWilliams, W. (1987) Probation, pragmatism and policy. *The Howard Journal of Criminal Justice,* **26**(2).

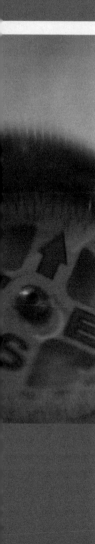

Chapter 2

Knowledge in vocational education

Towards an understanding of change

The history of the probation service and the history of training and preparation for work in the probation service is a history of changing discourses. These changing discourses are about the nature of knowledge, the relationship of knowledge to vocational preparation and professional values and, more recently, about the relationship between knowledge and learning. In this chapter some of these key ideas are explored before presenting a detailed and critical discussion about knowledge and learning in the current probation officer qualifying training arrangements.

McWilliams (see Chapter 1) describes the journey of probation from an activity underpinned by religious faith, through a period of 'professionalisation' around an eclectic knowledge base, to an output-driven activity increasingly drawing on management science. However jaundiced a view of the present this model implies, it describes changes in values that are reflected more widely in western industrial society and, closely related to this, changes in how knowledge is used in the process of decision-making in policy and practice. The 'faith-based' activity of the early probation missionaries did not occur in a vacuum of knowledge. Indeed the attraction to courts and, in due course, to legislators of the work of the missionaries was that they did bring experience and information to the process of sentencing. We know little about the knowledge base that individual missionaries brought to their calling but we do know that their knowledge about the circumstances of individual offenders was increasingly valued by sentencers. The problem for the missionaries was neither lack of knowledge, nor their faith, but rather that they applied their knowledge and faith too indiscriminately. Their information and knowledge and their commitment to rescuing 'lost souls' was not enough for a system that recognised the value of the work but wanted to identify the most 'tractable' offenders. It might be said, therefore, that the notion of training and a specific knowledge base for probation emerged from an early (1930s) question about 'What Works'. The social casework that emerged could not answer this question but could address it. Now unfettered by notions of universal forgiveness, through social casework probation officers could apply a systematic approach to the assessment and treatment of individuals and began to draw on a range of theory to explain crimes and rehabilitation. The change then from mission to new profession in probation is characterised by the emergence of the notion of a body of circumscribed and relevant knowledge, distinct from universal truths claimed by religion. This relevant knowledge, although eclectic, had two important characteristics; first, it was rational and offered explanations for the phenomenon of crime and, second, it was discriminatory and allowed for diagnosis, prognosis and treatment in relation to individual offenders. Psychology offered a wide framework for the analysis of individual history, drawing on notions of stages of human development and on scientific explanations about individual behaviour. Treatment might variously be based in helping individuals to accommodate previous trauma and unresolved transitions or in techniques of positive and negative reinforcement of particular behaviour. Sociology, on the other hand, offered some structural and sometimes intrinsically political explanations for crime and a treatment approach based on supporting individual escape routes from structural disadvantage. Contained in what are essentially the processes of social casework, this eclecticism and range of relevant knowledge has continued until recent times so that probation has drawn on theories and approaches variously humanistic (e.g. counselling; 'getting alongside' the offender) and scientific (e.g. behaviourist approaches; diagnosis and treatment); functional (e.g. welfare approaches; budgeting, training and employment support) and critical (e.g. community approaches, consciousness raising, anti-oppressive work).

In the same way that the modernisation of the missionaries became necessary as probation became legitimised within the criminal justice system it was the climax of the 1991 Criminal Justice Act that led to a need for a more focused probation knowledge base. Crucially the new Act made the probation service an instrumental part of the sentencing framework. The Probation Order became a sentence of the court and no longer an alternative to a sentence of the court. As a result, the Probation Order had to be framed, at least in part, as punitive. Perhaps even more significantly the Probation Order could not be made in terms of a merciful decision of the court. Notwithstanding the modernisation of the missionaries, right up until 1991 probation officers were making special pleas for the mercy of the court in individual cases. Sentencers would often make reference to this special pleading and to their decision to make an exceptional disposal. This special pleading was only different to the special pleading of the missionaries in that it was pleading for faith in the professional rather than faith in God and humanity. The plea was still a plea and the mercy was still mercy. The rational 'just deserts' sentencing framework introduced by the 1991 Act and the placing of community sentences firmly in a tariff-based framework may be said to have affected this special relationship between the probation officer and the court. The pressure on the knowledge base was clear. If sentencing was to be a more scientific process, then information and proposals for the court would have to be similarly scientific. The rationalism based on trust in a profession working in good faith was no longer enough. Subsequently, much has been made of the 'nothing works' debate of the 1970s and the failure of the probation service to establish a scientific evidence base for its work. However, it has been the changing legitimacy of the probation service that has required a different and more positivist articulation of probation knowledge.

It could be argued that the recent development and organisation of probation knowledge has been as much about the harnessing of knowledge-as-power as about extending the boundaries of understanding of crime and offenders, knowledge shaped by the changes in organisational legitimacy. Knowledge organised around faith gave way to knowledge organised around the notion of professionalism which, in its turn, has given way in most recent times to knowledge organised around the activity of a publicly funded, centrally controlled criminal justice agency.

Knowledge and competence

This new order of accountability for the probation service has been the driver for a range of signal organisational developments. Accountability to central government as an integral part of criminal justice policy has necessitated a strong centralising process and a new national apparatus and bureaucracy. Alongside this has been the articulation of the vision, aims and objectives for the organisation. The need for consistency and measures for performance has seen, first, the defining of National Standards and the setting of Key Performance Indicators and annual targets. Arguably these developments represent the apotheosis of McWilliams' (see Chapter 1) vision of a managerialist service and certainly represent an important strand of knowledge in probation. However, perhaps most significant in relation to probation knowledge has been the emergence of Occupational Standards.

Occupational Standards attempt a detailed articulation of the competences involved in particular jobs and are also expressed in terms of level and range. Occupational Standards are arrived at through an arcane process of wide consultation and expert specialist involvement. They have a number of uses. In the first place they are a standardisation process and establish clear boundaries and expectations in relation to particular groups of employees in relation to particular sets of competences. As such they can be tools in organising the workforce in functional ways. They can be used to identify recruitment, training and development need and to focus effort in relation to identified target areas of work for priority and effort. They can also be used as a basis for accrediting competence.

The Occupational Standards can be used alongside processes of assessment and verification to certify individual and groups of competences through the awarding of NVQ certificates. Originally this process was intended to be a way of giving credit to people who had developed and were using competences in their work that were previously unrecognised and unrewarded. A development from this has been the use of Occupational Standards as the basis of requirements for particular jobs and in the case of the probation service also as a basis for a process of qualification as a probation officer.

Every competence described in Occupational Standards includes reference to the knowledge requirements of that competence. These knowledge requirements are not detailed discussions but list a range of knowledge headings necessary for the competence. This requirement implies on one hand the need to acquire or develop this knowledge to be competent and also the need to assess this knowledge when accrediting the competence. Knowledge in this system is essentially a constituent part of competence. Knowledge exists in Occupational Standards only to the extent that it can be seen to inform observable behaviour. An individual candidate's knowledge can be assessed in a number of ways but often much of the required knowledge will be implicit in the competent and consistent behaviour of the candidate. Where this is not clear the assessor might question the candidate or the candidate might provide other evidence. In probation officer qualifying programmes, this other evidence might be a written product from the parallel degree programme that is designed to complement these knowledge requirements.

In many ways the model that describes knowledge in relation to professional practice is not new. The social work training with which probation was previously tied, traditionally described professional practice in terms of a combination of the right skills, values and knowledge. Here knowledge was assessed academically, skills assessed in practice and values integrally with both. The difference is in the codification of the prescribed knowledge base in recent probation qualifying training, in the generation of a large part of the academic curriculum and the whole of the practice curriculum from the Occupational Standards. One of the aims of this book is to clarify, illuminate and make more accessible this codified knowledge base but before doing so it is appropriate to identify some of the problems associated with this approach to knowledge for practice.

The knowledge economy

The establishment in the 1980s of the National Council for Vocational Qualifications and the steady spread of the codification of knowledge in terms of Occupational Standards across different employment sectors has also represented a development in the notion of knowledge as an important economic commodity linked to the efficient management of the workforce. The associated NVQ awards, and the expertise involved in delivering them, have been the subject of marketing and their growth has been supported by the government-endorsed Sector Skills Councils (or what used to be known as National Training Organisations). This employability-based knowledge is now a strong presence in schools in the delivery of GNVQs and can be discerned in the shaping of the National Curriculum. At the same time the notion of lifelong learning has gained currency and again the underlying theme is that of continual/lifelong learning for the world of work and the maintenance of employability. Higher Education (HE) has been the last or slowest sector to respond or to be required to respond to this 'new vocationalism' (Symes & McIntyre, 2000).

The debate in HE has been and continues to be around various approaches to the academic accreditation of workplace activity, skills and learning with the new universities being generally more prepared to contain vocational codifications of knowledge. The establishment of subject benchmarks across the sector has seen HE accountable to national codifications of knowledge and learning, here not driven by vocationalism but by the attempt to make the HE market more transparent to potential customers. Most recently there have been attempts to articulate the added value of university education, to identify the components of graduateness and to assure their delivery. Again these are focused on graduateness primarily as improved employability expressed in terms of the transferable skills acquired.

What is this knowledge that is economically important? Amid the rhetoric about a knowledge society it is tempting to believe that there are particular bodies of (no doubt rapidly changing) knowledge that are central to economic success and need to be acquired by large numbers of individuals in the workplace. This argument seems to be largely overstated with only comparatively small sectors of the workforce in the post-industrial economy needing these special skills and knowledge, with a large majority only needing basic skills in predominantly service industries (Sieminski, 1993; Avis et al., 1996).

> The knowledge economy is a myth, whose main function is to feed fears of future mass unemployment and to spur learners on to new and still higher levels of attainment.
>
> COFFIELD, 2000, p. 241

Ironically there may be arguments to suggest that the vocationalisation of knowledge and the marketing of knowledge codified in this way lead to a learning economy characterised by mass production, division of labour and price sensitivity.

Theory and practice: Knowledge for work

For a long time there has been a popular conception that vocational preparation requires the acquisition of two types of knowledge: knowledge of
theory and knowledge for practice. This distinction and the relationship
between these types of knowledge have been developed in a number of interesting ways. For example, Nellis (2001) describes overarching and underpinning theory for probation officers. In this paradigm for vocational
knowledge, practice knowledge offers frameworks for the what, where, when
and how of practice, and theory offers frameworks for understanding the
why of practice. Through an understanding of theory, practitioners can contextualise organisational policy and practice and have a critical and analytical perspective on development and change. However, in a vocational
knowledge economy it is not difficult to imagine that such benefits of theory
are not always seen as necessary prerequisites for many jobs. For example,
learning theory constitutes only a minimal part of the prescribed curriculum for the post-graduate qualifying award for teachers.

The knowledge requirements of the Occupational Standards for Probation
are largely non-theoretical and this is for the very good reason that the
knowledge described is the knowledge needed and implicit in observable
work behaviour. Furthermore, knowledge is required to achieve only competent or good enough practice. The need to know why is largely an unnecessary luxury. In the Regulatory Framework for Probation, qualifying
training the undergraduate degree sits alongside the NVQ process but it is
a degree that is required to give one-third of its credit for the achievement
of the level 4 NVQ and a prescribed curriculum generated principally by the
knowledge requirements of the NVQ. It is an undergraduate degree that
is both supporting and accrediting NVQ achievement and, as such, its
theoretical content is severely constrained.

However, this separation of theory and practice is a flawed paradigm for two
reasons. First, theory and practice are much more closely entwined and
interchangeable than the paradigm suggests and, second, this twin-track
model overlooks the notion of knowledge in the different but important
sense, as good thinking.

In *An Introduction to Social Work Theory*, David Howe (1987) adopts the
notion of theory for asking why but connects this directly to practice as a
central question for dealing with complexity. For Howe, 'why?' becomes
'what's going on here?' and is the leitmotif of professional skill as opposed
to artisan skill. 'What's going on here?' is a question that prepares the worker
for the unexpected, and in the complex world of the social is a guard against
the inappropriateness of routine responses and interventions. Furthermore,

theory for Howe is personalised knowledge – drawing on fashion, personal preference and acceptability. Knowledge of theory can be the source of personal and professional animation. Finally, 'what's going on here?' becomes the cornerstone question of ongoing reflection and the professional researcher-practitioner. This view of the integral nature of theory and professional practice resonates strongly with an important element of current probation practice. Central to 'What Works' in probation is the focus on cognitive-behavioural approaches around which a strong evidence base has been presented. Cognitive-behavioural programmes now constitute an important strand of probation intervention. These programmes require high levels of quality control and their integrity depends on consistency of delivery. Training and accreditation are required to deliver the programmes and sophisticated systems are required to monitor delivery. Most programmes are delivered by non-probation officer staff. The irony is that successful cognitive-behavioural interventions are built upon a joining process with the offender in addressing the question 'what's going on here?' Successful interventions will involve animated practitioners applying high levels of skill to motivate offenders around that question.

Second and separate from this suggestion – i.e. that the separation of knowledge of theory and knowledge for practice is unhelpful – is the proposition that this separation omits the crucial and relevant phenomenon of what might be called 'process knowledge'. In this process knowledge the process of learning becomes the central consideration. As early as the 1950s Reg Revans (1998) was proposing that prefabricated (or codified) knowledge had limited use in helping people to solve the real practical problems of the workplace or to provide a framework for individual development in the workplace. For Revans successful organisations needed to match the pace of change of the external environment with comparable rates of organisational and individual learning. This learning happened most effectively when groups of individuals were given properly structured and supported opportunities to address and solve their own real workplace problems. Revans was proposing a moral view of knowledge in which workplace knowledge is grounded in experience and is indeed inseparable from experience. His 'action learning' resonates with androgogical theory where the relevance of knowledge and the safety of the learning environment are central to successful learning taking place. Reg Revans died in January 2003 but his principle of 'teaching little and learning a lot' is a significant contribution to the debate about vocational knowledge.

Another important thinker in relation to learning for work is Donald Schon. Schon (1987) recognises that in complex social spheres the workplace is characterised by the unexpected, by surprise. He proposes that practice in such circumstances is a form of 'artistry' and an artistry that can be developed through the development of reflective approaches to practice, reflection on practice (learning from practice) and reflection in practice. Reflecting in practice is the key to professional artistry and is developed through self-discipline, critical awareness and a commitment to a cycle of learning through practice and reflection. Like Revans, Schon is describing a knowledge process that is grounded in practice. Here knowledge is not codified but is the very currency of continuing personal and professional growth and development.

The concept of reflection has its place in the probation qualifying programme. At their best, academic programmes work hard and imaginatively to help trainees to make connections between the curriculum and lived experience at work. This process of making connections is central to reflection. Reflection becomes a much lower-level activity when reflective pieces are generated to provide specific evidence for the NVQ process. Here reflection is sometimes used to meet the need for evidence of particular knowledge requirements. Such pieces are seldom extracts from ongoing reflective processes but are constructed particularly to meet the evidence need. As a result, the pieces are driven by the codified knowledge not by the actual learning from practice.

More recently Soden and Pithers (2001) have pointed to the dangers of focusing vocational education on 'procedural' knowledge. They describe the increasing demand in the workplace for people who think well and who can solve problems:

> . . . vocational education as a vehicle for developing a thinking workforce rather than as a training in the application of specific procedures.
>
> SODEN & PITHERS, 2001, p. 219

It is not clear that post-school teaching institutions or the (G)NVQ processes have been able to consistently deliver these thinking skills to students, partly because expertise in teaching thinking is not widely held and partly because the various codifications of knowledge fail to articulate 'thinking well' as an aim or objective. Soden and Pithers base their work on the body of cognitive research that indicates two key factors in the development of critical and effective thinking. First there is strong evidence to suggest that deep understanding of subject matter does lead to superior thinking and problem-solving skills. A key feature of this deeper understanding is 'connectivity' or the extent to which students can connect and map the elements in the particular domain of knowledge. This will be encouraging to those particularly in HE who argue that thinking skills can be developed through traditional academic scholarship. Second, students need to be given opportunities and encouragement to gain awareness of their thinking, their knowledge and their thinking strategies and how these can be orchestrated to achieve 'task performance' ('meta-cognition'). This awareness can be encouraged and developed by first making sure that it is transparent in the learning content and then by applying techniques such as modelling, 'scaffolding' and 'epitomising' to encourage meta-cognition.[1]

Other factors that will affect the success of such learning processes will be the nature of assessment that will need to reflect the desired outcomes: the understanding of teachers/facilitators of the cognitive processes involved; their commitment to the outcomes; and attention to the moulding of students' perceptions and expectations of learning.

This aspect of knowledge as cognition and thinking skills is significant for both HE and practice inputs to the probation qualifying programme. In particular, for Practice Development Assessors (PDAs) consideration needs to be given to the value ascribed to thinking skills in the learning process at work and the extent to which the development of self-knowledge and deep subject understanding is not sacrificed to the acquisition of predominantly procedural knowledge. If thinking skills are important, then there are also implications for the knowledge base and skills for PDAs and HE staff involved in delivering them.

From codification to learning

In the Skills Foresight Analysis produced by the Community Justice National Training Organisation (CJNTO, 2003) it is interesting to note that although some of the sector training and development needs are expressed in terms of knowledge gaps or updating, there is a strong emphasis from practitioners on the need to feel more confident in their roles, in particular to be more confident about the legitimacy of their roles. Codified knowledge often fails to accommodate notions such as confidence and legitimacy (we discuss confidence and legitimacy as part of a model for professional development in Chapter 7). Meanwhile in the same report managers in the sector express concern about lack of innovation in practice. Innovation is a crucial part of any complex business and to some extent you would expect innovation to thrive in environments where practitioners are encouraged to learn with and from others in tackling difficult problems in the workplace (cf. Reg Revans) and/or where reflective techniques are made available and encouraged (cf. Schon). However, it is far from certain that, even in such circumstances, innovations and developments in practice can penetrate the process of a revision of Occupational Standards and it may be that this particular type of codification of knowledge does have the effect of driving out innovation.

[1] For more on these techniques, see Soden and Pithers (2001).

In the case of probation, a national, centralised agency, more sensitive than ever to political necessity and expediency, is concerned to achieve two main objectives. First, to drive up standards and, in particular, to be able to demonstrate that rise in standards in measurable ways. From this imperative we get target-setting and targets connected to cash from the centre. The second big objective is consistency, and here the tools are the National Standards against which services are inspected and Occupational Standards against which probation staff are trained and developed. It is here that we see the power of the managerial agenda. National Standards, Occupational Standards and indeed the notion of programme integrity in the delivery of probation programmes are all framed as baseline essentials. National Standards are the baseline procedures for staff, Occupational Standards are the baseline competences for staff and programme integrity is a requirement that all programmes are delivered by staff in the same way. These rules and baselines allow for measurement, comparison and for numerical target-setting but it would be a mistake to believe that they are based on any infallible truths about best practice, the most appropriate skills and knowledge or the most effective programmes. They are all codas for the policing and managing of consistency. The processes of if, how and why these codas are changed and developed are therefore significant.

Changes in National Standards are made through a centralised process and changes to date have all been about closer articulation of the 'when' and 'what' of practice and a tightening of deadlines and, in particular, enforcement procedures. Here we see the drive to raise standards and achieve consistency, but perhaps also to reflect political considerations such as public perceptions of the probation service, and government need to present themselves as tough on crime. Changes in existing programmes and the development of new approved probation programmes are subject to arcane national processes. Since programmes must be delivered according to the rubric, there is little opportunity for local experimentation or improvisation. Resources are stretched to meet the demands of programmes and National Standards with the result that there is little scope for new approaches to be developed by individuals and teams of practitioners. The incentive to work up new approaches is constrained by the centrally controlled process of national approval and accreditation and, indeed, by the very language of nationally approved accredited programmes.

Our main concern is with Occupational Standards, which should be reviewed at least every three years to ensure that they reflect contemporary practice in the occupational area. This minimum requirement is barely adequate to meet the needs of occupational worlds where change is almost continuous. In fact the current Occupational Standards for probation were produced in 1997 and in 2004 the first (limited) review of those standards will be completed. This unresponsiveness to change runs the risk of Occupational Standards not, in fact, being fully relevant to practice. Perhaps, more dangerously, torpid standards could serve to entrench probation knowledge. Certainly the processes involved in creating and codifying probation knowledge are increasingly centralised: the National Probation Service, the national Sector Skills Council, the national awarding body (City and Guilds), the national accreditation panel and the very small number of universities still involved in qualifying training are all striving hard for increased consistency and may find it increasingly difficult to marry this with the complexities of sustaining an eclectic, imaginative and innovative knowledge base.

However, as a basis for qualifying training the biggest problem with Occupational Standards is not the currency of their content and structure (Stevenson, 2001). Their limitations are intrinsic to the project of codifying vocational knowledge. Codification certainly facilitates explicitness about knowledge.

> ... it allows us to talk about our knowledge, to inspect it, to assist in sharing it with others, to assist others in acquiring it, to engage in an appraisal of its coherence and utility, to attest to knowledge development, and to give credit in subsequent studies for previous learning.
>
> STEVENSON, 2001, p. 648

The problem is in what codification leaves out:

> ... we need to be wary of assuming that we can verbally express all of what we know, the most important aspects of what we know, or any of what we know, accurately.
>
> STEVENSON, 2001, p. 648

To be a probation officer we need to draw on knowledge that is often tacit, implicit or indeed ineffable:

> The capacities to contribute, innovate, create, adapt, solve problems, fit in, add value, ask and solve the right questions, and so forth are often difficult to express, and it is usually difficult to work out how they might be acquired and transferred.
>
> STEVENSON, 2001, p. 650

Recent debate about the nature and purpose of HE has seen a focus on the delivery of non-discipline-based, transferable skills and a debate about whether the qualities of 'graduateness' are intrinsic to a traditional academic scholarship. If anything, however, the problems of codified knowledge are more acute and complex in HE than in vocational standards. The codification of academic disciplines in the articulation of curricula in HE programmes has been contained to some extent by the emergence of subject benchmark standards, but still involves much debate in deciding the appropriate content, weighting, learning outcomes, assessment, etc. The benchmark standards and the processes of these debates tend to exclude consideration of the implicit and tacit in the same way. Furthermore, in HE the different and hybrid academic disciplines, the different schools, faculties, departments, institutions and indeed the different academic staff bring with them a complex of different contexts within which knowledge is interpreted and assessed and in which knowledge acquisition can be distorted by processes of assessment that emphasise particular conventions of academic writing.[2]

Codified knowledge, as expressed in Occupational Standards and academic programmes, is in some important sense incomplete knowledge and perhaps inadequate knowledge. Notwithstanding the need for a range of procedural and contextual knowledge, probation knowledge as a reflection of best and innovative imaginative practice and as a shape and direction for the development of competent and confident practitioners needs to be reframed and decodified. At the heart of this reframing we would place the practitioner and/or the learner. Vocational knowledge is only as good as the relevance it has for the practitioner. This means that vocational knowledge must be understood as mediated through the learner/practitioner. Unlimited by coda and notions of attaining a required standard in a prescribed timescale, probation knowledge must accommodate notions of learner need, embrace the diversity of learner experience and frame itself in terms of a career-long process.

Although current qualifying arrangements are not an ideal shape for such a conception of probation knowledge they contain two important elements that are potentially crucial and formative for trainees.

- *First*, in the very medium of the qualifying award and through a consciousness about the codified nature of the knowledge being assessed, trainees can learn much about the nature of the probation service and the political realities of the national probation agenda and the managerial realities of accountability, measurement and targets. For this reason it is important that trainees have opportunities to understand and critically evaluate this context.

- *Second*, in the role of the PDA lies the real opportunity for the mediation of codified knowledge through the trainee. PDAs face the

---

[2] See Lea and Street (2000) for an analysis of the problems associated with these academic literacies.

challenge of transcending the role of gatekeepers and assessors of codified knowledge through creating learning environments in which trainees' individual learning needs can be addressed and their different experiences and particular strengths can be valued. Crucially, PDAs can establish the context of probation knowledge as a continuous exploration in which the qualifying award contains some useful starting points and through the process of which there is much to be learned about the priorities and procedures of the service.

We will look in more detail at the role of the PDA in Chapter 6 and in Chapter 7 we look in more detail at models of knowledge development that transcend the codified knowledge of the Occupational Standards and the HE programmes.

Feelings: Last but not least

The science of psychology offers us a model for the analysis of behaviour in which action is understood alongside the thoughts and feelings that accompany it. An intrinsic problem in such analysis is in separating out these elements. However, as a model for understanding vocational development this notion of professional behaviour consisting of thoughts, feelings and actions is a useful tool for evaluating processes designed to prepare individuals for complex jobs. In particular, the inclusion of the emotional as a key element resonates with the lived experiences of doing such jobs. It would be difficult to deny that there is strong emotional content to probation practice. Powerful emotion is routinely associated with offending behaviour and the processes of engagement, assessment and purposeful work with offenders inevitably takes place in a context of the feelings of all parties. The impact of these feelings on the achievement of successful outcomes is extraordinarily complex. Feelings are invariably present but the extent to which they are transparent varies greatly, as does the extent to which the parties are able to recognise, articulate or understand them. Meanwhile feelings are often the reactive element in the reflexive processes of interaction. The problem for the practitioner is in recognising and understanding their own feelings and those they are working with and in walking a sophisticated tightrope between controlling/hiding feelings and expressing feelings towards positive outcomes. Notwithstanding the increasingly scientific base for probation practice and the drive for consistency and programme integrity, the reality of probation practice still involves the engagement of the unique emotional narratives of offenders and workers.

Although there is a useful theory to help practitioners to understand the place of emotions in behaviour, a vocational notion of emotional intelligence or competence is impossible to describe, inappropriate to prescribe and very difficult to assess. Such a notion of emotional competence is thus absent from the codified knowledge for probation.

HE has much to learn about creating an environment in which students can engage on an emotional level with the content and process of an academic discipline. However, for TPOs it is the learning environment in the workplace that is critical. There are two crucial elements to such a positive learning environment. First there must be encouragement to engage with the emotional content of the work. Trainees need to know that there is not just permission but an expectation to review and reflect upon how they feel. This sort of confidence is unlikely to be realised unless experienced practitioners and supervisors disclose something of their own emotional experience of the work in appropriate settings. Central to such a working climate is an acceptance that not only is it healthy and formative to engage with the emotional content of experience but also that such experiences of the world are different and that this difference is to be valued. Feelings are not right or wrong but can contribute to understanding and to an identification of need.

The second element necessary to contribute to an emotional learning environment for trainees consists of more formal contexts within which to explore the emotional content of probation work. On the one hand, this will involve regular sensitive and supportive supervision and, on the other, the routine consideration of feelings in reflective exercises.

For trainees, much of this environment is currently provided by those PDAs for whom emotional engagement is a central part of their sense of legitimacy. This in turn will be a function of both the PDAs' own professional identities and the particular service or team climate within which they are set. Once again then we find that those parts of probation knowledge that fall between the large cracks in the codified knowledge in academic programmes and occupational standards fall to the PDA to recover. In the same way that the PDA mediates the knowledge and understanding requirements of standards and curriculum through individual learners and their unique needs, it is again the PDA to whom we look to mediate between the realities of the work and emotional knowledge and understanding.

Where, for whatever reasons, the emotional is not engaged with formally and/or implicitly in the workplace, trainees will need to support one another and seek out other opportunities to share and explore this part of their development.

Summary

This chapter begins with a mapping of the changes in the knowledge underpinning probation practice against the broad framework of probation history detailed in Chapter 1. It is suggested that, as ever, current probation knowledge reflects a wider and a specific discourse that reflects the context of and controlling influences on probation today.

Part of the context is the ubiquitous concept of competence that is explained and discussed. In particular the role of knowledge in Occupational Standards is discussed and, more broadly, the place of knowledge in the degree and NVQ elements of the probation qualifying award. The relationship between theory and practice is discussed together with the artificial distinction between knowledge for theory and knowledge for practice. Knowledge for the degree and NVQ is described as codified knowledge.

The advantages and disadvantages of this codified knowledge are discussed and in the process a range of ideas is explored. There is a brief critique of the so-called knowledge economy. The works of Donald Schon (knowledge through reflection) and Reg Revans (action learning) are used to illustrate potential gaps in codified approaches to vocational knowledge. The ways in which codified knowledge functions well for central and controlling agendas are described alongside an analysis of the apparent drawbacks, e.g. innovative approaches to practice may be discouraged. More fundamentally, codified knowledge fails to include those parts of what we need to know for practice that are tacit, implicit or indeed ineffable. These limitations inherent to codified knowledge apply generally to both HE programmes and to Occupational Standards. Knowledge as consisting of transferable skills such as communication skills and thinking and problem-solving skills is articulated in HE programmes but is only an implicit part of demonstrating competence against the Occupational Standards.

Knowledge for probation is only as good as it is relevant to the practitioner. This means that knowledge for the NVQ and for the degree needs to be mediated through the individual learner. This may be a central and crucial role for the PDA and will be explored in more detail in Chapter 6.

Finally, the central importance of feelings and emotional knowledge in successful practice is discussed, and again the importance of the PDA role is highlighted, as is the notion of a learning environment.

> Probation work, because it involves engaging with people, has the capacity to invoke strong emotions, particularly in those who have developed the emotional intelligence to empathise with the human condition of those with whom they work and who have a refined conception of justice.

Further reading

Relevant to this chapter are the Occupational Standards for Community Justice (especially level 4) and you will have access to these as soon as you are registered for the NVQ.

Coffield, F. (2000) Lifelong learning as a lever on structural change? *Journal of Educational Policy*, **15**, debates the relationship between knowledge and the economy.

Nellis, M. (2001) The new probation training in England and Wales: Realising the potential. *Social Work Education*, **20**(4), 415, is an important elucidation of a particular way of recognising different kinds of knowledge in probation.

The importance and relevance of theory to practice has been debated widely in the world of social work, and Howe, D. (1987) *An Introduction to Social Work Theory*. Aldershot: Wildwood House presents a strong argument that will seem relevant to probation officers.

Revans, R. (1998) *The ABC of Action Learning*. London: Lemos & Crane, and Schon, D. (1987) *Educating the Reflective Practitioner*. San Francisco: Jossey-Bass, have both played an important part in stretching the notion of knowledge for practice in relation to problem-solving in the real world and inspired and creative practice.

For a route into further reading about the notion of codified knowledge, begin with Stevenson, J. (2001) Vocational knowledge and its specification. *Journal of Vocational Education and Training*, **53**(4), 647.

Chapter 3

The Diploma in Probation Studies

Introduction

In 1997/98 the Dip.PS became the required qualification for probation officers. It replaced the Diploma in Social Work, a generic award for social
work-based professions. It had long been argued that the Diploma in Social
Work (and before that the Certificate of Qualification in Social Work) had
not served the preparation and training needs of probation officers. The specialist element of these courses had been restricted to one or two academic
units and the availability of probation practice placements. The arguments
for change were based on both the need for a broader specialist underpinning knowledge and, by some, on the need for a more distinct probation
value base (see Nellis, 1995) – for example, one founded on clear principles
of anti-custodialism. However, in the event this practitioner, probation
service and academic pressure for change and development was less significant than a range of other largely external factors and influences:

- the changing legal context of probation (in particular following the
  1991 Criminal Justice Act[1]);

- the managerial reframing of the probation service in terms of, pro-
  gressively, National Standards, 'What Works', target-led management,
  moves towards more central control and a National Probation Service,
  and a more clearly articulated mission (Home Office, 2001);

- the political reframing of criminal justice issues in the run-up to the
  1992 General Election in the aftermath of the James Bulger murder
  and the subsequent trial and conviction of the 11-year-olds Robert
  Thompson and John Venables in 1993.[2]

A clearer sense of location and direction for the probation service emerged
from this maelstrom of influences, while in parallel to these developments
the service was drawn into the national movement towards the definition
and application of Occupational Standards (see Chapter 2). If the probation service was becoming ever more clear about its role and mission, if it
had articulated National Standards for performance and was increasingly
wanting to describe its activity in terms of 'What Works', then it should

---

[1] The 1991 Act made the Probation Order a sentence of the court rather than an alternative to a
sentence. As a result, community disposals had to be thought of more clearly as in part punitive
and restrictive of liberty. Probation now stood within the main framework of criminal justice agencies, alongside rather than standing outside of the courts, police and prisons.

[2] Public and press reaction to this crime was extreme and created a volatile climate of moral panic
captured well by Blake Morrison in *As If* (1997).

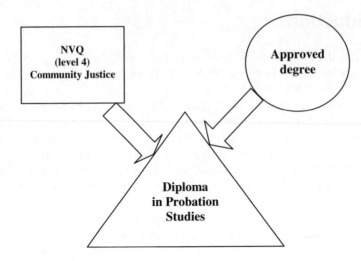

Figure 3.1 Route to diploma in probation studies

increasingly be able to describe the work of probation staff in terms of the competencies required.

The Dip.PS was built around the notion of Occupational Standards and from the outset a Regulatory Framework and Core Curriculum were pre-scribed for the process and content of the award. The Dip.PS is a composite qualification awarded on successful completion of both the NVQ level 4 in Community Justice and an approved degree programme (see Figure 3.1). It represents a unique and challenging integration of vocational and academic experience and structure. As a result it should be an award that is directly and intensely relevant to probation practice.

Interestingly in the process of setting up the award there was a highly self-conscious separation from the social work tradition to the extent that HE providers were advised that the probation programme delivery could not be through social work departments (presumably for fear of infection from an imagined social work disease). In broad terms there were three elements to social work training in HE that were dispensed with or heavily diluted in the new probation arrangements:

- the emphasis in social work training on an eclectic theory base and the development of a range of associated communication and intervention skills;

- the opportunity in social work training to choose specialist areas for study and development;

- the allowance in social work training for the relevance of structural explanations for individual circumstances and behaviour.

In this chapter we describe the key processes of Occupational Standards and NVQs. In particular we discuss the assessment of NVQs and the knowledge and understanding requirements in that assessment process. We discuss the synergies and tensions that underpin the integration of a degree with NVQ. Finally, we analyse the underpinning knowledge and understanding requirements of the NVQ and describe how that analysis can be helpful to NVQ candidates and assessors (PDAs) in assuring both excellence in practice and high-quality assessment of performance.

Occupational Standards

The construction of Occupational Standards is an arcane process and involves specialist skills. Standards are based on the notion that any occupational sector will be able to describe what it does in terms of the competences required to do the jobs involved. The range of these broad competences is mapped and then articulated in precise and fine detail. For example, the starting question in drawing up Occupational Standards for probation officers was: 'What do probation officers do?' Detailed consultations took place with relevant stakeholders, draft standards were produced, further consultation sought until, in due course, agreed standards were adopted by the CJNTO[3] and offered to the NVQ awarding bodies to deliver as NVQ awards. The devil is in the detail. These are not generalised ideas about the skills needed to be a probation officer but are competences that are described and broken down into enough detail that they can be objectively assessed with confidence. This process of detailed articulation is made more complex by the notion of levels of competence. Occupational Standards describe sets of competences required for particular employment sectors in terms of a variety of levels. There are five levels of Occupational Standards and in the Community Justice awards the probation service officer standards are set at level 3 and probation officer standards at level 4. Broadly speaking these levels represent decisions about the levels of responsibility, autonomy and complexity relating to particular jobs. Overlap between standards is common so that the level 3 Community Justice standards contain competence units that are also part of the level 4 award. Competence in these common units must be assessed at the appropriate level (although it is possible to transfer relevant completed units at level 3 onto the level 4 award).

---

[3] The CJNTO is now part of a broader-based Sector Skills Council.

An important part of the detailed articulation of each competence is the underpinning knowledge and understanding. In relation to each part of a competence (known as an element) the competence unit descriptor lists the knowledge and understanding required. As the level of the standards rises, this knowledge and understanding becomes an increasingly significant factor and the competence can only be judged in the context of the candidate's knowledge and understanding of the situation and his or her rationale for action.

Occupational Standards are reviewed on a regular basis to reflect changes and developments in particular employment sectors. In fact for probation this process of review has seemed slow so that the standards for probation workers have lagged behind substantial developments and changes. This question of the responsivity of Occupational Standards to sector development and change is crucial for the probation service. On the one hand, there is simply the historic fact of change being an ongoing feature of probation practice. For the Occupational Standards to be credible and indeed useful in terms of identifying development need and recognising relevant competences, they need to reflect change and, further, to be a live reflection of real occupations they often need to predict change. In the current standards it could be argued that there are important competence gaps, for example, in relation to the processes of case management and the issue of offender resettlement. Neither of these subjects is new to probation practice and their increasing importance was predictable, but the processes of Occupational Standards development have lagged behind changes in practice. Without this quality of responsivity the credibility of Occupational Standards is damaged. However, if they become increasingly a description of generalised competences they lose much of their occupational identity and flavour and, perhaps more importantly, become less easy to assess objectively.

Meanwhile, as well as the danger that changes and developments in probation practice can overtake the Occupational Standards, the very process of applying Occupational Standards to the organisation also brings with it the risk of further dissonance. The Occupational Standards have applied to all probation officers who have commenced training since 1998. Graduates of the new Occupational Standards-driven framework have been entering practice since 2000. Expansion of probation officer numbers has meant that the proportion of these differently trained officers is significant. However, they join an experienced probation officer workforce untouched by notions of required competence. The extent to which the Occupational Standards have impacted on the appraisal, supervision and development of this old school of existing officers is not known and certainly varies from area to area. Meanwhile the current middle and senior management of the probation service have not had to engage with demonstrating competence and the processes of assessment of competence except in those few services that have engaged with the level 5 Management Award. This assessment experience has largely been abrogated to a new specialist cadre of PDAs, who are still almost exclusively recruited from the old school and specially trained (and assessed) in the arcane world of NVQ. The potential value of Occupational Standards as a tool for managers to identify and focus on training and development needs of staff, or indeed as a tool to identify and focus organisational or team effort, is largely unexploited. As things stand, the impact of Occupational Standards in developing and changing probation practice is limited to their impact on new TPOs. The old school will continue to be untouched and even the post-2000 Dip.PS cohorts will be largely unaffected by any changes and developments in the standards. These issues present significant questions and problems if the probation service seeks to establish a true competence culture. The net result may well be an almost subconscious resistance to the formal reframing of probation work that Occupational Standards development represents – a need to keep things static while the organisation gets to grips with the full implications that touch on the culture and very identity of the probation service. The process may take a long time to work its way through the service, with unknown factors influencing the pace and direction towards more coherence and confidence. For example, we know very little about the dynamics when new school meets old school. Research into the relative impact of vocational training and workplace culture in other areas of work (for example, teaching) seem to show quite clearly the overriding influence of the latter. At what pace can we expect new school probation officers to become a significant voice in middle and senior management of the service, and to what extent will they bring changed understandings, perceptions or values? Can we expect different retention rates for new school probation officers being recruited increasingly at a younger age and for old school probation officers trying to adapt to a different sense of identity?

Underpinning these issues and problems lies a fundamental tension in the probation qualifying award. Occupational Standards are intended to describe the competences that constitute a particular job. They are not designed to be a template for time-limited qualification training. They are designed to clarify occupations, to provide a tool to identify training and development need and to offer the opportunity to recognise competence in those already performing a job. In the current probation service the level 3 standards have been applied to and used by current staff to demonstrate existing competence and to steer development, but are now increasingly being used as a template for time-limited probation service officer training. The level 4 standards are the template for an intensive two-year programme delivered to experienced and non-experienced alike, that leads to a non-time-limited licence to practice as a probation officer.

NVQs

Through a highly assured process of assessment and verification, candidates for NVQs must demonstrate and evidence their competence in units and elements of the Occupational Standards and have that competence certificated by an NVQ awarding body. NVQs are for people already working in a particular occupational sector. The very notion of assessing competence implies that candidates will already be doing the job. Opportunities to demonstrate competence will occur naturally in the process of doing that job. With the help of a properly qualified assessor, candidates plan such opportunities and engage in a process of reviewing their practice until the competence has been properly evidenced. Candidates are either competent in a particular area or not yet competent. Competence is not an issue of success or failure but, of course, may well be an issue of employability. In practice it is also often an issue of opportunity with some competences more rarely applied or needed in particular individual work situations. The process is generally described as candidate-led, with the candidate deciding both the pace and direction of the work and drawing on the assessor as required.

As part of the Dip.PS the NVQ assumes a very different nature. Candidates, whether experienced in probation work or not, are required to evidence the full range of competences over the two years of the traineeship. Some may bring a small part of this evidence from level 3, but even for these candidates the bulk of the level 4 award must be achieved during the two years of the programme. In effect this demonstration of competence across the full range of the job has to be done in something less than 18 months. The first six months of the programme are designated in the Regulatory Framework for the Dip.PS as for foundation practice, i.e. pre NVQ. This begins to accommodate the idea that NVQ is for people already doing a job. The reality for trainees in their first six months is variable, but is generally characterised by a long period of induction and acclimatisation; for most there is a substantial academic programme and, in the workplace, highly structured learning experiences. Furthermore, the process of assessment and verification means that completion within the two years actually requires the completion of all NVQ units well before the end of the programme. Within this tight timeframe trainees must accommodate their learning and development through experience and the wide range of experiences required to provide the necessary evidence, and must devote half of their time to the pursuit of the undergraduate degree. The result of these particular constraints and pressures is that the NVQ in qualifying training does not 'fall out' of naturally occurring evidence as trainees engage with the job. Rather, experiences at work need to be carefully planned around the NVQ requirements, the process of learning from experience needs to be intensive and well planned, and the academic curriculum needs to be closely integrated with, and relevant to, the evidence gathering. In terms of traditional NVQ this would seem unworkable and is made feasible in practice by trainees' intensive engagement with the programme and through the special role of the PDA.

PDAs

PDAs are experienced probation practitioners (in some cases senior practitioners). They are either full-time or part-time specialists, and their role combines responsibility for the assessment of the NVQ competences with planned and progressive learning opportunities in the workplace. PDAs are required to obtain specialist NVQ assessor accreditation. This involves the demonstration and evidencing of two specialist NVQ units. It is a role fraught with tensions. First, there is the professional challenge of successfully combining the promotion of learning and development with responsibility for assessment. This is a classic tension: how to create a learning environment in the workplace in which candidates feel confident enough to admit doubts, make mistakes and express uncertainty at the same time as being responsible for the assessment of practice. Second is the tension resulting from accountability. PDAs are accountable in their assessor role to the NVQ Assessment Centre. In addition, they are line managed either through the probation consortium or through their area service. They are usually accountable for the work undertaken by the trainees they supervise and this accountability can be to a range of different service managers. They often have direct responsibility in relation to the delivery or facilitation of particular parts of the academic programme and/or a programme of in-house trainee development events. They also often feel an overriding sense of accountability to the trainees to ensure that individual learning needs are identified and met and that the right opportunities to learn and to evidence competence are offered at the right time. The third central tension is in managing the inevitable levelling process of the programme. Whether experienced in practice or not, with a strong academic background or not and whether fast-tracked through the early part of the programme on the basis of previous NVQ/academic experience or not, all trainees must complete the award within the two-year timeframe. As well as the range of individual learning needs that the PDA is trying to accommodate, there is also an underlying pace towards completion that means processes of practice development (particularly for inexperienced trainees) must be compressed and carefully managed. In a traditional NVQ process of naturally occurring evidence, the order and pace at which particular units of competence are planned can be led by both the specifics of the candidates' working situation and by their particular learning needs. Here the pace and direction of the NVQ are highly individualised. For PDAs working within tight time constraints and working with trainees with a wide range of experience and ability, an important role has been to manage the pace of NVQ achievement and development alongside a coherent and comprehensive programme of experience. (Chapter 6 is devoted to developing these preliminary thoughts about the role of the PDA.)

Assessment and knowledge

At level 3 and in particular at level 4 of the NVQ in Community Justice, knowledge and understanding are key components of competence. The assessment of this knowledge and understanding becomes both more important and more difficult in the higher-level NVQs. This is particularly true when the competences are related to the social sphere such as in probation, where there is potentially a range of appropriate action and the context of a level of uncertainty. The transparency of a candidate's knowledge and understanding contextualises his or her action and is a crucial indicator of competence or of developmental need. The importance or priority given to this issue is directly related to the professional status of a probation officer. A useful model for considering relative professional status is in relation to accountability and the extent to which, in particular jobs, one is accountable variously before and/or after the event. In other words, to what extent is competent practice prescribed? This is an interesting model to apply to the work of a probation officer. Clearly in recent years the growing public and central accountability of probation work, National Standards, target-led management and evidence-based practice have all tended towards increased prescription of probation work. Certainly the autonomous probation officer, accountable largely after the event to the court, to the line manager, to the client and to conscience has become increasingly problematic. Nevertheless probation practice is still overwhelmingly characterised by the unique individual experience of offenders and by the unexpected and new in engagement with offenders. Do probation officers still need to bring creativity and problem-solving skills to their work? The alternative may have some attraction in terms of assuring consistency across a national service. However, the price is not simply the dumbing-down or deskilling of the probation officer role but innovation and practitioner research will also be jeopardised. Perhaps even more importantly the loss of significant professional accountability (after the event) will jeopardise practitioner animation. Ownership of elements of decision-making and practice are central to motivation. It is this motivation and animation in practitioners that gives quality to relationships with offenders and success in motivating offenders. In turn, it is constructive relationships and offender motivation that are central to the successful delivery of effective programmes of work.

The assessment of knowledge and understanding in the NVQ presents the PDA with a complex task, and evidencing that knowledge and understanding presents the candidate with a considerable challenge. There are a number of ways in which knowledge and understanding are evidenced.

Although the following does not constitute an exclusive list (for example, knowledge and understanding evidence can be generated by the observation of candidate presentations to other trainees, to probation colleagues and to other agencies), the four methods described represent the principal sources for evidence of knowledge and understanding.

Implicit knowledge and understanding

A central tenet of NVQ assessment is the concept of implicit knowledge and understanding. The assessor can conclude that a candidate has particular knowledge and understanding from all sorts of evidence but, in particular, from observation of practice. The level and quality of practice is seen to imply specific levels of knowledge and understanding. Knowledge and understanding evidenced in this way are unlikely to be assured without repeated observation over time that demonstrates consistency. This notion of implicit knowledge and understanding will only tend to be useful when assessing particular kinds of knowledge, specifically what we might call functional knowledge, knowledge about what, when and how. At the lower level of NVQ this is the scope of the knowledge requirements. In higher-level NVQs, and certainly in the level 4 Community Justice standards, the knowledge required is more about understanding and the question of 'why'.

Questions

Another important source of knowledge and understanding evidence is generated after observation of practice. Here the assessor and candidate plan to address knowledge and understanding questions and in a structured way can explore the context of the observation, identify knowledge gaps and explore the candidate's understanding. Sometimes candidates are given written questions by the assessor and provide knowledge evidence in the form of written answers.

Reflection

Reflective journals, logs and one-off pieces are also routinely used to evidence knowledge and understanding. Reflection can mean a range of different things and is most effective if it has a clear focus, e.g. analysis of process, self-evaluation or analysis of critical incidents. They are invaluable learning tools in all these forms and can also provide the opportunity for the candidate to make connections between units of competence and with academic theory and learning. The danger in using reflective journals for evidence of knowledge and understanding is that their value as a learning tool can be compromised by the need to show particular knowledge. Whereas evidence of knowledge and understanding from reflective journals and logs can be very powerful and valid, reflective pieces generated specifically to demonstrate particular knowledge and understanding elements, unless carefully constructed, can be a much less convincing form of evidence.

Academic assessments

The degree programmes that runs alongside the NVQ process in the Dip.PS have sought to integrate their curricula and assessment regimes in different ways. The Regulatory Framework for the award requires degrees to give academic credit for workplace learning and increasingly this has seen provider universities give direct academic credit for NVQ achievement. It has been argued that some of the processes involved compromise the integrity of both the degree and the NVQ (Thompson, 2000). Notwithstanding these debates, the academic curricula have variously been built around or sought to reflect the main strands of the knowledge and understanding requirements of the NVQ. Indeed increasingly assessment schedules in HE have been designed to provide such evidence directly in relation to specific NVQ units.

Analysing the knowledge requirements

Knowledge and understanding, and the associated cognitive skills, are part of competent performance and not something separate from it. Evidence of an individual's knowledge can be drawn from formal and written and oral tests, informal questioning and directly from performance. Knowledge is about knowing what should be done, how it should be done, why it should be done and what should be done if circumstances change. It includes:

- *Knowledge of facts and procedures*
- *Understanding of principles and theories*
- *Ways of using and applying knowledge in competent performance*

QUALIFICATIONS AND CURRICULUM AUTHORITY, 1998, p. 20

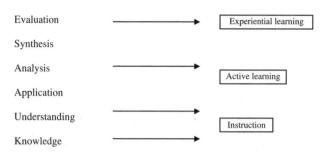

Figure 3.2 Bloom's levels and the learning process in NVQ

The methods by which this knowledge is assessed in NVQ have been discussed. It is clear, however, that in terms of Bloom's taxonomy of cognitive level (Bloom, 1964) the NVQ level 4 Community Justice is demanding more than simple knowledge and understanding but seeks application of that knowledge and understanding. Furthermore, both in the process of the NVQ and in a specific unit of competence (F307), evidence of the higher levels of cognition (analysis, synthesis and evaluation) is also required (see Figure 3.2).

The processes of learning and development are different at the various cognitive levels. Candidate and PDA have the challenge of moving through the necessary instruction phase, creating and using opportunities to apply knowledge to practice through active learning and reach a point at which trainees are reflecting, reviewing and planning autonomously as experiential learners. As implied in this model, however, the higher-level cognitive skills are dependent on a firm foundation. An analysis of the knowledge and understanding requirements for the NVQ level 4 in Community Justice helps us to clarify these knowledge foundations, to plan how best to access and deliver this foundation, and to assure some consistency in knowledge standards.

The NVQ component of the Dip.PS comprises 12 complementary units with a total of 202 underpinning knowledge and understanding (UKU) items, ranging from 11 items in unit F407 to 34 in unit E205. This is an average of 16.8 per unit. However, for the purposes of this analysis it has been decided to exclude unit F307, which has 31 items, on the grounds that:

- it can be perceived as a discrete and stand-alone unit because of the way in which it tends to reflect the other 11 units and has to be undertaken either concurrent to or after other units;

- it focuses on developing knowledge and practice in relation to the other 11 units;

- it brings together material found in other units.

For these reasons it could be argued that this unit distorts the analysis. It is not excluded because it is unimportant but rather because it represents in the NVQ a rather different order of knowledge, arguably reflecting the higher levels of Bloom's taxonomy. It draws on the application of knowledge and requires the candidate to move to a higher level of cognitive ability. The significance of this unit is discussed further, and related to learning beyond qualification, in Chapter 7.

The remaining 11 units comprise 171 underpinning knowledge items and it is possible to group the knowledge items to produce 11 key themes using 168 of the 171 items (98%) (see Table 3.1). This leaves a small residue that has been incorporated into the text.

It is interesting to note that most of the NVQ units require a wide range of thematic knowledge and that some seem to draw particularly heavily on the notion of knowledge and understanding. This has particular significance in relation to structuring learning to support the NVQ achievement. As candidates will need to draw on a range of knowledge to demonstrate competence, there will be problems with learning programmes that deal with themes in a linear way, i.e. one theme at a time. A common frustration expressed by trainees is wanting to know everything immediately and then feeling frustrated at learning that seems to take place too late.

Chapter 4 presents a detailed resource in relation to the key knowledge themes identified in the analysis of the required underpinning knowledge for the NVQ. It is intended that such a resource will be of direct benefit to trainees and assessors in planning learning and assessment opportunities. However, it is also hoped that this analysis can be the basis for ongoing debate. The generation of these themes from the underpinning knowledge and understanding requirements begins to describe what might be seen as a central or managerial view of a knowledge base for probation that was previously less clear, and lost in the detail of defining probation in terms of competence. There is potential for significant and important debate about important omissions, for different ways of shaping the analysis and for articulating the limitations of the way NVQ processes relate the notions of knowledge, understanding and competent performance.

Table 3.1 Knowledge themes mapped against NVQ units (NB numbers in boxes refer to the specific knowledge items from the unit)

UKU themes	B103	D308	D102	D103	D202	D302	E409	F403	F407	E203	E205
Victims	1	1	1	1	1	1					17
Explaining offending behaviour	2	2	2	2	2	2	1, 2, 3			7	15, 16, 17, 20
Probation service legislation	9	13	11	11, 13	9	10	10	13	1, 2, 3, 5, 7, 9	11	1, 2, 5, 8, 9
Local area policies and guidelines	3, 4, 6, 7, 10	14, 17	12	14	11	11	11	1, 3, 4, 5, 8, 11	10	12	
Professional values	12	18	5, 8, 9	5, 8	4, 8	4, 8	9	7, 9, 12	6	5, 9, 10	10, 28
Risk assessment			4, 5, 6	4, 5, 6, 9, 10, 15	4, 5, 12	5, 6				5	3, 10, 13, 14, 19, 21, 25, 29, 31, 32
Effective practice/methods	5	4, 5, 6, 7, 8, 9, 10, 12	3, 10	3	3, 7	4, 7	4, 5, 6	10			18, 22, 23, 27, 32
Communication			7	7		3	7, 8	2, 6	4, 8	1, 2, 3, 4, 6, 8	33, 34
Enforcement and compliance		3, 11			6, 10						
Self-reflection and personal development	13	19	14	16	13	12	12	14	11	13	
Confidentiality		15	13								4

Summary

In this chapter we have traced the development of the Dip.PS and described how this unique award is structured. The separation of the award from social work and the significance of this split are discussed.

Occupational Standards are introduced and the capacity of such standards to accommodate change in policy and practice is discussed. It is suggested that there could be a relationship between the adoption of Occupational Standards and the capacity to accommodate change or to adapt and innovate in the light of new research, practice and policy. It is also suggested that the introduction of standards-based management and training will generate tensions between the new and the old, and that we know very little about whether such tensions exist in probation and how any such tensions are being resolved.

The chapter also describes the relationship between Occupational Standards and NVQs. We discuss the concept of competence and the central role of the PDA in ensuring that the demonstration of competence is a learning experience. In particular we discuss the issue of assessing knowledge and understanding as an integral part of assessing competence and the methods commonly used as part of that assessment. Bloom's taxonomy is used to help us to understand what characterises the knowledge being assessed.

Finally, an analysis of the knowledge requirements for the NVQ level 4 in Community Justice is offered in which the majority of the items fall into one of 11 subject areas. These blocks of knowledge form the structure of the resource for candidates and PDAs in Chapter 4.

Further reading

For an insight into the debate about probation values before the inception of the Dip.PS, read Nellis, M. (1995) Probation values for the 1990s. *The Howard Journal of Criminal Justice*, **34**, 19–44. The Occupational Standards themselves and the candidates guidance, both of which you should have access to when registering for the NVQ, will illuminate this chapter. It is the Qualifications and Curriculum Authority (QCA) that oversees NVQ nationally and their website explains the context and processes of NVQ in some detail. http://www.qca.org.uk/adultlearning/610.html

Chapter 4

Knowledge resources for trainees: Help with the NVQ

Introduction

The previous chapter identified some of the salient knowledge themes that weave their way through the NVQ level 4 units in Community Justice (see Table 3.1). It is the task of the present chapter to consider some of the resources that illuminate these themes that will assist candidates to get to grips with underpinning knowledge demands. Additionally it is anticipated that these resources will raise the level of awareness of other staff (established probation officers; NVQ level 3 and prospective level 4 candidates; NVQ Assessors and Internal Verifiers; service managers) who want a deeper understanding of the contemporary knowledge base of practice. It should be reiterated that trainees can evidence UKU demands in the following ways: knowledge inferred from practice (for example, a PSR can demonstrate knowledge of risk assessment); answering assessor-devised questions; witness testimony evidence; self-report and self-reflection. Consequently the following resources can be utilised by trainees as part of an interactive process to demonstrate to the PDA that they have the required knowledge and understanding to function as level 4 candidates, and are therefore prospective probation officers.

Victims

During the previous three decades it may be suggested that victims of crime have gradually taken centre stage and assumed an importance previously not seen within the criminal justice system, and this change has implications for probation practice. According to David Garland we have moved from a system in which the individual victim was not the focus of attention, to a very different situation in which the rights of the victim are seen as sacrosanct in the sense that they must be appreciated and protected; have their voices heard; have their memory honoured; have their anger expressed and their fears addressed (2001, p. 11). This escalating sense of importance is reflected in a letter from the National Probation Directorate on 4 July 2001 that reaffirmed a probation service target to reduce crime of offenders under supervision by 5% which, if achieved, equates to one million fewer victims. Furthermore, section 2 of the Offender Assessment System (OASys), and section B7 of National Standards, which concerns the preparation of presentence reports, draw attention to the impact of crime upon victims. It is important for trainees and other staff to be aware of the growing significance of victims within the probation service and wider criminal justice system. Therefore, the following chronological outline plots certain changes over recent years.

1964   Criminal Injuries Compensation Board established in the UK.

Late 1960s and early 1970s: Beginning life as a local initiative in Bristol in 1974, Victim Support grew dramatically in the following years.

1982   Criminal Justice Act – Compensation Orders as a penalty in their own right were introduced.

1984   Probation Rule 37 – the probation service has a duty to participate in arrangements concerned with crime prevention and the relationship between victims and offenders.

1986   Government Circular – advises the police on the treatment of rape and domestic violence victims.

1986   Victim Support – receives political recognition and funding.

1988   Criminal Justice Act – requires the courts to give reasons for not ordering Compensation Orders because it was expected that the courts would make such an order in every case of death, injury, loss and damage.

1988   Government Circular – instructs the police to provide victims with feedback on their case.

1990   The Victim's Charter – published by the Home Office, requires the probation service to contact victims and/or their families in life sentence cases.

1991   Criminal Justice Act – increases the maximum sum of compensation from £2000 to £5000.

1995   Probation Circular 61/95 – issued by the Home Office and requires the probation service to contact victims of sex and violence offences.

1995   Victim Support, *The Rights of Victims of Crime* – a policy document providing a statement of rights to which Victim Support believes victims are entitled.

1996   The Victim's Charter – a revised edition extending contact to victims of offences of a violent and sexual nature where the offender is sentenced to imprisonment of four years or more.

1997   Protection from Harassment Act – deals with stalking, domestic abuse, racial harassment and neighbour disputes.

1998   Crime and Disorder Act – contains important measures regarding
        victims. For example, it introduced the Reparation Order (s. 67)
        that requires young offenders to make reparation to their
        victims.

2000   *The Victim Perspective: Ensuring the Victim Matters* was published by
        Her Majesty's Inspectorate of Probation. This was based upon a
        thematic inspection during 1999.

2000   Probation Circular 108/2000 – emerged from the HMIP report just
        alluded to.

2000   Section 69 of the Criminal Justice and Court Services Act placed a
        statutory duty on local probation boards to work with the victims of
        crime and extended victim contact. Probation now has a legal duty to
        contact victims of violent and sexual offences in cases where the
        offender has been sentenced to a term of imprisonment of 12 months
        and over.

2001   Probation Circular 62/2001 – provides guidance on the
        implementation of the above legislation.

2001   Home Office Circular 35/2001 – victim personal statements were
        introduced on 1 October 2001.

2003   Probation Circular 29/2003 – is important because it clarifies that
        when an offender is sentenced to imprisonment for 12 months or
        more for sex and violent offences, the Victim Liaison Officer (VLO)
        must consult the victim within two months of sentence. If the victim
        requests ongoing contact with the VLO he/she should be consulted so
        that representations can be made about release arrangements. The
        VLO should also take steps to inform the victim of, for example,
        appeals or temporary release, and if the offender is moved to an
        open prison.

Therefore, it is clear that the importance attached to victims over recent
years has escalated considerably and good communication is essential
between practitioners and VLOs to make the system work effectively. It is a
stretch objective in the document *A New Choreography* and since April 2003
has also been a cash-linked target (first contact between the VLO and victim
must be within two months of sentence). It is interesting to speculate on
whether the scope of victim work will expand beyond sex and violence
offences in the next few years (for example, dwelling-house burglary victims).
Importantly, probation practitioners must be concerned with victims and
offenders.

Further reading

Ashworth, A. (2000) *Sentencing and Criminal Justice* (3rd edn). London, Dublin and Edinburgh: Butterworths. This book contains references to victim issues that are worth perusing.

Garland, D. (2001) *The Culture of Control: Crime and Social Order in Contemporary Society*. Chicago: University of Chicago Press.

Home Office (2001) *A New Choreography, 2001–2004*. London: HMSO.

Spalek, B. (2003) Victim work in the probation service. In W.H. Chui & M. Nellis (eds), *Moving Probation Forward*. Harlow: Pearson Longman.

Zedner, L. (2002) Victims. In M. Maguire, R. Morgan & R. Reiner (eds), *The Oxford Handbook of Criminology* (3rd edn). Oxford and New York: Oxford University Press.

Finally the Home Office website is an important source of information on victims and other related areas: www.homeoffice.gov.uk.

Explaining offending behaviour: The search for patterns

In its work with offenders who are the subject of community sentences and licence supervision, in addition to the preparation of PSRs for the magistrates' and crown courts, the practitioner has a professional duty to provide a coherent explanation of each offender's behaviour. Moreover, practitioners need to be able to undertake this task in order to intervene effectively within the lives of offenders and to protect the public. The UKU item that captures this theme, which runs through most of the units at level 4, is articulated as follows: 'the ways in which the physical, social, psychological and emotional development and functioning of individuals affects their behaviour and its associated patterns'.

Even though it may be discerned that the word 'childhood' does not appear in this item of UKU, it is nevertheless being inferred because it should be acknowledged that practitioners cannot begin to explain patterns of adult behaviour unless attention is given to those significant influences and events during the early years of development. Everyone is influenced for good or ill by childhood experiences: whether parents or guardians were present or absent; how adults within the family related to their children; the experience of stability, security, continuity or disruption; attachment; whether there was significant trauma such as physical, emotional, sexual abuse and neglect. Offending is part of antisocial behaviour that normally begins in childhood and tends to persist into adulthood. Farrington (2002, p. 658) says that there is

> *significant continuity over time since the antisocial child tends to become the antisocial teenager and then the antisocial adult, just as the antisocial adult then tends to produce another antisocial child.*

Therefore, the practitioner needs to be aware that when attempting to illuminate current behavioural patterns it is the past, in all its complexity, that needs to be explored and understood.

During the period immediately following the 1991 Criminal Justice Act, which emphasised the current offence rather than the biographical details of the offender (a shift of emphasis reflecting the justice rather than the treatment model), it should be recalled that probation court reports became temporarily impoverished because they tended to overlook the importance of undertaking an assessment of the individual offender that included childhood and adolescent experiences. The reason for drawing attention to this point can be illustrated, for example, by turning to explanations of violence. The research indicates that violent offending is linked to childhood experiences of violence within the family. Furthermore, domestic violence has the highest occurrences in those households where offenders experienced a violent and abusive childhood, so that those who have witnessed violence between their parents are more likely to proceed to be abusers themselves. By using violent episodes as an example, practitioners need to ask the right questions about current patterns of adult behaviour which may involve the possibility that an explanation can be traced to childhood experiences. This insight also has implications for intervention strategies in the sense that uncovering serious trauma during the offender's formative years could well necessitate specialist resources beyond the scope of probation. The message for practitioners is that knowledge of the past informs the present.

Furthermore, it should be considered that where this item of UKU is concerned – focusing on explaining patterns of behaviour – the probation service has recourse to a number of overlapping theoretical frameworks that are designed to illuminate the aetiology of offending episodes (which should be covered during the academic component of the Dip.PS). First, criminology, a term that surfaced towards the end of the nineteenth century, has been defined as being;

> part of the apparatus of control in modern societies, as well as being concerned with the study of control. It is a body of knowledge developed to help the day-to-day work of police, courts, prison governors and medical officers, probation officers, social workers, and forensic psychiatrists, as well as to inform legislators and policy makers.
>
> HUDSON, 2002, p. 234

Second, sociology sheds light upon human behaviour as Anthony Giddens (1989, pp. 7–8) explains:

> Sociology is the study of human social life, groups and societies. It is a dazzling and compelling enterprise, having as its subject-matter our own behaviour as social beings. The scope of sociology is extremely wide,

*ranging from the analysis of passing encounters between individuals in the
street up to the investigation of global social processes.*

Third, psychology, which was established as an academic discipline in British
universities by the early 1900s, 'has been defined as the study of the mind,
as the study of behaviour, as the study of human information processing,
or just simply as the study of why human beings act as they do' (Hayes,
1998, p. 1). Therefore these disciplines provide practitioners with some of
the theoretical tools that inform the phenomenon of offending behaviour
they are trying to explain. In fact David Howe (1987, p. 12) says that 'a
theory may be defined as a set of concepts and propositions that present an
organised view of phenomena' by allowing their users to describe, explain,
predict and control. Criminological, sociological and psychological perspectives help practitioners to answer the question that needs to be posed
when attempting to make sense of offending episodes: What's going on here?
These disciplines help the practitioner to make connections between the
present and the past.

Let us conclude this section by introducing a caveat intended to remind practitioners that it is not always straightforward to ascertain, with precision, why
offending has occurred. This is because offending is often a consequence of
a multiplicity of factors that conspire to produce antisocial behaviour and
include: genetics, temperament, child rearing and socialisation, learned
behaviour from inappropriate role models, respondent and operant conditioning, thought processes, opportunities to offend, disinhibitors such as
alcohol and drugs, unsuitable accommodation, educational deficits, unemployment, poverty, and lack of recreational facilities. Disentangling these
factors to provide a coherent explanation for each unique individual offender
is complex, so we must be careful about what we think we know. Often we
know much less that we claim to know, which implies that, more often than
not, practitioners proceed on the basis of hypotheses rather than certainty.

Further reading

Downes, D. & Rock, P. (1998) *Understanding Deviance: A Guide to the Sociology of Crime
    and Rule Breaking*. Oxford: Oxford University Press.
Farrington, D. (2002) Developmental criminology and risk-focused prevention. In
    M. Maguire, R. Morgan & R. Reiner (eds), *The Oxford Handbook of Criminology*
    (3rd edn). Oxford and New York: Oxford University Press.
Giddens, A. (1989) *Sociology*. Cambridge: Polity Press.
Hayes, N. (1998) *Foundations of Psychology: An Introductory Text* (2nd edn). Surrey:
    Nelson.
Henry, S. & Einstadter, W. (1998) *The Criminology Theory Reader*. New York: New York
    University Press.
Hollin, C.R. (1989) *Psychology and Crime: An Introduction to Criminological Psychol-
    ogy*. London and New York: Routledge.

Home Office & HM Prison Service (2002) *Offender Assessment System (OASys) User Manual*. Home Office.

Kerfoot, M. & Butler, A. (1988) *Problems of Childhood and Adolescence*. London: Macmillan.

Smith, D. (1995) *Criminology for Social Work*. London: Macmillan. This is an excellent book for TPOs.

Smith, D.J. (2002) Crime and the life course. In M. Maguire, R. Morgan & R. Reiner (eds), *The Oxford Handbook of Criminology* (3rd edn). Oxford and New York: Oxford University Press.

The probation service and legislation 1861–2001

It is law and statute that gives the probation service its legitimacy. Probation officers are officers of the court and some knowledge about the legal context of probation practice is very important. It is also important to understand the structure and processes of the courts and the roles of the different agencies involved. Risk assessment and report writing form a particularly important part of the probation service contribution to the sentencing process, and these are dealt with separately and at greater depth in Chapter 5.

Andrew Ashworth (2000, p. 27) says that:

> Statutes passed by Parliament establish the framework of English sentencing law . . . Statutes lay down a maximum sentence for almost every offence. Legislation lays down the terms of the orders which a criminal court can make after conviction.

TPOs and other practitioners must have an appreciation of the legislation that underpins practice, primarily because the probation service is part of the criminal justice system and its work is undertaken within a legislative framework (from writing reports to the implementation and supervision of court orders). Trainees need an appreciation of this knowledge to complete the NVQ in a competent manner and to justify their claim to professionalism. Therefore this section maps out some of the most important items of legislation from mid-Victorian society until the present day in a way we hope is helpful.

1861   Offences Against the Person Act

1871 and 1879   Prevention of Crime Act

1879   Summary Jurisdiction Act

1887   Probation of First Offenders Act

1895   Gladstone Committee Report

1901   Borstal experiment introduced

1907   Probation of Offenders Act – This legislation formalised a system of
        probation that had been introduced during the 1870s as a voluntary
        scheme to keep people out of prison by the Police Court Missionaries
        of the Church of England Temperance Society. The 1907 Act was
        amended by the Criminal Justice Administration Act 1914; CJA 1925;
        CYPA 1933.

1908   Prevention of Crime Act – This legislation consolidated the Borstal
        system and Preventive Detention and empowered the court to impose
        upon an offender with three previous felony convictions since the age
        of 16, a sentence of PD between 5 and 10 years. The aim was to
        protect society from the more dangerous offenders.

1908   Children Act – This Act introduced separate courts for young offenders
        and restrictions on imprisonment for children.

1914   Criminal Justice Administration Act

1925   Criminal Justice Act

1933   Children and Young Persons Act – In this Act, Industrial and
        Reformatory Schools were abolished and replaced with Approved
        Schools for young offenders, and courts had to have regard to the
        'welfare' of the child. This legislation introduced Schedule 1 Offences.

1948   Criminal Justice Act – This legislation abolished birching, penal
        servitude, prison with hard labour and whipping, thus dismantling the
        Victorian system. Introduced the Attendance Centre Order and
        encouraged courts to use Borstal instead of prison for young offenders.
        It introduced the Detention Centre for 14- to 21-year-olds, and
        Corrective Training. The maximum period of Preventive Detention was
        raised from 10 to 14 years. This Act reflects a 'get tough' attitude in
        the immediate post-war period, but there are also elements of
        rehabilitation within the newly created welfare state. It replaced
        previous measures as the basic legislative framework for the probation
        service.

1952   Prison Act

1956   Sexual Offences Act

1959   Penal Practice in a Changing Society (Cmnd 645)

1959   Mental Health Act – This Act established arrangements for joint
       working between Health, SSD and, to a lesser extent, the criminal
       justice system.

1960   Report of the Committee on Children and Young Persons – Ingleby
       Report

1961   Criminal Justice Act – This Act increased the maximum level of fines for
       juveniles; and the minimum age for ACO was reduced from 12 to 10
       while hours were increased. Attempts were made to compel courts to
       use non-custodial sentences. The minimum age of imprisonment was
       raised from 15 to 17. Greater use of Borstal was encouraged instead of
       prison for offenders who were under 21 and the Act reduced the
       minimum age for a Borstal sentence from 16 to 15.

1963   Children and Young Persons Act

1964   Crime – A Challenge to us All – Longford Report

1965   The Child, Family and Young Offender (White Paper)

1967   Criminal Justice Act – Attempts made to compel courts to use non-
       custodial sentences; Preventive Detention and Corrective Training
       abolished; the Suspended Sentence and discretionary Parole to reduce
       the prison population introduced; the notion of rehabilitation in prison
       and subsequent release when there were signs that treatment was
       working. This Act also introduced the extended sentence to protect
       the public.

1968   Children in Trouble (White Paper)

1969   Children and Young Persons Act – The introduction of Care Orders,
       Supervision Orders and Intermediate Treatment for young offenders,
       instead of custody. Approved Schools replaced by Community Homes
       with Education. The 1969 Act, which built on the 1933 CYPA, was
       based on the notion that children who offend should, on the whole,
       not be treated differently to children in need or those in need of care
       and control.

During the mid-1960s the Home Secretary made a request to the Advisory Council on the Treatment of Offenders to consider ways of expanding the range of non-custodial sentences. A sub-committee was established under Baroness Wootton and reported in 1970. The central position of the probation service was confirmed in relation to the provision of non-custodial sentences. Wootton proposed Community Service Orders.

1971   Misuse of Drugs Act

1972   Criminal Justice Act – This legislation introduced the CSO; the Suspended Sentence Supervision Order; Bail Hostels; and Day Training Centres; in addition to the Deferred Sentence. Alternatives to custody introduced due to increased pressure on the prison system.

1973   Powers of the Criminal Courts Act

1974   Rehabilitation of Offenders Act (amended 1986)

1974   Health and Safety at Work, etc., Act

1975   Sex Discrimination Act – This outlawed treating people less favourably because of gender or marital status in areas of employment, education and housing.

1976   Bail Act

1976   Race Relations Act – It is unlawful to discriminate on the grounds of race, colour, nationality or ethnic origin in areas of employment, education and housing (amended in 2000).

1977   Criminal Law Act – Allowed a court to suspend a sentence of imprisonment in part.

1980   Magistrates' Court Act

1982   Criminal Justice Act – Replaced the indeterminate Borstal sentence with Youth Custody and a new minimum sentence of three weeks in DC. Introduction of statutory criteria relating to seriousness of offence which had to be satisfied before custody could be imposed. The Act also provided for an expanded range of conditions in Probation Orders. Suspended Sentences were abolished for offenders under 21 (and the 1991 CJA, in addition to the 2000 PCC(S) Act, retained the Suspended Sentences in a restricted form).

1982   Mental Health (Amendment) Act

1983   Mental Health Act

1984   Police and Criminal Evidence Act

1985   Prosecution of Offences Act – Established the Crown Prosecution
        Service.

1986   Public Order Act

1988   Criminal Justice Act – Youth Custody and Detention Centres were
        replaced with Young Offender Institutions. This Act introduced stiffer
        criteria into section 1(4) of the 1982 Act, which resulted in custody
        levels declining even further for young offenders. Courts were
        instructed to give reasons for not ordering compensation.

1989   Children Act – Belief in the effectiveness of an early severe sentence for
        young offenders had now given way to an approach based on
        minimum intervention, an important theme in the 1989 and 1991
        Acts. There was also emphasis on the welfare of the child.

1991   Criminal Justice Act – Main emphasis on strengthening statutory
        sentencing guidelines, reform of the parole system and introduction of
        a wider range of community penalties. Proportionality and Bifurcation
        – the punishment should fit the crime (commensurate with offence
        seriousness) and custody for the most serious cases only to protect the
        public from serious harm. Less emphasis on previous convictions.
        Restrictions on the use of the Suspended Sentence. Introduction of the
        Combination Order and Probation becomes a sentence in its own
        right, rather than an alternative to punishment. Introduction of the
        Unit Fine (linked to income) and Curfew Order that could be enforced
        by electronic monitoring. Increase in maximum compensation from
        £2000 to £5000. Also provided for the Extended Supervision of sex
        offenders following release from prison.

One of the central aims of the 1991 Act was to reduce the use of custodial
sentences for low/medium-range offences and to replace them with community sentences. Desert and proportionality became the primary rationale
of sentencing, except for rare cases when an incapacitative sentence for
public protection was required – s. 2(2)(b) 1991 Act; now Powers of Criminal Courts (Sentencing) Act 2000, s. 80(2)(b).

1993   Royal Commission on Criminal Justice (Runciman)

1993   Bail (Amendment) Act

1993   Criminal Justice Act – Amended the 1991 Act. Abolished the Unit Fine
       and instructed sentencers that when considering the seriousness of the
       offence they were permitted to take account of previous convictions
       and failure to respond to previous sentences, thus watering down the
       1991 Act.

From 1993 we begin to see the development of a more (populist) punitive
approach under the Conservatives when Michael Howard was appointed
Home Secretary (his 27-point plan on law and order). It persisted under
Labour after 1997. We begin to see the increased politicisation of sentencing policy.

1994   Sexual Offences Act

1994   Criminal Justice and Public Order Act – Secure Training Orders for 12-
       to 14-year-olds; revised bail law; right to silence redefined. This Act
       gave the police powers to tackle hunt saboteurs, raves and 'new age'
       travellers, that created outrage among civil liberties groups.

1994   Police and Magistrates' Courts Act

1995   Learmont Report on Prison Security

1996   Criminal Procedure and Investigations Act – This Act introduced new
       rules on disclosure of evidence and timing of pleas.

1996   Family Law Act

1997   Protection from Harassment Act

1997   Sex Offender Act – This Act established the sex offender register to
       keep track of sex offenders. This legislation encouraged the creation of
       multi-agency public protection panels that were put on a statutory
       footing by the Criminal Justice and Court Services Act 2000.

1997   Crime (Sentences) Act – Life imprisonment was mandatory for adults
       convicted of a second sexual or violent offence; seven years for a third
       offence of trafficking class A drugs; and three years for a third
       dwelling-house burglary offence. Therefore, this Act, and the CJPO Act
       1994, increased prison sentences for certain categories of offender.
       Consent was no longer necessary for a community sentence (s. 38).

The Crime (Sentences) Act 1997 introduced the first mandatory minimum
sentences since the mandatory sentence of life imprisonment for murder.

However the caveat is that there could be exceptional circumstances and that it may be unjust to impose the mandatory minimum. We may also question how this legislation fits with the Human Rights Act 1998.

1998　Crime and Disorder Act – Extended Sentences ss. 58–60, now s. 85 PCC(S)A 2000; Sex Offender Order (s. 2); DTTO. This legislation facilitated a collaborative approach between agencies in relation to Multi-Agency Public Protection Panels – MAPPP (s. 115). The Act also introduced new offences to deal with racist incidents, for example, racially aggravated assaults (Chapter 5 expands on these offences).

1998　Human Rights Act

1999　Youth Justice and Criminal Evidence Act

2000　Powers of Criminal Courts (Sentencing) Act – A consolidating statute that brought together most of the relevant sentencing law scattered across other legislation. This Act is important for the probation service.

It should be acknowledged that there were many changes in sentencing law during the 1990s that resulted in confusion, hence the need for consolidation. This Act brings together relevant provisions from previous legislation: CJA 1991; Crime (Sentences) Act 1997; Crime and Disorder Act 1998. However, some legislative provisions have already been overtaken by the Criminal Justice and Court Services Act 2000.

2000　Child Support, Pensions and Social Security Act – Sections 62/66 deal with enforcement implications.

2000　Criminal Justice and Court Services Act – Various community punishments were renamed: PO/CRO; CSO/CPO; COMBO/CPRO. It created the National Probation Service and initiated new procedures for dealing with victims. It also created two new community orders: Exclusion Order and Drug Abstinence Order. Also s. 53 makes imprisonment the anticipated penalty for a second breach of a community sentence. Implications for public protection partnership procedures – ss. 67/68 – by legislating for closer cooperation between probation and police (MAPPP).

2001　Criminal Justice and Police Act

Supplementary resources

1.   Data Protection Act 1998 and Crime and Disorder Act 1998 have implications for Confidentiality, Disclosure and Consent issues.

2.   Family Law Act 1996, Protection from Harassment Act 1997, and the Children Act 1989, have implications for Domestic Violence.

3.   Equal opportunities and diversity issues:

Equal Pay Act 1970

Race Relations (Amendment) Act 2000 was part of the Government's response to the Stephen Lawrence murder enquiry

Disability Discrimination Act 1995

Sex Discrimination Act 1975 and 1986 as amended

Employment Rights Act 1996

Asylum and Immigration Act 1996

Working Time Regulations 1998

Human Rights Act 1998

Amsterdam Treaty (Article 13)

Health and Safety at Work Act 1974

Protection from Harassment Act 1997

4.   Additional comment on the Human Rights Act 1998 is required. This legislation came into force on the 2 October 2000 and it is destined to call into question certain features of current sentencing law and practice. It requires all public authorities, including the courts and the probation service, to act in conformity with the European Convention on Human Rights (see Ashworth, 2000, p. 79). In conclusion we now await the legislative implications of the Halliday and Auld reviews and the impact of the Criminal Justice Act 2003.

Further reading

Ashworth, A. (2000) *Sentencing and Criminal Justice* (3rd edn). London, Dublin and Edinburgh: Butterworths.

Downes, D. & Morgan, R. (2002) The skeletons in the cupboard: The politics of law and order at the turn of the millennium. In M. Maguire, R. Morgan & R. Reiner (eds), *The Oxford Handbook of Criminology*. Oxford and New York: Oxford University Press.

Rex, S. (2003) 'What Works' in theories of punishment. In W.H. Chui & M. Nellis (eds), *Moving Probation Forward: Evidence, Arguments and Practice*. Harlow: Pearson Longman.

Stone, N. (2000) *A Companion Guide to Sentencing: Part 1, Specific Offences*. Kent: Shaw & Sons.

Stone, N. (2001) *A Companion Guide to Sentencing: Part 2, General Issues and Provisions*. Kent: Shaw & Sons.

Local area policies and guidelines

Since 2001 the work of the 44 area services has been heavily influenced by the creation of the National Probation Service. Even though area services have lost a degree of autonomy to the centre, in the form of the National Probation Directorate, nevertheless local areas are in possession of their own policies and best practice documents, sometimes referred to as practice guidelines. Therefore, in addition to trainees being required to have a working knowledge of underpinning legislation, it is equally important to understand the workings of each local service in relation to guidelines and multi-agency protocols; for example, domestic violence, public protection, child protection, sex offenders, and Schedule 1 offenders. For NVQ purposes trainees must familiarise themselves with these documents, which should be located within every office.

An increasingly important aspect of local practice is the role that probation plays in local and regional partnerships; as part of Crime and Disorder Reduction Partnerships, as partners in Drug Action Team strategies and in other partnership arrangements with voluntary and statutory agencies to deliver specific services or as part of particular social strategies, e.g. Multi-Agency Public Protection. Working competently and successfully across professional boundaries requires a particular and challenging set of attitudes, knowledge and skills. Furthermore, such work highlights relative power, differences in agency culture and contrasts in the structure and organisation of collaborating parties (Loxley, 1997).

Further reading

Leathard, A. (ed.) (1994) *Going Interprofessional: Working Together in Health and Welfare*. London: Routledge. This text offers a useful range of insights, theory and analysis.

Loxley, A. (1997) *Collaboration in Health and Welfare: Working with Difference*. London: Jessica Kingsley. This provides a useful context, analysis and practical guide to collaboration and partnership.

Payne, M. (2000) *Teamwork in Multiprofessional Care*. Basingstoke: Macmillan. This relates the task of working across professional boundaries to good practice in team building, team maintenance and team dynamics.

Professional values

This section conflates and considers the following overlapping UKU themes that can be found in the Occupational Standards for Community Justice: Equal Opportunities; Diversity; Anti-Discriminatory and Anti-Oppressive practices; Stereotyping and Bias; Culture and Gender; Ethnicity and Race.

It seems to us that several NVQ knowledge themes can be linked together because they help to locate probation practice within a clear ethical framework. It is important for all probation staff to have an understanding of the ethics and values that permeate the organisation and the resources being considered in this section establish certain parameters. It should initially be acknowledged that probation work can be enriched by personal values, perhaps of diverse origin, that may be brought into the organisation by its employees. Furthermore, there is often a high degree of compatibility between personal and professional values and this may be one of the reasons for working in a people-focused organisation. Nevertheless, it is important for all staff to have an understanding of, and commitment to, those distinctive professional values that shape probation practice. This section is concerned to yield insights, raise awareness, and develop an understanding of ethics and values.

It is a core ethical principle that no one should be denied the facilities and services provided by staff of the National Probation Service because of age, class, gender, race, religious beliefs, disability or sexual orientation. In fact it may be argued that it would be unjust and therefore unethical to favour one individual over another, or one group over another, and to do justice to some but not to others. This would neither be fair nor right, and to resort to this type of language reinforces the point that probation work with offenders is a moral enterprise of some significance. Nevertheless, trainee probation officers must be aware that while it is important to consider the notion of equal opportunities and equal access to services, offenders are not a homogeneous but rather a heterogeneous group. Therefore a balance needs to be struck between equal opportunities and the principle of diversity (respect for difference) that is concerned to respond to the differing needs of different offenders. In addition to the need to unpack the principles of equal opportunities and diversity, the ethical framework of practice must also take cognisance of anti-discriminatory practice (not to block opportunities or act on the basis of prejudice but to be aware of the professional demands of fairness and justice) and anti-oppressive practice (avoid being harsh, tyrannical, unjust and overbearing). These principles can be expanded by exploring the following related terms.

To stereotype is to perceive that an individual or group of people is considered to typify or conform to a specific pattern; for example, perceiving that

all offenders are heroin addicts, which is patently not the case as any practitioner will testify. To stereotype is to fail to treat each individual on his or
her own merits; it is a failure to differentiate between people. When turning
to the related notion of bias then it may be said that this is a preference or
inclination that inhibits impartial judgements to be made about someone. It
is linked to prejudice, which is an adverse judgement or opinion formed
beforehand about someone without being aware of all relevant information
or having a close examination of all the facts. Prejudice is a preconceived
preference that militates against an accurate and fair assessment of an
offender, which would be unprofessional. Consequently, TPOs, in addition
to all other practitioners, must be aware of the possibility of stereotyping,
bias and prejudice, because these attitudes do not contribute to professional
probation practice and run counter to those ethics and values that are important within the contemporary probation service, and of course the wider
society within which probation is located.

Within this section, in which we are considering a lexicon of significant
terms, we arrive at 'culture', which refers to the values, ideas and beliefs that
exist within different social groups. These values, ideas and beliefs help to
shape our experience in addition to helping us to make sense of the world
in which we live. Therefore within a multi-cultural society practitioners need
to be aware of and sensitive to the norms and values of people from other
cultures and races, which links with the professional duty to respect individual differences and cultural diversity. Next there is the concept of gender,
which can be contrasted with the term sex: sex equates to biological and
anatomical differences; the physical differences of the body. However, gender
equates with psychologically, socially and culturally constructed differences
between males and females. This distinction is important because some of
the differences between males and females are obviously not biological in
origin. Prior to concluding this section we should comment on ethnicity, race
and the specific issue of racial discrimination which, if promoted, would
offend the ethical framework of probation practice. Consequently, racial discrimination exists when the members of an ethnic minority are disadvan-
taged in some way and when one group has rights and opportunities denied
to others.

Therefore this section, essential for trainees within the context of working
towards the NVQ, has introduced a lexicon of terms that help to illuminate
the ethical context and value orientation of probation work with offenders.
It is clear that probation work is a moral enterprise in the sense that there
is a right and wrong, acceptable and unacceptable, way of engaging with
individuals who have committed offences. Moreover, this section has, by
implication, drawn attention to the importance of self-knowledge among
trainees, which involves possessing the insight, awareness and understanding that enables them to realise when practice does not conform to or

promotes the professional code of ethics that should prevail within the organisation. This point may be illustrated by accepting that, for a variety of complex personal reasons, it is not possible for practitioners to 'like' all offenders with whom they work; nor are they expected to. Nevertheless, regardless of one's own feelings about certain offenders it should be forcibly stated that there is an organisational expectation that judgements are arrived at and decisions made that adhere to a framework of professional values that may transcend personal values. This is the framework articulated within this section. Finally, at a much wider level it should be acknowledged that since 1997 the newly elected Labour Government has been committed to the principle of a more inclusive and fair society which, of course, has implications for all public services, including probation, with the result that there is a political dimension to the themes considered in this section that weave their way through the NVQ in Community Justice.

Further reading

Giddens, A. (1989) *Sociology*. Cambridge: Polity Press.
Home Office (2003) *Heart of the Dance: A Diversity Strategy for the National Probation Service for England and Wales, 2002–2006*. HMSO.
Phillips, C. & Bowling, B. (2002) Racism, ethnicity, crime, and criminal justice. In M. Maguire, R. Morgan & R. Reiner (eds), *The Oxford Handbook of Criminology* (3rd edn). Oxford and New York: Oxford University Press.

Risk assessment

Risk assessment has become as important as victim issues within probation practice over recent years. It has two main dimensions: risk of re-offending and risk of harm, which of course has implications for public protection. Farrington explains that 'Risk factors are prior factors that increase the risk of occurrence of the onset, frequency, persistence, or duration of offending' (2002, p. 664). The National Probation Service uses the OASys that enables staff to assess the risk of re-offending and harm, and identify offender's needs, by considering both static and dynamic factors. It facilitates the matching of offenders with appropriate interventions that are designed to reduce re-offending and manage the risk an offender poses to the public. It can also measure change over time. Therefore OASys is important but we would like trainees to reflect on the following discussion.

Practitioners must understand that OASys should not be endowed with a status it does not inherently possess. What we mean by this is that risk assessments produced by OASys (of re-offending and specifically harm) are only as accurate as the information fed into the instrument by the person who has interviewed the offender. In other words, the emphasis when making an assessment should be placed upon the professional skill of the practitioner:

- to engage with and relate to offenders;

- to interview insightfully and ask appropriate open and closed questions;

- to be aware of and understand what is going on in someone's life, which critically depends upon the ability to 'read' the whole person by giving and receiving verbal and non-verbal cues;

- to be able to communicate and weigh the significance of the information gleaned.

Therefore, the efficacy of an OASys assessment is predicated upon practitioners acquiring a range of skills associated fundamentally with interviewing and communicating. We should not confuse an instrument, important as this can be, with the dynamics of practice. Notwithstanding these important qualifications, the OASys manual rightly says that,

> OASys is a central part of evidence-based practice. It is designed to be an integral part of the work which practitioners do in assessing offenders; identifying the risks they pose, deciding how to minimise those risks and how to tackle offending behaviour effectively. OASys is designed to help practitioners to make sound and defensible decisions.
>
> HOME OFFICE, 2002, p. 3

We will turn to the tenets of evidence-based practice in the next section.

At this point let us turn again to the work of David Farrington (2002), which illuminates the issue of risk under discussion in this section. When looking at risk factors associated with offending behaviour he draws attention to: impulsivity, attention problems, low school attainment, poor parental supervision, parental conflict, an antisocial parent, young mother, large family, low family income and broken home. However, he goes on to say that the causal mechanisms linking risk factors and offending are less well established. In fact it should be remembered that many children at risk proceed to have successful lives, which raises the issue of the presence of compensatory protective factors. Farrington (2002, p. 680) also states that the Cambridge study found that it was generally true that each of the six categories of the following variables – impulsivity, intelligence, poor parenting, criminal family, socio-economic deprivation, child antisocial behaviour – predicted offending independently of each other category. Finally, if we return to OASys, the main criminogenic risk factors that practitioners need to be aware of when undertaking an assessment are: accommodation; education, training and employability; financial management and income; the quality of relationships; lifestyle and associates; drug and alcohol misuse; emotional well-being; thinking and behaviour; attitudes. The OASys manual helpfully reviews the empirical research into these areas associated with offending behaviour.

Consequently assessment involves formulating judgements and making decisions about the level of risk based upon all relevant information to reduce re-offending, protect the public from serious harm, and determine whether the probation service can intervene to manage these risks. The important areas of practice to draw attention to in relation to harm are domestic violence, child protection, sex offenders and Schedule 1, which have important implications for public protection procedures and multi-agency cooperation, informed by OASys, which enables practitioners to make defensible decisions. Moreover, probation assessments and risk-management strategies are contained within the conclusion of PSRs and then linked to supervision plans.

Further reading

Farrington, D. (2002) Developmental criminology and risk focused prevention. In M. Maguire, R. Morgan & R. Reiner (eds), *The Oxford Handbook of Criminology* (3rd edn). Oxford and New York: Oxford University Press.

Hollin, C.R. (2002) Criminological psychology. In M. Maguire, R. Morgan & R. Reiner (eds), *The Oxford Handbook of Criminology* (3rd edn). Oxford and New York: Oxford University Press.

Kemshall, H. & Pritchard, J. (1996) *Good Practice in Risk Assessment*, Volume 1. London: Jessica Kingsley.

Kemshall, H. & Pritchard, J. (1997) *Good Practice in Risk Assessment*, Volume 2. London: Jessica Kingsley.

The OASys manual contains lots of useful information on risk assessment, including the distinction between clinical (based upon the practitioner's experience and expertise) and actuarial (derived from methods used in the insurance industry that focus on the statistical calculation of probability).

Raynor, P. (2002) Community penalties: Probation, punishment and 'What Works'. In M. Maguire, R. Morgan & R. Reiner (eds), *The Oxford Handbook of Criminology* (3rd edn). Oxford and New York: Oxford University Press. It should be acknowledged that Raynor, from page 1190, refers to the Level of Service Inventory (LSI-R); Assessment, Case Management and Evaluation instrument (ACE); OASys; and the Offender Group Reconviction Scale (OGRS).

Robinson, G. (2003) Risk and risk assessment. In W.H. Chui & M. Nellis (eds), *Moving Probation Forward*. Harlow: Pearson Longman.

Effective practice/methods of working

Risk assessment and risk management strategies are associated with effective practice and specific methods of working (intervention logically follows

assessment). Some years ago (1970s to the early 1990s) the methods of intervention used by probation officers reflected the training that was undertaken
alongside social workers. For example, during the period of the CQSW (see
Chapter 1 for further information) the theory and practice of probation
interventions included the psychosocial approach that was part of the casework tradition, in addition to behaviourism, and even radical practice (see
Howe, 1987, for an excellent summary of these diverse methods of working).
By contrast, contemporary probation practice, detached from social work
training, has evolved in a cognitive-behavioural direction and put all its eggs
into one basket of accredited programmes/'What Works'. Effective practice
is about achieving intended results and outcomes, predominantly understood as reducing offending behaviour. The effectiveness research indicates
that (a) the higher the risk of re-offending, the more intensive and extended
the supervision programme should be (risk principle); (b) programmes that
target criminogenic needs are likely to be more effective (need principle); (c)
programmes that match the learning styles of staff and offenders, and
engage the active participation of offenders, are likely to be more effective
(responsivity principle). Research by Crow (2001, p. 73f) indicates that the
most effective programmes contain the following components:

- multi-modal (use a variety of methods that address criminogenic
  needs);

- skills-oriented (cognitive-behavioural, vocational, literacy and
  numeracy);

- model pro-social behaviour;

- programme integrity;

- community based;

- address social needs, which means that rehabilitation is associated with
  an awareness of wider social factors that impinge upon offenders such
  as education, training and employment, which is an important point
  to make;

- monitored and evaluated.

At this stage it may be helpful to touch upon the historical background and
theoretical framework for the cognitive-behavioural approach within probation. The term cognitive-behavioural, at first sight not easily accessible, is
a conflation of two psychological traditions stretching back into previous
centuries. First, the cognitive tradition is associated with Wilhelm Wundt,
William James, Herman Ebbinghaus and Piaget, who suggested that

behaviour is a consequence of mental processes. Alternatively, the behaviourist tradition associated with J.B. Watson and B.F. Skinner examined concrete observable idiosyncrasies such as mannerisms and verbal behaviour rather than what is purportedly and subjectively occurring within the mind and consequently hidden from view. Therefore, human behaviour within the behaviourist tradition is explained in terms of a stimulus–response (S–R) association in the sense that something happens in the environment to which the individual learns to respond, which is referred to as classical or respondent conditioning. Later Skinner pointed to learning as a process that follows the individual operating on the environment which results in certain consequences, the point being that actions with pleasant consequences are more likely to be repeated (operant conditioning). Both the cognitive and behaviourist approaches are trying to explain human learning and behaviour. The theoretical model that emerged from the conflation of these two traditions during the 1970s, and is currently used to underpin the effective practice agenda within the probation service, may be outlined as follows (McGuire, 2000):

$$S \quad - \quad O \quad - \quad R \quad - \quad C$$

Stimulus   Organism   Response   Consequences

The gist of the model is that a stimulus (an event in the environment) impacts upon the individual and elicits a behavioural response (S–R), which in turn results in certain consequences that have implications for reinforcing and shaping behaviour (C; or the ABC sequence of antecedents, behaviour, consequences). However, the model is incomplete unless we add the unique individual or organism (O) which involves the way in which the person responds to events because of the following factors: attention, perception, thought processes, memory and meanings attached to events. Moreover, it is said that the organism can be understood as having three distinct modalities:

- *Cognitive* – associated with thinking skills and processes, reasoning and problem-solving;

- *Emotional* – concerned with insight, awareness, self-expression and self-control;

- *Behavioural* – associated with pro-social ways of behaving.

According to this model, human behaviour is a result of the complex interplay of thoughts and feelings. However, if we can change the way people think, then we can change the way they feel and behave. In other words, if offending behaviour has to some degree been learned (by repeated S–R associations; actions eliciting pleasant consequences; Bandura's learning through imitation; cognitive processes) then it can be unlearned by a cognitive-behavioural approach that teaches problem-solving, thinking and social skills. Therefore the approach draws upon the psychological theories of behaviourism, cognitive theory and social learning theory.

It is assumed and expected that an individual learns to manage these complex facets – cognitive, emotional, behavioural – by experience and the positive example of other people during the process of growing up. However, the process of socialisation to which each individual is subjected may result in certain deficits which reinforce antisocial behaviour, but these deficits can, to some degree, be modified by appropriate interventions situated along the following cognitive-behavioural continuum, some of which resonate with the content of accredited programmes:

- Behaviour modification

- Behaviour therapy

- Social skills

    - Instruction

    - Modelling

    - Role-play

    - Feedback

    - Coaching

- Self-instructional training

- Problem-solving training

    - Problem awareness

    - Problem recognition

    - Differentiate facts and opinions

    - Generate alternative solutions to problems

    - Means–end reasoning

  –   Consequential thinking

  –   Perspective taking

•   Rational-emotive therapy

•   Cognitive therapy

In due course the probation service will establish a menu of accredited programmes: Think First, Priestly One-To-One, Aggressive Replacement Training Programme (ART), Drink Impaired Drivers (DIDs), Addressing Substance-Related Offending (ASRO) and Programme Reducing Individual Substance Misuse (PRISM). Nevertheless, it should be acknowledged that probation practitioners work with acutely impoverished people who have a range of individual and social problems. Therefore, in addition to accredited programmes other strategies will need to be utilised to encourage, facilitate, support and motivate offenders to engage in a process of change. Practitioners need to be aware of the cycle of change, motivational interviewing, relapse prevention, crisis intervention, task-centred approach, solution-focused therapy and pro-social modelling, and, in addition, should give assistance with employment, accommodation and basic skills.

Further reading

Chui, W.H. & Nellis, M. (2003) *Moving Probation Forward: Evidence, Arguments and Practice.* Harlow: Pearson Longman. Chapters 4, 5 and 8 provide excellent material for TPOs.

Crow, I. (2001) *The Treatment and Rehabilitation of Offenders.* London: Sage.

Chapman, T. & Hough, M. for HMIP (1998) *Evidence Based Practice: A Guide to Effective Practice.* London: HMIP.

HMIP (1998) *Strategies for Effective Offender Supervision: Report of the HMIP What Works project.* London: HMIP.

Hollin, C.R. (1989) *Psychology and Crime: An Introduction to Criminological Psychology.* London and New York: Routledge.

Hollin, C.R. (2002) Criminological psychology. In M. Maguire, R. Morgan & R. Reiner (eds), *The Oxford Handbook of Criminology* (3rd edn). Oxford and New York: Oxford University Press.

McGuire, J. (2000) *Cognitive-Behavioural Approaches: An Introduction to Theory and Research.* London: HMIP. This is an extremely useful background text for trainees on the theory and practice of cognitive-behavioural approaches.

Raynor, P. (2002) Community penalties: Probation, punishment and 'What Works'. In M. Maguire, R. Morgan & R. Reiner (eds), *The Oxford Handbook of Criminology* (3rd edn). Oxford and New York: Oxford University Press.

Miller and Rollnick (1991) is the authoritative text on motivational interviewing and is often looked at in conjunction with Prochaska and DiClemente (1983). The father of solution-focused approaches is de Shazer (1985), and O'Connell (1998) also provides an excellent introduction.

Communication

The rationale of probation work can be articulated in terms of achieving clearly defined organisational objectives and, over recent years, cash-linked targets. Within this framework it should be acknowledged that probation practice, at its core, is about people (in the form of trained practitioners) working with other people (offenders with a range of personal and social problems). Therefore it is important that trainees, in addition to all practitioners, must be able to communicate with colleagues and clients in pursuit of service targets. In fact effective communication is a fundamental prerequisite of practice from assessment skills and interviewing, to methods of intervention; it is an essential building block of effective practice that concerns the transmission of information from one person to another. We need to be aware of four important features of communication:

- *Verbal* – What we say by word of mouth; selection of words; asking questions and interviewing skills. Verbal communication involves asking closed questions that invite a 'yes' or 'no' answer (e.g. Are you employed?); open questions that facilitate the exploration of problems and situations from the client's perspective (e.g. What concerns you at the moment?).

- *Non-verbal* – Aspects of behaviour including body language, eye contact, facial expressions, posture, gesture and touch.

- *Written* – Trainees must acquire the skill of writing PSRs for courts, writing letters, completing case records, and OASys.

- *Symbolic* – This is an important dimension of communication that involves, for example: the way we dress, conveying a professional attitude (or not) to the job; being on time for appointments as a courtesy to colleagues and clients; not being disturbed by the telephone when interviewing a client, as this can communicate discourtesy and should be avoided.

It should be emphasised that interviewing is a significant aspect of communication within probation work and trainees need to be aware of the importance of attentive and active listening; reflecting back to clients what we think they have communicated to clarify that we have understood the meaning of what they have conveyed; summarising; and being alert to verbal and non-verbal cues that aid the process of understanding and assessment.

If practitioners are involved in interviewing an offender to prepare a PSR for the magistrates' or crown court, then good communication is essential to produce an accurate assessment of the offender's circumstances that must be conveyed to the court to facilitate the sentencing process. Therefore, it is critically important to listen carefully and be aware of what the client is communicating both verbally and non-verbally. In fact the skill of listening to other people appears to be a dying art form in many human encounters, and in our experience there are more talkers than listeners in probation. On this point Lishman says that 'In order to understand our clients and their problems we must be able to attend and listen to them' (1994, p. 58). The implication of this is that practitioners must be conscious of being disciplined in the interview situation: ask pertinent open and closed questions; be clear about the result you want to achieve; wait until the client has finished replying to your question before continuing; don't interrupt in your anxiety to progress the interview; try to be relaxed and keep calm because if not you will communicate anxiety that is not conducive to the interview. In other words, you speak by posing relevant questions, but then you listen while the client replies; and don't be afraid of silence. This is an art of conversation that needs to be practised to facilitate an effective interview.

One caveat to which we need to draw attention when communicating with offenders is the distinction between the world of objects and subjects, elucidated by David Howe (1987). Think about the following: when communicating with an offender in order to undertake an assessment (for example, preparing a PSR for court) do we think we are (a) describing the real objective nature of things as they exist and are understood by the client; or (b) imposing meaning on the client derived from our theoretical frameworks (for example, criminological theories, sociological perspectives and psychological insights)? There seems to be a profound difference between perceiving that we are objectively describing what is real and important for the client; and imposing onto clients some patterns and meanings that are derived from our own frame of reference and favourite theoretical perspective. This is a distinction to be aware of, and it is important, as far as we are able, to pose clear questions when interviewing. We should check things out, reflect back and clarify the meaning and level of understanding. Furthermore, the OASys instrument includes an opportunity for the client to complete a self-assessment form that helps to narrow the gap between the objective and subjective distinction elucidated by Howe. This section on communication is intended to yield insights, develop awareness and facilitate understanding of an important skill within probation practice, in addition to providing underpinning knowledge resources for the NVQ.

An important aspect of communication is the relationship within which the communication takes place. Probation officers need to be clear in their own minds – and clear to offenders and others with whom they are communicating – what the boundaries are to that relationship, i.e. what kind of relationship it is. This involves being transparent about, for example, the purpose of assessment, the objectives of programmes and the consequences of failing to comply with requirements. The great art is to forge constructive and positive relationships in such a context. Inevitably such relationships bring tensions and sometimes conflict, therefore probation officers need to be able to model assertiveness as opposed to aggression and be aware of the impact of their own emotions (including anger) on the relationship. They also need to learn skills in relation to handling aggression, to understand how to listen for and spot cues for aggression and to learn good practices in terms of maximising their own physical and emotional safety.

Further reading

Hayes, N. (1998) *Foundations of Psychology: An Introductory Text*. Surrey: Nelson. Chapter 15 includes helpful information on non-verbal communication.

Howe, D. (1987) *An Introduction to Social Work Theory*. Aldershot: Wildwood House. See, particularly, Chapter 4 on the world of objects and subjects.

Lishman, J. (1994) *Communication in Social Work*. Basingstoke: Macmillan. This is a highly recommended book for trainees because it explores the following practice issues: types of communication; the communication skills necessary for building and maintaining helping relationships (genuineness, warmth, acceptance, encouragement and approval, empathy, responsiveness and sensitivity); attending and listening. These are the practical skills required for effective practice.

For a good guide to aggression, assertiveness and best practice in handling aggression and potential violence, see Gillen (1998) and Leadbetter and Trewar (1996).

Enforcement and compliance

There is an expectation that offenders who, rather than being given a custodial sentence, are made the subject of a community sentence and are provided with an opportunity to atone for their behaviour within the community, should adhere to the basic requirement of such a sentence, which is to maintain regular contact with the probation service. The rationale underpinning regular contact is: (a) to ensure that offenders comply with the sentencing decision imposed by the court; (b) to uphold the rule of law; and (c) to protect the public. Moreover, if an offender does not serve the community sentence in the manner expected by the court, for example, by not maintaining weekly contact with the supervising officer during the first three months, in addition to any other requirements that may be imposed, then it is obvious that the sentence cannot have the required impact, which militates against the reduction of crime and public protection (Home Office, 2001, p. 29).

While it is reasonable to expect offenders to adhere to the requirements of a community sentence imposed by the courts, supervising officers are nevertheless well aware that the issues of enforcement and compliance are fraught with moral dilemmas. It may be argued that a high proportion of offenders have not been inculcated with a disposition to conform to the basic tenet of a community sentence, which is to maintain regular and planned contact. This could be explained by a history of family difficulties; poor socialisation into the norms of appropriate behaviour, including time-keeping; impoverished childhood and adolescent experiences culminating in alienation and apathy concerning conventional norms of behaviour; lack of appropriate role models from whom to learn the importance of keeping appointments at the required time; impoverished education; unstable relationships and accommodation; in addition to problems with drugs, alcohol and mental illness. Furthermore, Mair and May (1997, p. 30) state that 'the poverty and deprivation exhibited by those on probation is an important factor which is likely to have implications for supervision and should not be forgotten or dismissed'. Consequently, these are some of the factors associated with offending behaviour in the first instance and which also constitute an explanatory framework for understanding why a proportion of offenders find themselves the subject of breach action. Therefore, while the probation service does not and should not condone missed appointments by offenders, there is little doubt that supervising officers readily understand why certain offenders struggle to comply with the basic requirement of a community order, which is to keep regular appointments at the appropriate time. Indubitably the proper enforcement of orders is important, for the reasons already alluded to above. Furthermore, the national target for breach action in accordance with National Standards is 90% of relevant cases, and it is a cash-linked target. Therefore, the next section will turn to National Standards to clarify probation practice on enforcement.

National Standards and enforcement

National Standards (2000, revised 2002) at section D deals with the required levels of contact for those offenders aged under 22 or serving 12 months or more in custody; offenders released on licence; community rehabilitation and punishment orders. It is reinforced that minimum levels of contact, in addition to enforcement, serves two main functions: (1) to satisfy the court and wider community that a credible level of disciplined supervision is taking place, and (2) ensuring that all offenders have the opportunity to engage in effective supervision. Therefore, any failure to comply by not keeping appointments demanded by community sentences or licence supervision shall be deemed to be unacceptable unless the offender provides an acceptable explanation. It is unnecessary to duplicate the text of National Standards; nevertheless it is necessary to refer to the process that is invoked when appointments are not kept, particularly where community sentences are concerned:

- Where no explanation is provided to the supervising officer within two working days of an apparent failure to keep an appointment, the supervising officer will send a final warning letter explaining that if an acceptable explanation is not received within a further five working days of the date of the letter, the failure will be deemed unacceptable and that further failure could lead to breach action.

- If the offender provides an acceptable explanation within the above timescale of seven days, the supervising officer should rescind the warning and withdraw it from the file.

- The supervising officer must fully record every apparent failure within seven working days of the failure.

- If the explanation is unacceptable or no explanation is given within seven working days of the failed appointment, record it as an unacceptable failure to comply and place copies of the written warning in the case record.

- When breach action is required, usually a consequence of two unacceptable absences during a 12-month period (and subsequent to a final warning and intention to breach letters), the supervising officer must instigate breach action within ten working days of the failure to comply (which is the cash-linked target). Although it should be acknowledged that, in appropriate circumstances, breach action is permissible after one unacceptable absence rather than the normal two.

- In normal circumstances supervising officers should continue to offer appointments when a breach is pending before the court.

Sanctions for breach of community orders and licences

In those circumstances where offenders fail to adhere to the requirements of community sentences, supervising officers must be clear about the appropriate application to make to the court. In cases where offenders *will not* comply, the supervising officer proceeds with a prosecution/breach. By contrast, if an offender *cannot* comply, for whatever reason, then the procedure will be revocation rather than prosecution. This important distinction – which is sometimes confused in the minds of supervising officers, primarily because revocation can also be an outcome of prosecution proceedings – is clarified in Figure 4.1.

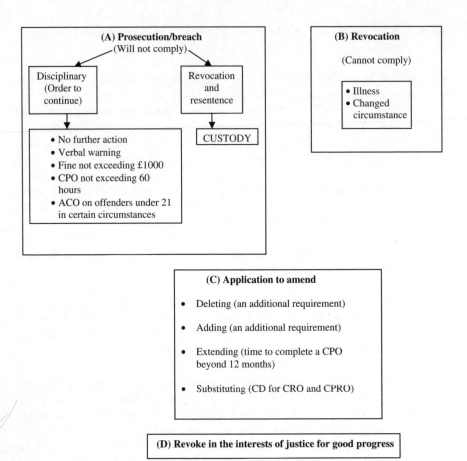

Figure 4.1 Distinction between offenders who will not/cannot comply

Where licences are concerned it is not our intention to delve into detail about available sanctions. This is because the service has access to numerous documents which discuss licence enforcement practice (for example: National Standards – Stone, N. (1999) *A Companion Guide to Enforcement*, 3rd edn) which obviates the necessity for duplication. However, it can be briefly stated that, depending upon the type of licence – No Further Action, Financial Penalty, Custody, or Recall to Prison – constitutes the main sanctions either through the courts or the Sentence Enforcement Unit.

Likely consequences of breach action for offenders subject to community sentences

Even though the probation service has a professional duty to initiate breach action in appropriate circumstances, it should be acknowledged that such action may have serious consequences for offenders, thus militating against a central objective of probation practice, which is to facilitate the rehabilitation of offenders within the community. In fact there are three main points to establish. First, if offenders do not keep their appointments or comply with other reasonable requirements, this could culminate in the loss of all or part of their benefit entitlement for up to four weeks (the benefit sanction that operates in certain areas at the time of writing). However, this will only occur if the offender is aged between 18 and 59 and subject to a community rehabilitation, community punishment, or community punishment and rehabilitation order. Moreover, the offender must be claiming Jobseeker's Allowance and Income Support, or claiming the following training allowances: Work Based Learning for Adults, New Deal for Young Persons, Intensive Activity Period, Intensive Activity Period 50 Plus. The sanction to lose all or part of one's benefit is a consequence of ss. 62/66 of the Child Support, Pensions and Social Security Act 2000. Second, according to s. 53 of the Criminal Justice and Court Services Act 2000, a custodial sentence may result for a second breach of a community order, thus contradicting the original intention of the court, which was to deal with the offender in the community. Third, the breach of a community sentence will appear on the offender's criminal record. Therefore if, in future, the offender re-offends following the termination of the current community sentence and the matter is adjourned for the preparation of a PSR, the author of the report has a duty to analyse the offender's response to previous sentences. This means that a previous breach will be viewed as an aggravating factor that could reduce the possibility of another community sentence being imposed. Therefore, it is clear that breach action initiated by the supervising officer in response to the behaviour of an offender can have serious consequences. At this point we want to turn to the equally important issue of reducing the likelihood of breach proceedings by encouraging compliance.

Improving compliance

Compliance is the act of yielding to a wish, request or, within the context of this discussion, a demand enshrined within legislation, supported by National Standards. However, an interesting paper by Tony Bottoms (2001) provides a conceptual framework for understanding the mechanisms of compliant behaviour by identifying four main types:

(a)   Instrumental/prudential compliance (based upon self-interested calculation);

(b)   Normative compliance (based on a felt moral obligation, commitment or attachment);

(c)   Constraint-based compliance (derived from some form of constraint or coercion);

(d)   Compliance that is based on habit or routine.

With this framework in mind the following suggestions should be carefully considered as the means by which compliance can be facilitated and improved by probation practitioners.

Clear communication

At the commencement of a community order (and licence) it may be suggested that it is important to have clear communication between the supervising officer and the offender. Section D9 of National Standards states that offenders must receive a leaflet which clarifies expectations during the supervisory period, including standards of behaviour: to ensure that the order or licence has been signed; to explain that appointments with partnership agencies, if not kept, can also be enforced (D10). It is at this initial stage of the supervisory process that the supervising officer must reinforce the importance of maintaining regular contact and discuss the consequences of non-compliance, particularly where the benefit sanction is concerned. Even though it is important to consider the significance of clear communication at the commencement of a court order to encourage compliance, it should also be acknowledged that good communication should be a feature of effective probation practice at the PSR stage, specifically if a community sentence is being proposed, in addition to court procedures immediately following the imposition of an order. In other words, at certain key stages of probation service–offender contact, the importance of complying with court orders should be clearly communicated to offenders.

How to engage with and relate to offenders

In 1971 Ian Sinclair examined data from 46 Approved Probation Hostels which revealed that 'failure rates', while offenders remained at the hostels, varied from 14% to 78%, and that this variation was only partially accounted for by differences in previous offences and the social histories of offenders. However, when explaining this variation Sinclair referred to the modus operandi within the hostels and found that successful hostels had staff that combined emotional warmth, kindness, and an understanding of residents' problems, in addition to administering the rules of the hostel in a fair and consistent manner. Furthermore, Lishman (1994) says that those features which are important when building a relationship are: genuineness, respect, warmth, acceptance, encouragement, approval, empathy, responsivity and sensitivity. Therefore, the point being established here is that *all* probation staff who engage with, and relate to, offenders (from administrators and clerical staff, to trainees and other supervising) should reflect carefully upon how probation work is undertaken, and how they interact with offenders, in order to create the conditions that are conducive to facilitating compliance. The issues being alluded to here relate to the notions of practitioner legitimacy and credibility. See Appendix 6 for a fuller discussion on the 'what' and 'how' of practice.

Respond to offenders' needs

Within the context of thinking about 'What Works' and effective interventions within the probation service, Iain Crow (2001, p. 86f) engages in a discussion that has implications for improving compliance. The main points alluded to may be summarised as follows:

- The type and level of intervention must be matched to the individual offender, which is premised upon accurate assessment (facilitated by OASys) and means that more intensive programmes are directed at higher-risk offenders.

- Be responsive to offenders' needs, which means that supervising officers should discover what offenders respond to best. It is more effective to be interactive, inclusive and engaging, than didactic.

- Focus on criminogenic needs such as drugs, alcohol, accommodation, literacy and employment. Therefore, it is important to supplement and complement a cognitive-behavioural approach to working with individual offenders by giving attention to addressing wider social issues.

- Adopt a multi-modal approach, which means that we should use more than one approach when working with offenders, in addition to addressing various problems.

The point being suggested here is that, as the probation service becomes more sophisticated in its work with offenders, then by refining effective methods of working this could have a positive impact upon compliance rates. This point can be elaborated further in the next section.

Methods of working

Under this heading we want to refer to three specific areas of work. First, *cognitive-behavioural approaches* hold out the prospect that if we can facilitate change within offenders' thinking patterns, then behaviour associated with offending episodes will be changed. Consequently it is theorised that the probation service should address the following areas within supervision: impulsivity; consequential thinking; empathy; conceptual rigidity manifested in the way some offenders resort to repetitive patterns of self-defeating behaviour; poor interpersonal problem-solving skills; egocentricity; and poor critical reasoning. Second, *pro-social modelling* is about the supervising officer modelling anti-criminal behaviour and reinforcing pro-social attitudes and responses. Accordingly, the supervising officer acts as a role model in relation to appropriate relationships; problem-solving attitudes; attending appointments and good time-keeping; thinking about other people. Third, *motivational interviewing* embodies a directive but non-confrontational approach that encourages offenders to accept personal responsibility for change. It also accentuates dissonance and explores ambivalence between where offenders are now and where they want to be in future. This involves considering advantages and disadvantages of situations with a view to exploring the consequences of offending behaviour. Therefore, it is considered that working with offenders that employ these approaches will help to reduce re-offending and, by implication, improve compliance. This section can be supplemented by referring to Appendix 5.

Flexibility

Attention should be given to facilitating and encouraging a flexible approach when working with offenders which means, for example, reflecting on the most appropriate way of responding to the following situation. If an offender has an appointment for 10 a.m. Monday morning but arrives at 3 p.m. instead, is this apparent failure to keep a scheduled appointment being classified as an unacceptable absence by supervising officers? It is not unreasonable to assume that by 3 p.m. the supervising officer is no longer located at the office but attending to other duties and thus unable to see the offender. However, in this situation the offender could be seen by the duty officer and provided with a new appointment to prevent the drift towards enforcement action being initiated. The issue here is responding imaginatively and flexibly to varying needs and circumstances, which takes account of the needs and problems of offenders. Linked to this flexible approach are two related points. First, supervising officers should think carefully about the provision of sensible appointment times for certain offenders that coincide with their daily routines. However, it should be acknowledged that a balance must be struck between offender needs and supervisor responsibilities and availability. Second, there should be a balance between office and home visits to facilitate compliance. Occasionally practitioners must go the extra mile and visit the offender at home.

Enlisting appropriate help

Some offenders need all the help they can get to comply with the demands of National Standards. Therefore supervising officers need to think about enlisting the help of family members, partners, or any significant other people in this process. This should be explored with offenders at the commencement of the order to enhance the likelihood of compliance.

Technological solutions

Is it possible that alarm clocks, and mobile telephones for the sending of text messages, could be used to facilitate compliance? The imaginative use of technology should be considered, and could complement the current practice of contacting the offender by telephone to remind him/her of his/her appointment. In fact it may be suggested that there is the scope to broaden the practice of reminding an offender by telephone to keep his/her appointment. To argue that offenders should be responsible for remembering appointment days and times is good theory, but unimaginative and unhelpful practice if it results in breach proceedings.

Weekly tasks

One method to encourage offenders to comply with court orders and therefore maintain their interest in the process of supervision could be for supervising officers to set specific tasks between appointments, related to the supervision plan. This method of working is a feature of the Priestly One-to-One accredited programme, which could be utilised more widely.

Incentives

It may be argued that to revoke a community sentence for good progress provides an incentive for offenders sentenced at the magistrates' court to comply. Moreover, the probation service should, in the interests of justice and compliance, initiate a debate with crown court judges to explore similar opportunities for developing revocation practice. The point being suggested here relates to the type of compliance referred to by Bottoms (2001) as instrumental or prudential, which means that offenders comply with orders because of self-interest. In other words, revocation for good progress, prior to the expiry date on the order, provides them with an incentive to comply. Additionally, this practice is consistent with pro-social modelling that praises and rewards manifestations of pro-social behaviour.

Consequently it appears that a number of initiatives (no doubt this list can be expanded) can be usefully considered which could improve compliance and thus reduce the necessity for enforcement proceedings leading to breach action which can create enormous problems for the clients of the service.

Further reading

Bottoms, A.E. (2001) Compliance and community penalties. In A. Bottoms, L. Gelsthorpe & S. Rex (eds), *Community Penalties: Change and Challenges*. Devon, UK: Willan Publishing.

Crow, I. (2001) *The Treatment and Rehabilitation of Offenders*. London: Sage.

Hedderman, C. (2003) Enforcing supervision and encouraging compliance. In W.H. Chui & M. Nellis (eds), *Moving Probation Forward: Evidence, Arguments and Practice*. Harlow: Pearson Longman.

Home Office (2001) *A New Choreography: An Integrated Strategy for the National Probation Service for England and Wales, Strategic Framework 2001–2004*. Home Office.

Lishman, J. (1994) *Communication in Social Work*. Basingstoke: Macmillan.

Mair, G. & May, T. (1997) *Offenders on Probation*, HORS 167, HMSO.

National Standards (2000; revised 2002) *National Standards for the Supervision of Offenders in the Community*. Home Office.

Sinclair, I. (1971) *Hostels for Probationers*, HORS 6, HMSO.

Self-reflection and personal development

This theme is dealt with separately in Chapter 7.

Confidentiality

If there is one area of practice that is determined to create tension for trainees it is the responsibility to disentangle the demands of confidentiality from the disclosure of information in circumstances not requiring consent. The premise operating in probation is that information will normally be shared with offenders except in those circumstances where it could result in harm to others. Furthermore, probation records should be perceived as open documents in the sense that offenders are entitled to view them, unless the stored information could inflict harm, in which case it would be stored in the confidential section of the case file. Consequently, it may be stated that there is a predisposition to share information with offenders, and that client confidentiality should be respected. Nevertheless, certain qualifications apply. Therefore, potential tensions and conflicts can be dealt with professionally if practitioners adhere to certain principles of good practice that will now be considered.

- Always have a care to respect the confidentiality of offenders (in addition to members of staff).

- Operate on a need-to-know basis when sharing information with staff in other agencies. However, protocols should exist for the sharing of confidential offender information.

- It is good practice both at the PSR stage and then subsequently with offenders on community orders to obtain their consent if information is required from a variety of sources, particularly for assessment purposes. An appropriate consent form can be used to facilitate this process if signed by the offender that is designed to alleviate any potential confidentiality problems.

- Remember that the service has an open record policy that has implications for OASys and case records. Nevertheless confidential information that should not be disclosed to an offender can be stored in appropriate confidential sections.

- In certain circumstances information on offenders can be disclosed to other agencies without their consent under s. 29(3) of the Data Protection Act 1998; also s. 115 of the Crime and Disorder Act 1998. Additional information will be provided on this legislation below.

- If you are contacted for information by, for example, someone who purports to be from the Social Services Department, do not provide information unless you can verify the status of the caller (usually by taking details of the caller and ringing back).

- Remember that breach of confidentiality can result in disciplinary proceedings. Therefore the issue needs to be treated with respect and you must consult with a senior officer if you are at all concerned or unsure about the correct procedures.

Relevant legislation

(a) Section 29(3) of the Data Protection Act 1998 says that disclosure can be made, without consent, if it is for the purpose of the prevention or detection of crime, apprehension or prosecution of offenders, and where failure to disclose would be likely to prejudice these objectives.

(b) Moreover s. 115 of the Crime and Disorder Act 1998 ensures that all agencies have a power to disclose where it is necessary or expedient for the purpose of any provision of the Act. A provision of the Act is the prevention and detection of crime, reducing crime or the fear of crime.

The National Probation Service is in the business of working with offenders to rehabilitate, manage risk and protect the public. To achieve these objectives trainees and other practitioners have to balance the right of the offender to confidentiality and respect, with wider responsibilities to other agencies and the community that may involve the disclosure of information without the consent of the offender. It is permissible to do the latter in certain circumstances, specifically when the issues concern public protection and child protection.

Further reading

Each area service will have its own guidelines and protocols on confidentiality that should be consulted.

Conclusion

This chapter provides resources for trainees (and other practitioners) on the following NVQ underpinning knowledge themes: victims; explaining offending behaviour; legislation; local area practice guidelines; professional values; risk assessment and effective practice; communication; enforcement and compliance; confidentiality. We envisage that these resources can be utilised primarily as a basis for discussion between the trainee and PDA on UKU, but they will also complement the academic component of the Dip.PS. The next chapter continues to provide knowledge resources by turning to the preparation of PSRs, an important probation task that requires detailed knowledge.

Summary

This chapter addresses 11 knowledge themes that emerge from an analysis of the knowledge and understanding requirements of the NVQ level 4 in Community Justice. Each theme is discussed separately and suggestions are made for further reading and learning in relation to each one.

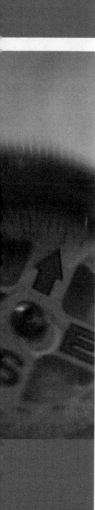

Chapter 5

Knowledge resources for trainees: Writing quality Pre-Sentence Reports

Introduction

According to Joan King (1964, p. 5) the work of the Police Court Missionaries before the Probation of Offenders Act 1907 involved attending police
courts, visits to homes and prisons, helping offenders to find or keep employment. Additionally, some magistrates in London were using missionaries to
report on the homes and other circumstances of offenders. Building on this
last point William McWilliams (1983) says that around 1889, missionaries
were being used to undertake pre-sentence investigations even though they
did not have the legislative authority (also see Herbert & Mathieson, 1975,
p. 10). Some years later the Probation Rules of 4 June 1926 made by the
Secretary of State under the Probation of Offenders Act 1907, and Part 1
of the Criminal Justice Act 1925, says that: 'Rule 37: A Probation Officer
shall make such preliminary enquiries, including enquiries into the home
surroundings, as the court may direct in respect of any offender in whose
case the question of the making of a Probation Order may arise' (Le
Mesurier, 1935, Appendix 3).

During the 1930s Le Mesurier provides intriguing details of the information
required in a (juvenile) court report under the heading of the Environment,
that included: home conditions, family, father and mother details, other relations, employment record, recreation, associates, religious influences, and
school record. Additionally under Personal History there are four main
headings: childhood, behaviour and habits, temperament, physical and
mental ability. It is of historical interest to give the reader a taste of the
information required at this period – relating to behaviour and habits – that
the probation officer needed to consider:

> *Personal cleanliness; incontinence; any pilfering habits; wandering; record*
> *of truancy and causes; temper displays; lying, whether protective or appar-*
> *ently meaningless. Sex: masturbation; promiscuous intercourse; prostitu-*
> *tion; perversions. Tobacco; drink or drugs, extent of habits; betting and*
> *gambling, state form and extent. Method of spending leisure time; is it*
> *habitual, e.g. cinema attendance? Reading: type of book. Peculiarities in*
> *speech, dress, etc.*
>
> LE MESURIER, 1935, p. 94

This reads like an early attempt to establish National Standards for court
reports.

Moving on, paragraph 336 of the Streatfield Committee (Home Office, 1961)
stated that 'our cardinal principle throughout is that sentences should be
based on reliable, comprehensive information relevant to what the court is
seeking to do' (which takes us beyond the rationale of a report, during the

early years of practice, to determine the suitability of an offender for a probation order only). The period following the Streatfield Committee witnessed an increase in Social Enquiry Reports which, by the time we arrive at the Statement of National Objectives and Priorities in 1984, were understood as important documents in the process of diverting offenders from custodial sentences. Then, as a consequence of the Criminal Justice Act 1991, Social Enquiry Reports were renamed Pre-Sentence Reports (PSRs) which TPOs must learn how to write during their training. The following is an attempt to facilitate the process of acquiring relevant knowledge and skill of what may be perceived as one of the most important pieces of work practitioners undertake and which encapsulates core probation skills, namely: the ability to engage with and relate to offenders; interviewing and posing the right questions; communication; assessment; selecting effective methods of intervention; self-reflection and evaluation. Consequently we need to look at the knowledge resources for this piece of work in some detail.

Rationale

Section 162(1) of the Powers of Criminal Courts (Sentencing) Act 2000 states that a PSR is 'a report in writing which, with a view to assisting the court in determining the most suitable method of dealing with an offender, is made or submitted by an appropriate officer'.

Moreover, National Standards clarifies that 'The purpose of a PSR is to provide information to the sentencing court about the offender and the offences committed and to assist the court to decide on suitable sentence' (National Standards, 2000; revised 2002). This is a view echoed by the Magistrates' Sentencing Guidelines and the New Choreography document published in 2001. Therefore PSRs are documents that fundamentally contribute to the sentencing process.

Defining quality

In all areas of probation practice from community supervision and resettlement, to hostels, prisons and court work, the National Probation Service is charged with the responsibility of delivering quality services. Where PSR writing is concerned, quality may be defined as the aspiration to prepare first-class, excellent documents, written to the highest possible standards. This means that a quality report is one where the content demonstrates to the reader that the author has a clear grasp and insightful understanding of the sometimes complex reasons why a person has offended and what, if any-thing, the probation service can do about it to reduce offending and prevent harm to others. Furthermore, the notion of quality includes the identifica-tion of present and future risks, and proceeds to explain how such risks posed by an offender can be managed. Therefore quality in PSR writing is premised upon the notion of sound assessment, which is a process that eval-uates and judges a person's character, offending behaviour, attitudes, and risk to the public. A quality PSR is informed by the academic disciplines of psychology, sociology, criminology and law. Quality also depends on the report writer's knowledge and experience of offenders and the criminal justice system, in addition to coaching and feedback received during super-vision by a service manager (not forgetting consultation and the sharing of ideas with peers). There will be occasions when, faced with competing demands, practitioners prepare reports that are classified as 'good enough'. Nevertheless the aspiration should be to produce quality documents, a notion informed by National Standards in the next section.

Process

The process of report writing is informed by National Standards which specify that reports must:

- be based on at least one face-to-face interview with the offender;

- specify the sources of information;

- be prepared within 15 working days;

- be objective, impartial, free from discriminatory language and stereo-typing; balanced, verified and factually accurate;

- utilise the OASys to provide a systematic assessment of the nature and causes of the defendant's offending behaviour, the risk the defendant poses to the public, and the action that can be taken to reduce the like-lihood of re-offending;

- pay attention to grammar, spelling, punctuation and language (avoid jargon).

The National Probation Service does not, as a matter of usual practice, prepare reports in circumstances where an offender has not been inter-viewed. However, it may be possible that situations occur in which it is appropriate to submit a report when the offender has not been recently interviewed. Prior to doing this the report writer should seek the approval of a service manager. It should also be acknowledged that a home visit, where appropriate, is good practice, because it will facilitate the assessment process and therefore enhance the credibility and quality of a report.

Content of PSRs

The content of reports is determined by National Standards, which specifies the following format.

Frontsheet

The frontsheet contains basic factual details about the offender: name, address, date of birth, offences, etc. Furthermore, in the Introduction report writers must acknowledge and consider, along with other sources of information, any Preliminary Indications made by the commissioning Bench or even Judge.

Offence analysis

This section provides an analysis of the offence(s) and focuses upon the 'why' question (the court knows *what* the offender has done, but it is the report writer's task to evaluate *why*). This section also analyses the key features of the nature and circumstances of the offence(s) in addition to culpability and level of premeditation. It should include an assessment of the consequences for other people, specifically the victim, exploring the offender's attitude towards the offence and victim, and any steps taken by the offender to make reparation and/or address offending behaviour. Furthermore, report writers need to be alert to the possibility of, for example, domestic violence, child protection and racist incidents underlying offences of criminal damage and assault, all of which have important sentencing implications.

It should be acknowledged that there are occasions when reports are requested in circumstances where the offender maintains his or her innocence. This usually occurs following a trial. In such circumstances report writers must, as far as they are able, analyse the offence(s) in order to submit a full report on the basis of the facts outlined by the prosecution. It is recognised that the protestation of innocence will inevitably limit the scope of the author's analysis but attitude, coupled with effects upon the victim, can still be commented upon. It is not an option to refrain from preparing a report in cases where offenders maintain their innocence. If the court has requested a report then it must be prepared, albeit in a qualified manner.

Offender assessment

This section begins with an analysis of the offender's basic skills in respect of accommodation, employment, literacy and numeracy. Additionally this section should assess the implications of any special personal circumstances relevant to offending (for example, family crisis, substance abuse, mental illness). It is important to analyse the defendant's previous convictions for patterns and assess whether there was a racial element to what occurred. The report writer should also consider the offender's response to previous sentences.

The aim of this section is to produce a succinct biography of the offender who is appearing before the court. It pieces together significant events in the offender's life which have a bearing upon his or her offending behaviour (significant childhood events; family background; school attendance; adolescence; behavioural patterns; transient and unstable accommodation; negative and pro-social factors; work record; relationships). In other words, it explores the ways in which the social, psychological and emotional development and functioning of individuals affects their behaviour and associated patterns.

Assessment of risk of harm to the public and likelihood of re-offending

This is an important section that focuses upon the following issues:

- assessment of the offender's risk of causing serious harm to the public;

- assessment of the offender's likelihood of re-offending based upon the current offence, attitude to it, and other relevant information;

- risk of self-harm.

It should be emphasised that the author's judgement in this section of the report must be based upon the facts of the case; the nature and level of offence seriousness; previous convictions and associated patterns; the attitude of the offender; and any other pertinent information that is informed by OASys. It is important to think clearly about the level of risk posed by an offender, which involves distinguishing between different types of offenders, offences and the circumstances in which offences were committed. On the one hand are those offences committed in specific situations that have a degree of inevitability and predictability. This may be illustrated by those offenders who commit offences when they have consumed an excessive amount of alcohol in the company of like-minded peers at the weekend (situation specific). In other words, if they avoid alcohol in future (and drugs) it is unlikely that they will re-offend. By contrast report writers are aware of a minority of offenders who have the capacity to behave unpredictably and inflict harm regardless of the situation in which they find themselves, or in the presence of alcohol and drugs. This distinction has implications for risk assessment and the subsequent classification of offenders when community sentences are imposed. Both scenarios are serious but the former could be classified as potentially dangerous, and the latter dangerous. What we are trying to allude to here is the distinction between situation-specific offences, manifested by discernible patterns, and a more serious level of dangerous unpredictability.

Conclusion

The final section must evaluate the offender's motivation and ability to change, and assess how offender motivation can be improved. The report writer must address the question: Is the offender suitable for a community sentence, in addition to articulating a clear sentencing proposal that is designed to achieve reparation, protect the public, and reduce offending? If the report writer concludes that a community sentence is appropriate, then the report must include a supervision plan which articulates the purpose of the sentence and methods of intervention on all such offenders, including ethnic minorities.

If a custodial sentence is a possibility, then the report writer should evaluate the implications for the offender, the offender's family, accommodation and employment. However, there are occasions, particularly at the Crown Court, when a custodial sentence is inevitable because of the seriousness of the offence. In such circumstances the report writer should acknowledge this in order to avoid unrealistic proposals for community sentences. It should also be added that if the report proposes a curfew order, details of the suitability of the proposed curfew address and the likely effects on others living at the offender's address should be included. Reports also have an obligation to provide advice on the appropriateness of extended supervision in cases of serious sexual or violent offences (see below for further details). A PSR should conclude with a single preferred proposal which is commensurate with the nature of the offence(s), level of seriousness, previous convictions, aggravating and mitigating factors, in addition to the offender's response to previous disposals and motivation to change. While deviation from these five headings is proscribed they do not limit the inclusion of additional headings, and the analysis and professional interpretation of material which the author considers relevant.

Key features in report writing

Report writers should focus upon analysis rather than description. In other words the author's emphasis should be on *why* rather than *what* (why has this person behaved in this manner at this particular point in time?). It is critically important to provide an analysis, explanation, assessment and evaluation of the offence(s), and associated patterns, to assist magistrates and judges to understand the person before them.

Additionally, report writers should explore the offender's sense of personal responsibility and attitudes; think about the aetiology of offending episodes; and locate current offences and previous convictions within a biographical context. Reports look at offending in relation to background factors, context and circumstances.

Report writers have a professional obligation to: produce balanced judgements based upon all relevant information which avoids discrimination; display insight and awareness; provide a dispassionate analysis; and weigh the relevance of different information. If the authors of PSRs engage in this process by taking notice of these features, it may be suggested that they will make a creative contribution to sentencing, including the process of justice, within the criminal justice system.

Furthermore, it should be acknowledged that reports, as far as possible, should be factually accurate (make sure you write about those offences the offender is charged with, in addition to providing accurate offender details). However, the report writer's professional task is to interpret the salient facts of an offender's life; to locate them within an explanatory framework; and to assess the significance of certain life events with a view to explaining why a person has offended. A form of words that can be used to facilitate assessment and interpretation of information may be suggested as follows:

- In my opinion . . .

- In my view . . .

- In my judgement . . .

- It seems to me that . . .

- I am led to the view that . . .

- I am minded to suggest that . . .

As a brief word on what may be described as the 'Test of Relevance' when assimilating and assessing information prior to writing the report, it is possible for PSR interviews to generate copious amounts of information (particularly when trainees are in the early stages of acquiring report writing skills), some of which is more relevant than others. Therefore to discriminate between relevant and irrelevant information the following questions may be posed:

- Does the information in the report analyse the offence(s)?

- Does the biographical information locate the offender within an explanatory context that sheds light on the offender's development in relation to offending behaviour?

- Does the information deal with the seriousness of the offence and provide a risk assessment in relation to re-offending and harm?

Reports and race

The probation service has a professional duty because of its commitment to anti-discriminatory and anti-oppressive practice to work with all offenders regardless of age, class, gender, race, sexual orientation, disability or religion, and according to the principles of equality and fairness. Consequently quality reports should be prepared, and the same level of service and resources made available to *all* offenders, while being sensitive to the differential needs of individual offenders (the diversity principle). Furthermore, the Crime and Disorder Act 1998 introduced new offences to deal with racist incidents (racially aggravated assaults, criminal damage, public order offences and racially aggravated harassment) to ensure that racist features in offending are not overlooked. Therefore, where reports are concerned, Crown Prosecution Service (CPS) documents will clarify whether a racist crime has been committed. Subsequently the PSR must take this type of offence seriously and understand that a racially motivated offence is an aggravating feature (s. 153 PCC(S)A 2000). The central issue is awareness of the possibility of a racist element in offending episodes. A current cash-linked target is that 95% of all reports on offenders from ethnic minorities must contain a clear and unambiguous recommendation.

After exploring a number of salient features of report writing in the above sections, the next section proceeds to explore the sentencing context within which reports are prepared for the courts. The reason for doing this is to clarify the contribution made by reports to the sentencing process. In other words, sentencing documents must be located within the sentencing framework.

The sentencing framework

The sentencing framework within which reports are prepared remains the Criminal Justice Act 1991, consolidated by the Powers of Criminal Courts (Sentencing) Act 2000. The 1991 Act proposed that offenders should be sentenced according to the seriousness of the offence before the court (just deserts). In other words, they would not be sentenced to a more substantial penalty simply because they had offended in the past. Consequently, the primary task of the court is to select the most appropriate sentence that is commensurate with the level of seriousness involved in the offence(s). Therefore with this point in mind the following summary should be considered.

Custody threshold (discretionary prison sentences)

Section 79 of the Powers of Criminal Courts (Sentencing) Act 2000 says that the court cannot normally impose a prison sentence unless it accepts that the offence is *so serious* that only custody can be justified. When considering the issue of offence seriousness the court must take into account all available information as to the circumstances of the offence, including any aggravating and mitigating factors – s. 81(4) PCC(S)A 2000. For example, s. 151(2) states that an offence committed while on bail is an aggravating feature; by contrast s. 152 put the longstanding process of giving credit for a guilty plea on a statutory footing, which is a mitigating factor.

Previous convictions and response to previous sentences

The intention of the Criminal Justice Act 1991 was to exclude previous convictions when determining the most appropriate sentence. However, this principle was amended by the Criminal Justice Act 1993, and s. 151(1) PCC(S)A 2000 says that 'In considering the seriousness of any offence, the court may take into account any previous convictions of the offender or any failure to respond to previous sentences.' Once again these features can be interpreted as aggravating factors.

Furthermore, s. 80(2)(b) PCC(S)A 2000 provides for longer than normal sentences to protect the public from serious harm from sexual and violent offenders. Otherwise s. 80(2)(a) requires that the sentence is commensurate with the level of seriousness of the offence.

Mandatory sentences and the Crime (Sentences) Act 1997

It is now possible for offenders to receive a mandatory life sentence (in addition to murder) if convicted of a second serious offence, unless there are exceptional circumstances – s. 2 Crime (Sentences) Act 1997, amended by s. 109 PCC(S)A 2000. Offences in this category include conspiring to murder, manslaughter, rape or attempted rape, sex with a girl under 13, various firearms offences, and robbery. It should also be acknowledged that there is a minimum of seven years' imprisonment for a third offence of trafficking class A drugs, unless it would be unjust; and a minimum of three years' imprisonment for a third offence of domestic burglary committed after 30 November 1999 – s. 111 PCC(S)A 2000 – unless it is unjust.

Community sentences

A court shall not pass a community sentence unless it is of the opinion that the offence is *serious enough* – s. 35(1) PCC(S)A 2000. Moreover, the Crime (Sentences) Act 1997 removed the need for the offender's consent to a community sentence with the following qualification: consent is now only required in the case of orders that include alcohol and drug treatment, in addition to psychiatric treatment.

Extended sentences

Under the provisions of s. 44 CJA 1991, where the whole or any part of a sentence is imposed for a sexual offence and the defendant is liable to early release on licence as a short- or long-term prisoner, the court has the power to order that the licence can remain in force until the sentence expiry date, instead of the three-quarter point of the sentence. In making this order the court has regard to (a) the need to protect the public from serious harm and (b) the desirability of preventing crime and securing the rehabilitation of the offender. Furthermore, s. 58 of the Crime and Disorder Act 1998 introduced a new sentencing power applicable when a court (a) proposes to impose a custodial sentence for a sexual or violent offence and (b) considers that any period for which the offender would otherwise be subject to licence would not be adequate for the purpose of preventing further offences and securing rehabilitation. In these circumstances the court has the discretionary power to pass an Extended Sentence under s. 85 PCC(S)A 2000. In other words, this additional power provides for extended post-release supervision for two specific categories of offences. Where violent offences are concerned, the extended licence period must not exceed five years and the original custodial penalty must be at least four years. For sexual offences the licence period must not exceed ten years, and in both categories the total penalty must not exceed the statutory maximum for the offence(s).

Implications for reports: Points to emphasise

TPOs and other report writers need to be aware of this sentencing context. Additionally, it is important to reiterate that:

- Report writers have a responsibility to contribute to the courts' understanding and determination of what is a serious offence, particularly when custody is being considered. This is the *so serious* criterion that is determined by all relevant information presented to the court.

- Where community sentences are concerned and the criterion of *serious enough* is being considered, the PSR continues to be important. The report is a critical document in helping the court to form a view on the most suitable form of community sentence.

- Report writers in serious sexual and violence cases must provide advice to the Crown Court Judge on the appropriateness of *extended supervision* to reduce re-offending and protect the public following release from custody.

- Report writers must produce quality reports on all offenders, regardless of ethnicity, and be aware of the aggravating nature of racially motivated offences.

- Safeguards are built into the legislative framework against the use of custody for Mentally Disordered Offenders: s. 82(5) PCC(S)A 2000. In such cases the court should consider a report prepared by the probation service; a medical report; and consider the impact of sentence on the offender.

Nil reports

With its emphasis on the court as 'customer' the service has clear expectations that staffs' efforts to deliver a report on the date requested will reflect this. Therefore an officer's leave or sickness is not necessarily a valid reason for failure to prepare reports, which means that alternative arrangements should be considered at the allocation stage. However, it is also recognised that some offenders do not cooperate with this process, which means that when the service has been unable to deliver a report, a clear explanation of the circumstances is provided to the court. To facilitate and expedite the preparation of reports in circumstances where a nil report is being considered, the following procedure could be considered. We wish to raise two points.

First, if the author is submitting a nil report letter but considers, after briefly perusing relevant documentation (CPS, previous convictions, probation records), that it is necessary, and in the interests of justice, to prepare a full report after a further adjournment, then a new appointment date should be included in the letter. This may not always be possible, but such a process could be initiated in certain circumstances. Therefore, prior to submitting a nil report the matter should be discussed with the unit manager.

Second, if the author is submitting a nil report but considers, after briefly perusing relevant documentation, that matters could be disposed of without a further adjournment for a full PSR, then the nil report could suggest the preparation of a Specific Sentence Report by court liaison staff at the next hearing. Again this course of action should be discussed with the unit manager. It is envisaged that this process will be considered in less serious cases.

Conclusion

In addition to what has already been said, it should be acknowledged that PSRs have a role to play within the Breach Court, when community sentences and licence cases are in the process of being revoked in both prosecution and revocation proceedings. Next it is important to reiterate the role of Specific Sentence Reports which are designed to provide information about an offender and offence(s) to assist sentencers to determine the offender's suitability for a specific sentence envisaged by the court. Furthermore, reports are a critical link between the offender's court appearance and the ongoing process of supervision through the articulation of a clear supervision plan if a community sentence is imposed. It is the basis upon which initial work with an offender is undertaken in order to reduce the likelihood of re-offending and protect the public. Finally, PSRs have a central role within the criminal justice system at both magistrates' and crown courts. They are fundamentally sentencing documents located within a legislative framework and sentencing process. Therefore the National Probation Service has a duty to produce quality documents which facilitate the achievement of service objectives and cash-linked targets articulated within business plans, in addition to contributing to the process of justice.

Summary of available sentences

Custody

- Custodial sentences are governed by ss. 76–83 PCC(S)A 2000. Section 79(2) specifies two alternative justifications for a custodial sentence: (a) the so serious criterion and (b) the need to protect the public from serious harm at the hands of violent and sexual offenders. These are

- Available for offenders who are 21 years of age and over.

- The PSR is central in helping to determine the level of seriousness when custody is being considered.

- Power to impose a Young Offender Institution Sentence was incorporated in s. 96 PCC(S)A 2000, and is available for 18- to 20-year-old offenders.

- Hospital Order under ss. 37 and 41 of the Mental Health Act 1983.

Suspended sentences

- Section 118(4) PCC(S)A 2000 specifies that a court shall not deal with an offender by means of a Suspended Sentence unless it is of the opinion that (a) the case is one in which a sentence of imprisonment would have been appropriate even without the power to suspend and (b) exceptional circumstances. A sentence of imprisonment for an offence may only be suspended if it is for a term of not more than two years.

- Available for offenders 21 years and over at magistrates' and crown courts.

- Suspended Sentence Supervision Order – s. 122 PCC(S)A 2000.

- When passing a Suspended Sentence for a term of more than six months for a single offence the court may make a Suspended Sentence Supervision Order placing the offender under the supervision of a probation officer.

- Available for offenders 21 years and over, but only at the crown court.

Community sentences

- Community Rehabilitation Order: s. 41(1) PCC(S)A 2000.

  - Length: six months to three years

  - Availability: youth, magistrates' and crown courts

  - Minimum age: 16 years

- Community Punishment Order: s. 46

    – Length: 40–240 hours

    – Availability: youth, magistrates' and crown courts

    – Minimum age: 16 years

- Community Punishment and Rehabilitation Order: s. 51

    – Length: CRO element is 12 months to three years

        CPO element is 40–100 hours

    – Availability: youth, magistrates' and crown courts

    – Minimum age: 16 years

- Drug Treatment and Testing Order: ss. 52–58

    – Length: six months to three years

    – Availability: youth, magistrates' and crown courts

    – Minimum age: 16 years

- Curfew (may include electronic tagging): ss. 37–40

    – Length: up to six months' duration

    – Availability: youth, magistrates' and crown courts

    – Minimum age: ten years

- Attendance Centre Order: ss. 60–62

    – Length: 12–24 hours if offender is under 16;
        36 hours if 16 years or over

    – Availability: youth, magistrates' and crown courts

    – Minimum age: 10–20 for males

The offence must be punishable by imprisonment.

- Drug Abstinence Order – introduced by s. 44 of the Criminal Justice and Court Services Act 2000, amending PCC(S)A 2000, and currently being piloted. It seeks to combat drug-related crime by requiring the offender to (a) abstain from misusing specified class A drugs; (b) to provide, when instructed by the responsible officer, any sample mentioned in the instruction for the purpose of ascertaining whether the offender has a class A drug in the body. The power to make such an order is s. 58A PCC(S)A 2000. Available at magistrates' and crown courts for offenders aged 18 years at time of conviction.

- Exclusion Order – introduced by s. 43 CJCSA 2000 as an amendment to PCC(S)A 2000 (but so far not yet commenced). It is designed to extend statutory control over an offender's whereabouts, not by curfew confinement to a specified place, but by prohibiting an offender from entering a place specified in the order. Available at youth, magistrates' and crown courts and the minimum age is ten years. The prohibition should last for not more than one year.

Other disposals

- Deferred Sentence: s. 1 PCC(S)A 2000. Available at youth, magistrates' and crown courts, and period of deferment should not exceed six months.

- Absolute and Conditional Discharge: ss. 12–15

  The maximum period for a CD is three years; no minimum period.

- Financial Penalties: ss. 126–134

- Compensation Orders: courts are obliged to consider compensation in all cases of death, injury, loss and damage.

- Bind Over

- Restitution, Forfeiture, Confiscation and Destruction

Therefore there are three main sentencing bands (custody; community sentences; remaining orders) and the offender will be located within one of these bands depending upon the seriousness of the offence and other relevant sentencing information.

Additional requirements

Section 42 of the Powers of the Criminal Courts (Sentencing) Act 2000 says that a Community Rehabilitation Order may require an offender to comply with certain additional requirements to (a) facilitate rehabilitation and (b) prevent re-offending and protect the public. Schedule 2 of the PCC(S)A 2000 is the primary legislative source of additional requirements (formerly PCCA 1973, Schedule 1A). The powers under the PCC(S)A 2000, Schedule 2, includes six categories of additional requirements, augmented by a further two introduced by ss. 47–48 of the CJCSA 2000, which amend Schedule 2 by including curfew and the exclusion requirement:

- *Residence*, Schedule 2, paragraph 1

    (a)   Probation Hostels and other independent hostels

    (b)   To reside where directed by the supervising officer, in order to provide more control beyond the standard right to be informed of a change of address.

- *Participation in specified activities*, Schedule 2, paragraph 2

    (a)   A requirement to present himself to a person or persons specified in the order, or place so specified.

    (b)   To participate in activities required in the order. Should not operate for more than 60 days.

- *Requirement to refrain from activities* is a little-used option within Schedule 2, paragraph 2.

- *Community rehabilitation centre attendance*, Schedule 2, paragraph 3. This is the Accredited Programmes requirement ('Think First' and 'One to One') and probation officers can propose this by, for example, using the following form of words: My preferred proposal is for a 12 months CRO with a requirement to complete a general offending behaviour programme under Schedule 2, paragraph 3(1), of the PCC(S)A 2000.

- *Treatment for mental condition*, Schedule 2, paragraph 5. This is the facility that was popularly known as the psychiatric probation order. It requires that an offender 'shall submit, during the whole of the community rehabilitation period or during such part or parts of that period as may be specified in the order to treatment by or under the direction of a duly registered medical practitioner or a chartered psychologist (or both, for different parts) with a view to the improvement of the offender's mental condition'. The treatment includes:

- treatment as a resident patient in a mental hospital;

- treatment as a non-resident;

- treatment under the direction of a registered medical practitioner or chartered psychologist.

Note that the court should not impose such a requirement unless arrangements have been made for the offender's treatment (consulted appropriate person who will provide the treatment).

- *Treatment for drug or alcohol dependency*, Schedule 2, paragraph 6

- *Curfew*, Schedule 2, paragraph 7, inserted by s. 47 of the CJCSA 2000

- *Exclusion requirement*, Schedule 2, paragraph 8, inserted by s. 48 of the CJCSA 2000

Strategy for learning how to write reports

After providing some of the key ingredients that constitute underpinning knowledge where report writing is concerned in this chapter, the next step is to integrate these knowledge components into a strategy for the acquisition of essential skills required by trainees that will equip them to begin writing PSRs. At this point we must state that what follows is not presented as the definitive strategy for learning how to write reports; no one could claim to be so prescriptive. Rather, we simply want to sketch a framework that training units should consider when teaching trainees a critical skill that takes the service into the sentencing arena of the criminal justice system. The strategy is designed to enable trainees to acquire the basic skills within a period of three months (and they will only be basic skills at this stage), so that by the end of this period they are in a position to receive their first allocation along with qualified probation officers. Therefore, with these preliminary thoughts in mind, the plan that we suggest is detailed below, and is initially premised upon working with a group of trainees (a relatively large group should not constitute a problem at this stage).

Day 1

A full-day introduction to the principles of PSR writing by PDAs. During the morning session a substantial proportion of the material in this chapter can be introduced, from the rationale of reports to race issues. However, this input, which sets the scene, should only occupy the morning. During the afternoon session the trainees can be provided with an opportunity to write the first part of a report (the process of writing these documents should be built up slowly). Two PDAs role-play a PSR interview, but focus only on the offence and previous convictions. The next step is to divide the trainees into smaller subgroups (four or five would be ideal for this exercise) and encourage them to reflect on and discuss the interview with a view to writing the first part of a report. Later reconvene as a full group and get a representative of each subgroup to read the report they have been working on. Full group discussion can be facilitated to deal with any significant issues that have emerged during the day.

Day 2

The first part of the morning should be spent on exploring the sentencing framework, available sentences and additional requirements because trainees must have an understanding of the function of the report within the wider criminal justice system and the sentencing process. Therefore provide appropriate inputs that are based on the material in this chapter. The second part of the morning should be used to complete the PSR role-play interview that was started on Day 1 by focusing on offender assessment, risk assessment and the conclusion.

The afternoon session will allow subgroups of trainees to complete the process commenced during Day 1 by producing a completed report. Again it is important to provide opportunities for the trainees to discuss the role-play interview; think about the result they are trying to achieve; reflect on the principles of report writing; and arrive at a sentencing proposal. Feedback to the whole group will generate further discussion of the salient points, particularly the sentencing proposal, to which PDAs will contribute. By the end of Day 2 a full report has been prepared, but primarily as a consequence of a group exercise.

Day 3

Begin with another role-play but this time of a full PSR interview that the trainees observe and of course take notes. On this occasion they could be provided with an opportunity to pose questions to the 'offender', which contributes to the development of interviewing skills. However, by this stage the expectation is not to produce a report based upon four or five trainees working together, but rather individually. Therefore, if the first hour of the day is occupied by the interview, the remainder of the day allows the trainees to prepare their own reports in a relaxed environment. It may be helpful to encourage trainees to work in pairs, just in case they would benefit from consultation, discussion and reflection. PDAs should be available to provide appropriate support and guidance throughout this process. By the end of the day trainees will deliver their reports to PDAs who will provide both written and verbal feedback on an individual basis.

Day 4

The structure of Day 4 can be similar to Day 3 with the essential difference that, on this occasion, it is important to introduce the expectation to complete an OASys. In addition to PDAs providing feedback to individual trainees it may also be helpful, as part of the process of learning, to bring the whole group together to discuss any areas of concern when they have completed their reports.

By the end of Day 4 they have been involved in writing three PSRs based upon role-play interviews, and latterly complemented by OASys, and the expectations should be clearer by this stage.

The next step

The next step in this process is to continue to provide opportunities for TPOs to develop their knowledge and skill in this important area of practice. Therefore training unit staff should consider the following points:

- Create the opportunity for trainees to observe a PSR interview undertaken by a PDA. The TPO's report, based upon the observed interview, can then be compared with the PDA's report.

- Create the opportunity for trainees to observe a qualified probation officer interviewing an offender within a field team. The TPO's report can then be compared and discussed with the probation officer and the PDA.

- TPOs should continue to read reports prepared by different probation officers as part of the learning, thinking, reflection and knowledge-building process.

- TPOs should continue to refer to the material in this chapter so that they do not lose touch with the result they are trying to achieve, and the essential components of quality practice.

- TPOs should attend court to observe the role of the report in the sentencing process and, as much as possible, accompany their own reports to court.

- The guidance and support of the PDA within this demanding learning process is essential at all times. It takes a considerable period of time to acquire the confidence and skill to reach an acceptable standard, and experienced officers continue to work at refining report-writing skills after many years of service. Another way of acquiring knowledge is for the TPO and the PDA to share a PSR interview, so that the PDA begins the interview and then the TPO takes over at an appropriate point.

It should also be acknowledged that, prior to commencing the process of learning how to write reports (that in Teesside, for example, begins during November in the first year of training), the TPO should have been introduced to a number of issues that complement the theme of this chapter. In other words, these are some of the building blocks of quality PSRs:

- OASys training and risk assessment

- National Standards

- Interviewing and communication skills

- Assessment skills

- Supervision plans that flow from the concluding section of a report

- Ethics and values that differentiate the *what* from the *how* of probation practice and the notion of legitimacy (see Chapter 4)

- The preparation of a PSR interview plan; see the interview schedule contained in the OASys manual, from page 236, for a helpful guide

- Sentences available at the magistrates' and crown courts

- Methods of intervention including cognitive-behavioural approaches, motivational interviewing, the cycle of change and motivation, pro-social modelling

- Available resources for offenders that address criminogenic needs, including partnership arrangements.

These components contribute to the creation of a coordinated strategy for acquiring the skill of report writing which is a key feature of TPO training.

However, this framework simply allows the process of report writing to make a start, which of course continues beyond the initial period of training, which spans two years. Towards the end of this chapter the PDA has started to feature as the person who has an important role to play in the process of acquiring the knowledge resources to write reports. The next chapter begins to focus on the role of the PDA in some detail.

Summary

In this chapter knowledge for report writing is dealt with separately because of the way in which that task brings together a range of central and important probation skills and knowledge: engagement, communication, assessment, selecting effective methods of intervention, reflection and evaluation.

The current legal context of report writing and the features of a good report are discussed. Minimum standards and processes and the notion of high-quality reports are defined. Report content and the central task of risk assessment are explained, including the importance of considering the *why* as well as the *what* of offending. The chapter provides a checklist for the completion of reports.

A range of specific report-writing issues are discussed: racially aggravated offences, the sentencing framework, the role of previous convictions, mandatory sentences, community sentences, extended sentences and nil reports.

The chapter conclusion reflects on the central role of report writing in the sentencing process. A summary of all available sentences and additional requirements is included. The chapter concludes by describing a four-day strategy for trainees learning how to write PSRs.

Further reading

Ashworth, A. (2000) *Sentencing and Criminal Justice* (3rd edn). London, Dublin and Edinburgh: Butterworths.

Bottoms, A.E. & Stelman, A. (1988) *Social Inquiry Reports*. Aldershot: Wildwood House.

Davies, M. & Knopf, A. (1973) *Social Enquiry Reports and the Probation Service*. HORS 18, Home Office.

Gelsthorpe, L. & Raynor, P. (1995) Quality and effectiveness in probation officers' reports to sentencers. *British Journal of Criminology*, **35**, 188–200. The more thorough and better written, the more likely they were to have a beneficial effect upon sentencing. This was the finding of this study of reports prepared for the crown court.

Herbert, L. & Mathieson, D. (1975) *Reports For Courts*. London: National Association of Probation Officers.

Mathieson, D. & Walker, A. (1971) *Social Enquiry Reports*. Probation Paper No. 7. London: National Association of Probation Officers.

Nash, M. (2003) Pre-trial investigation. In W.H. Chui & M. Nellis (eds), *Moving Probation Forward: Evidence, Arguments and Practice*. Harlow: Pearson Longman.

Perry, F.G. (1979) *Reports for Criminal Courts*. Ilkley: Owen Wells.

Raynor, P. (1980) Is there any sense in Social Inquiry Reports? *Probation Journal*, **27**, 78–84.

Home Office (1961) *Report of the Inter-Departmental Committee on the Business of the Criminal Courts*. Cmnd 1289, HMSO.

Thorpe, J. (1979) *Social Enquiry Reports: A Survey*. HORS 48, HMSO.

Chapter 6

The Practice Development Assessor: Producing quality probation officers

Introduction

The main reason for writing this book is to benefit TPOs by facilitating access to knowledge resources that will enable them to negotiate the demands of the Dip.PS, particularly the NVQ component. Therefore the interests of the trainee are at the heart of this enterprise. However, we are also mindful of another audience that could benefit from additional assistance that leads us to conclude that this book would be incomplete unless we devoted a brief chapter to exploring the role of the PDA. In 1999 the Home Office published a document that was dedicated to the Dip.PS and is replete with various papers that were instrumental in the creation of the new arrangements for trainees (post-CQSW period). Section 10 of this document is referred to as 'Guidance documents on Practice Development Assessors (PDAs)'. Moreover Probation Circular 136/2001: Probation Staff, Recruitment and Training-Funding for Training Consortia contains guidance on the role and function of the PDA, located at Annex One. Therefore our first task in this chapter is simply to distil these documents with a view to clarifying the role of the PDA as it was envisaged towards the end of the 1990s, before broadening our theme to include other areas of interest. It should be unambiguously stated that the development of TPOs, for which the PDA has a responsibility, is premised upon the acquisition of knowledge and understanding that in turn contribute to effectiveness. Additionally the PDA requires knowledge to which this book makes a contribution.

The role of the PDA

The key functions associated with the role of the PDA may be enumerated in relation to the following four headings:

Practice development of trainees

- Identify learning needs and learning opportunities for each trainee;

- Support the trainee through the two-year course;

- Provide practice opportunities to trainees according to their individual needs and the requirements of foundation practice in the first year and subsequently the NVQ;

- Plan their timetable of work;

- Coaching and mentoring in relation to PSRs and cases;

- Feedback and review of progress.

Work-based assessment

- Preparing trainees for accredited prior learning assessments;

- Assessing the foundation practice portfolio;

- Assessment of NVQ level 4 in Community Justice;

- Contribute to the academic assessment of trainees when this is considered appropriate.

Liaison with stakeholders

- Liaison with the trainees' line manager;

- Liaison with the trainees' HE tutors;

- Attendance, when required, at assessment panels and boards, moderation, Internal Verifier, and consortium meetings;

- Liaison with specialist staff, Internal Verifiers, and those with overall responsibility for trainee development;

- Contribute to the evaluation of the whole programme.

Contribute to the teaching of trainees

- Facilitate group learning;

- Support work-based assessments through coaching;

- Design and deliver in-house training modules;

- Prepare material for use by individual trainees.

In addition to the above areas of responsibility we should also like to suggest that the following tasks are central to the PDA role in practice:

- Contribute to the induction period of each new cohort of trainees that sets the tone and professional expectations for the whole programme.

- Produce learning contracts and then assess progress against the contract in reviews undertaken on a regular basis.

- Plan, review, observe and assess the NVQ as a central component of the role.

- Supervise the trainee, initiate discussion and encourage reflection as part of the process of learning and the acquisition of knowledge.

- Relate theory to practice during supervision.

- Assist trainees to plan, manage and organise their work to ensure the successful completion of the Dip.PS by the end of the second year.

- Model best practice.

Furthermore, it is interesting to speculate on the changing nature of the PDA role in certain consortia because of the recent expansion of distance learning within the National Probation Service. One of the authors of this book works for a consortium that, for the last six years, has sent its trainees to the University of Northumbria to receive academic input. This arrangement is about to change radically and it is anticipated that under new distance-learning arrangements greater academic demands could be placed upon PDAs quite simply because they will be accessible in a face-to-face manner. Consequently, PDAs in these changing and challenging circumstances need to be flexible and ready to respond positively, for the good of the trainee. While there is an expectation upon the distance-learning provider to deliver the academic component effectively, there is equally a responsibility upon the PDA to acquire as much knowledge as possible about all substantive features of the Dip.PS to be effective in the role that will benefit the trainee, including relevant computer skills in order to access distance-learning materials via the internet. We also envisage an enhanced role, within a distance-learning framework, to facilitate theory into practice workshops, for example, on diverse methods of working with offenders (Appendix 5). Now that we have set the scene for the work of the PDA, the next step is a brief interlude that considers the responsibility of the assessor for the NVQ, in addition to Internal Verifier duties.

NVQ Assessor

It is clear from the above that the PDA has many tasks to undertake when working with TPOs within the parameters of the Dip.PS. Nevertheless a considerable amount of time is occupied pursuing the demands of the

NVQ, and it is therefore necessary to unpack this task because unless he or she successfully completes the NVQ then it is not possible for the trainee to work as a probation officer. The NVQ in Community Justice requires the trainee to demonstrate occupational competence by collecting naturally occurring work-based evidence in relation to the prescribed 12 units at level 4. Each of these 12 units comprises performance criteria, range statements, and of course UKU. It is the responsibility of the PDA in collaboration with the trainee to plan the collection of the evidence that meets the standards of each unit; review the plan to monitor progress; undertake observations of the trainee's work with offenders in different situations that will produce strong evidence for the portfolio; then assess the unit when the trainee considers that all the evidence requirements have been met, both quantitatively and qualitatively. Consequently the assessor must be satisfied that the evidence presented by the trainee clearly meets the required standards (transparent); that it is sufficient and replete with diverse evidence; that it is relevant to the unit being assessed (valid); and that it belongs to the trainee (authentic). It should also be stated that, until relatively recently, the rule of thumb in the North-East consortium was that trainees were expected to produce a minimum of three pieces of evidence to satisfy performance criteria; a minimum of one piece but preferably two for range; and a minimum of two pieces for UKU. However, towards the end of 2003 and subsequent to a visit by an External Verifier, the view was being expressed that less evidence was required to satisfy the requirements of the NVQ. Consequently the advice being given was that if one piece of evidence clearly meets the performance criterion then this would be sufficient. The implication of this advice, from the standpoint of producing quality probation officers, will be discussed towards the end of this chapter.

Internal Verifier

It is also necessary to allude, even more briefly, to the role of the Internal Verifier within the NVQ process and acknowledge that a number of PDAs also double up as verifiers. It is possible to summarise this role as follows:

Verifying assessment

(a)   Ensure that assessors are making consistent and reliable assessment decisions by sampling the evidence.

(b)   Monitor the quality of assessment decisions and highlight problems, trends and the development needs of assessors.

Monitor assessment practice

(a) Ensure that National Standards of assessment (clarified in the A1/A2 award that PDAs need to achieve) are adhered to by all assessors.

(b) Identify problems or areas where assessors require support, advice and/or development.

(c) Ensure that candidates (trainees) are aware of and are satisfied with the assessment process.

Standardise assessment judgements

(a) Ensure that each assessor consistently makes valid decisions to make certain that the required standards are being met.

(b) Ensure all assessors make the same decisions on the same evidence, which is the important principle of consistency.

(c) Ensure that all candidates are assessed fairly.

Therefore the Internal Verifier has an important role to play in maintaining the integrity of the NVQ process and quality assurance procedures by sampling a proportion of the evidence. Moreover the Internal Verifier has a critical role to play in supporting assessors and their candidates, the importance and value of which should not be underestimated.

Three PDA models

After clarifying the various functions that comprise the PDA role at the beginning of this chapter, and then touching on the NVQ Assessor and Internal Verifier tasks, the next step is to explore the different ways in which the role can be undertaken. This, of course, depends upon the exigencies of local probation services and consortia and it may be suggested that three main models can be identified. First, the semi-specialist or part-time PDA who, as a qualified probation officer, should maintain contact with practice by having oversight of a number of cases as well as continuing to write PSRs, alongside having responsibility for either one (preferably) or even two trainees (ambitious). The time allocated to each function will of course depend upon the workloads and resources that exist within area services, but it may be envisaged that the PDA role will occupy approximately one day each week for each trainee supervised. The part-time PDA role is attractive mainly because it enables the incumbent to maintain contact with practice that, in turn, will benefit the trainee's development. The main argument against the model is that there can be slippage in the way that time allocated to the PDA role is, often inadvertently and unwittingly, encroached upon by workload demands. Therefore this model is not without its problems, which means that all those involved (PDA, line manager of TPOs, managers in teams where the part-time PDA is based, and senior managers) need to adhere to agreements in order to allow the model to work effectively. Therefore good communication is essential. It should be made clear that the central task of the PDA within this model is that of NVQ Assessor because of obvious time constraints.

Second, a slight variation of the first model is to have semi-specialist middle managers or senior probation officers performing the role of PDA, in addition to their other managerial duties within the organisation. In this model a particular complication is that it is not appropriate for a candidate's work to be assessed by a direct line manager. The issues that services need to be aware of where the semi-specialist probation officer is concerned also apply to the semi-specialist middle manager. Nevertheless it is important to reiterate that in an organisation, which is subject to many competing demands, the time allocated to the PDA role can often get squeezed as other priorities create varying degrees of pressure. It could be argued that one of the reasons underlying this uncomfortable reality is that TPO training is not a cash-linked target, which could enable one to conclude that this is an area of practice where quality can be compromised (currently the cash-linked targets are in the areas of: timely information returns; reducing sickness absence; accredited programmes; Drug Treatment and Testing Order (DTTO) commencements; clear proposal in PSRs on minority ethnic offenders; enforcement; basic skills). As a riposte to this possibility we would argue that TPO training, which is fundamentally a commitment to the creation of quality probation officers, is of central importance for the long-term effectiveness and credibility of the organisation. Therefore we should not allow short-term thinking or today's priorities (which is not to deny the importance of cash-linked targets for area services) deflect us from a longer-term vision to produce the best probation officers possible. To achieve this objective there must be an appropriate investment in sufficient PDA resources and the commodity of time.

The third model is the specialist PDA who undertakes the full range of tasks enumerated above on a full-time basis, unencumbered by other duties. This is our preferred ideal-type, dedicated model, based upon observing all three models in operation within the North-East consortium. Nevertheless we accept that each probation area is different in terms of the staffing resource that can be allocated to TPO training, with the result that a mixed economy model may well be the pragmatic option that will be pursued (a nucleus of full-time PDAs who have a responsibility for all those tasks considered earlier, in addition to part-time PDAs who have responsibilities for one trainee and the NVQ component of the Dip.PS). Moreover, area services could well be forced into a mixed economy model as a direct consequence of the unprecedented increase in TPO numbers over recent years; not every service has sufficient numbers of probation officers to allocate to the PDA role on a full-time basis, even though this would be desirable.

When dealing with some of the practicalities of the full-time PDA role we are inclined to suggest, based upon our own experiences, that a ratio of no more that six trainees to one PDA is appropriate to ensure the delivery of quality service. Furthermore, a combination of three first-year and three second-year trainees is conducive to PDA time management. The time commitment of the PDA when working with second-year trainees particularly should not be underestimated, especially when 12 NVQ units must be completed to achieve the Dip.PS. One of the negative features of our preferred model is the need for full-time PDAs to keep in touch with practice. This, to some degree, is achievable when supervising trainees working with offenders (notwithstanding its vicarious second-hand nature). Additionally, the PDA should be encouraged to write reports (one every three weeks is sufficient) that would enable the assessor to maintain contact with assessment and intervention skills that are critical for trainees to acquire. Mechanisms need to be in place to ensure that full-time PDAs do not inadvertently drift away from the fundamental rationale of probation work that is to work with offenders. The issue being touched upon here is one of credibility within the PDA role.

Reflections on the role

After elucidating the various functions of the PDA role earlier in this chapter, it is clear that it is both diverse and demanding in equal measure, which requires a certain level of knowledge and understanding to work with trainees and subsequently facilitate the production of competent, effective, but also quality probation officers. It should be stated that the PDA is never far from the heart of this book because the successful negotiation of the Dip.PS and production of qualified probation officers critically depends upon the PDA planning, managing, coordinating, supporting, encouraging and organising the work of the trainee. Additionally the PDA must provide good advice on striking the right balance between academic study and practice opportunities. Consequently, PDAs should be encouraged to cultivate a vision of the result they are trying to achieve when working with trainees, which has implications for the knowledge base required in order to achieve key objectives.

Our analysis of the Dip.PS in Chapter 3, particularly the attention given to items of knowledge and understanding, draws attention to a number of key knowledge themes that trainees need to be aware of when working towards the NVQ. Equally PDAs must be familiar with these knowledge themes in order to appreciate, facilitate and searchingly test out the knowledge building of trainees in relation to, for example, victim issues, underpinning legislation, patterns and explanations of offending behaviour, risk assessment and effective interventions. PDAs should be aware of these knowledge themes because the level of knowledge that trainees must acquire and fledgling probation officers must possess depends, to a large extent, upon the knowledge base of the assessor. In other words, if the PDA does not possess relevant knowledge, how can the trainee be expected to know or be clear about service expectations? How can the knowledge base of the trainee be tested out effectively? How can the PDA make a judgement about the knowledge competence of the trainee? We would also express the view that the possibility of differential levels of knowledge among the PDA group will produce variable quality among the trainees. Once again we cannot overstate the importance of the PDA role in relation to the Dip.PS and subsequently the future of the organisation. Therefore this has implications for selection and training.

It may reasonably be assumed that the PDA is selected on the basis that, as a qualified probation officer (occupationally competent), valuable knowledge and experience have been accrued over a number of years that will benefit the trainee. It is stating the obvious that experience derived from undertaking the probation officer role for an appropriate period of time is a prerequisite for being selected as a PDA, and that experience of practice generates invaluable work-based knowledge. Nevertheless, we should not assume that acquiring work-based experience as a probation officer, or even senior probation officer, is tantamount to having the necessary knowledge base to function effectively in the PDA role. Therefore we should disentangle the experience of working as a practitioner that does produce relevant knowledge, from the additional knowledge required within the PDA role in relation to the demands of the Dip.PS. In our view the PDA will be of value to the trainee by having a working knowledge of, for example:

- historical and contextual issues, some of which are discussed in the first chapter of this book;

- the NVQ process;

- the themes identified in Table 3.1 and the diverse knowledge resources in Chapters 4 and 5;

- the insight, awareness, and understanding to make connections between theory and practice with a view to explaining offending behaviour and suggesting effective interventions (see Appendices towards the end of the book);

- how to help trainees to learn through planned input and practice opportunities and by encouraging reflection and offering dialogue on experience of practice;

- how to create a safe learning environment in which trainees can think things through and learn by mistakes;

- ethics and values; the 'what' and 'how' of practice; and the notion of legitimacy that gives credibility to the trainee and probation officer role (Appendix 6).

Therefore, the PDA must be committed to a process of learning and knowledge building that will benefit the TPO, in addition to the organisation as it pursues its objectives and targets. There are a number of knowledge features, already alluded to in this book, that we need to expand upon in the following section in order to develop our understanding of probation officer training.

Knowledge as a multifaceted concept

To work effectively as a TPO (and subsequently qualified probation officer) the aspiring practitioner needs to accrue various knowledge derived from different sources. The academic component of the Dip.PS provides some of these knowledge resources that are supplemented by the codified knowledge requirements contained within the NVQ. However, TPOs, due to the nature of the job, will find that they require access to additional knowledge resources when working with offenders. Even though knowledge derived from the academic course and accrued for the NVQ has a certain utility, this knowledge alone does not equip the trainee to deal with all possible workplace situations. Consequently, a much broader vision of knowledge within vocational probation practice than hitherto considered needs attention, although the ground has been prepared by the discussion in Chapter 2.

As we begin to feel our way into additional dimensions of knowledge it is not possible to be prescriptive in the sense of explaining exactly what constitutes its precise compass, which is in marked contrast to the approach of the NVQ. This is because the nature of probation practice is diverse and sometimes complex and involves attempts to make sense of, and then respond to, a range of human problems associated with adverse childhood experiences, emotional deprivation and abuse, disruptive behaviour, lack of opportunities, mental health concerns, alcohol and drugs, accommodation problems and unemployment, in addition to other socially and economically induced problems. Practice situations can be enigmatic and it is not always possible to specify in advance the precise nature of the knowledge and skill that will be required, which is why it should be clearly stated that it is unlikely that academic subjects and NVQ codified knowledge will have prepared the trainee to find a way through all the thickets of practice. Therefore we are clear that there is a body of knowledge beyond that contained within the twin parameters of the Dip.PS. With these preliminary thoughts in mind we want trainees and assessors to consider the following four-fold typology of knowledge that attempts to consolidate, clarify and expand what we are trying to articulate, which echoes some of the themes set out in Chapter 2.

Knowledge typology for probation practice

Academic knowledge

The first type of knowledge is provided to trainees by the academic component of the Dip.PS. As discussed in Chapter 2, academic curricula are in their own way codified knowledge and, in the degree supporting the Diploma, perhaps particularly so because of the requirements imposed on universities in relation to content. These requirements focus on knowledge content in order to assure a national consistency and a direct relevance to the occupation and, in particular, to the Occupational Standards. However, in our typology the distinguishing characteristic of academic knowledge is not content. Individual, commercial and state investment in HE are currently widely debated. Notwithstanding claims about the needs of a knowledge economy, much commercially and publicly useful knowledge is ephemeral. What such an economy and what modern society needs are people equipped with the thinking skills that enable them to critically evaluate information, communicate effectively, solve problems and deal with change creatively. The first characteristic we would claim for academic knowledge is that through the traditional academic processes of critical enquiry, debate and research, of reflection, planning and review of learning, come the development of these critical and flexible thinking skills.

The second characteristic of academic knowledge in our typology is that it is premised on the notion of a pursuit of excellence. At undergraduate level assignments are marked and degrees are classified. Trainees will qualify as probation officers if they achieve an appropriate degree at any level of classification and yet a wide range of achievement is available.

Knowledge for practice

This type of knowledge is represented in the Dip.PS by the NVQ. NVQs describe the knowledge you need to be competent. The emergence of these knowledge descriptors follows the articulation of particular practice competencies in terms of the evidence required to demonstrate them. This knowledge therefore is what is needed to demonstrate that you know and understand enough to be competent. We would argue that the way that the NVQ describes this knowledge for practice is inadequate and fails to capture the range of knowledge (from across our typology) that is required and implicit in good practice.

However, as in academic knowledge, in our typology the processes of the NVQ offer candidates the opportunity to develop what we would describe as knowledge for practice. As in academic processes it is opportunity for reflection, planning and review that is central to developing knowledge, but here it is practice knowledge; the reflection and learning is in relation to the instrumental need to perform the job. The quality of these processes around the NVQ will depend very much on the PDA and the extent to which he or she is competent and confident enough not to be constrained in approach by the codified knowledge in the NVQ and engage with the individualistic and holistic task of developing trainees' knowledge for practice.

We must pause at this juncture to state that types one and two are the essential knowledge constructs articulated within the Dip.PS, but, as we have implied, they describe a limited view of probation knowledge that is associated with competence and minimum standards of performance. These two types could be perceived as baseline or threshold knowledge. Types three and four attempt to articulate a broader and more holistic sense of probation knowledge – knowledge beyond codification.

Ineffable knowledge

Arguably the processes involved in the development of academic knowledge and knowledge for practice (the degree and the NVQ) can and do transcend the codified content of that knowledge. In transcending the content trainees begin to learn how to become, and how to be reflective, researcher-practitioners. This preparedness to deal with the new and unexpected and to continue to learn through practice in being a probation officer is discussed further in Chapter 7.

Beyond our codified knowledge and the processes of learning there remains a key question of motivation. Why do individuals seek knowledge beyond what is required for the job? How are organisations like the probation service to be successful in creating a learning culture?

Gherardi (2003) discusses the relationship of desire and passion to the pursuit of knowledge. For her, knowledge is not just 'problem driven' but also 'mystery driven'. Here myths are a form of knowledge, myths that are contained in the traditions, narratives and social relations of organisations:

> myth as a form of knowledge . . . not so much conveys factual knowledge as transforms a forma mensis: a perceptive grid used to interpret experience and which conditions the vision of the reality internal and external to both people and work communities.
>
> GHERARDI (2003, p. 353)

This mythical, ineffable knowledge is not instrumental but is an end in itself and motivates people and organisations. Here knowledge is anything but codified, it is knowledge as knowing and involves a desire to know and a passion for knowing.

> Passion about what one does, and about doing it well, is a sentiment that pertains to a community of practitioners and anchors its identity. However, if this sentiment is not kept alive, celebrated, and relived in the memory and stories, if it is not transmitted to novices, it will fade into routine, into passionless activity. Transmitting passion for a profession . . . for the mastery of practical situations, is an organizational practice for managing expert, tacit and collective knowledge.
>
> GHERARDI (2003, p. 354)

The motivation to continue to learn beyond instrumentality is then perhaps connected to desire; a desire to know, to understand and be part of the myth, a carrier of the tradition; to be part of a community of passion.

At times of major change there is clearly a challenge to this mythical knowledge and when, as in probation, this change involves reframing and structuring knowledge in terms of competence, that challenge is particularly strong. But this knowledge as knowing may be a critical element in not only motivating a learning community of practitioners but also to the passion of those practitioners. If so, how is it to be protected? Furthermore, is there any dissonance between the notion of a passionate practitioner and a managerial objective of minimum standards and consistent and competent performance?

In the universities, but perhaps more significantly in the workplace, the desire to know will be transmitted by an understanding of the history and traditions of the probation service, by the relationships and exchanges with practitioners and teachers, through stories and story-telling of practice and through the passion, both implicit and explicit, expressed in and about the work.

Self-knowledge

The final element in our typology attempts to acknowledge both the impact of the self on the practice of being a probation officer and the impact of the job on the self.

The medium of probation practice is largely relationships, and these relationships with offenders, colleagues and others are often intense. Many of them are central to successful and excellent practice. Generally these relationships are not friendships but rather professional partnerships and often depend for their success on shared understandings and trust. They can also be fragile, and it is therefore important to be aware of what you bring to these relationships in terms of how you present (your age, gender, size, clothes you wear, etc.) and the impact of how you communicate in those relationships. Self-knowledge here is not about prescribing how you should be, but about developing a sophisticated insight into how you are and a sensitivity to the impact of this on others. In part this involves consideration of the reflexive nature of communication, but it also involves expanding awareness of your emotional responses and their effect.

Meanwhile the work of the probation officer is not only stressful, but there is a strong emotional component to that work. It is important not to deny this emotional content and to know that anxiety, fear, anger, frustration or sadness are inevitable and natural consequences of the work. The knowledge involved in this instance is in how to deal with this emotional content, and there is a danger that the emotional content may not be dealt with, but will be bottled up. This will not only lead to increasing stress but is likely to mean that the emotional issues remain unresolved. We need to know how to talk about how we feel and how to be available and to listen when others want to talk about their feelings.

Finally, in relation to self-knowledge it is important to know what you believe, how this impacts on the values you bring to the work and the relationship of those values to the values of the probation service. This is part of having a sense of location and direction as a probation officer. Why are you doing this job? Where are you going with this job? This element of self-knowledge also involves identifying in more basic terms what it is you want from your job at different stages of your career (e.g. security, power, integrity, happiness, etc.). These issues are discussed further in Chapter 7.

Going beyond the NVQ

At this point we can expand the discussion a little further by saying that one of the concerns associated with NVQ knowledge codification specifically (and to some degree National Standards) is that trainees are inadvertently inveigled into a mind-set of working 'to' rather than 'from' the demands of the NVQ. Working 'to' the 12 units of the NVQ is tantamount to a minimum standards approach (this is the only knowledge you need to do the job attitude); working 'from' acknowledges that the NVQ primarily constitutes a baseline from which practitioners must travel beyond to achieve excellence (NVQ as base camp, not summit metaphor). This sense of 'moving beyond' the NVQ is required if PDAs want trainees to produce, for example, insightful assessments which demonstrate that they have a good understanding of those factors associated with offending by considering various hypotheses. This is knowledge as good thinking and reading the whole person that may be further illustrated as follows. Some of us who work as PDAs have witnessed trainees interview offenders for a court report with a copy of the relevant NVQ standards in front of them (D102/D103), and as soon as the evidence has been generated to meet the standards (sometimes allowing the standards to shape the questions during the interview) have moved on to other areas of concern, which is an example of working to the NVQ. This approach could well generate evidence to meet NVQ standards, but it could equally result in the trainee failing to pause, reflect, think, pick up on, and probe into certain areas (dynamics of childhood) that prevents the production of an insightful and accurate assessment, which is more likely to occur if trainees work *to* rather than *from* the NVQ. There are occasions within practice situations when the trainee will need to go beyond the minimum knowledge standards contained within NVQ codification to produce an insightful and accurate assessment that, in turn, will enable the completion of an accurate OASys; facilitate a clear view of the risk of re-offending and harm; yield insights into domestic violence, public protection and child protection issues; identify Schedule One offenders; and clarify effective interventions and use of resources. It is possible, for example, to meet all aspects of the NVQ standards yet fail to understand that the client was abused as a child, which compromises the entire assessment process. It needs to be made clear that the PDA has a central role to play in modelling the diverse knowledge resources required by the trainee, and what we are suggesting here is also applicable to the role of the middle manager when working with practitioners within the supervision process – particularly supervising those probation officers in their first year of practice after achieving the Dip.PS. As the practitioner engages in pro-social modelling with offenders, which is an integral component of the effective practice agenda, so the PDA has a role to play in modelling aspects of knowledge to trainees that will contribute to excellent performance and is therefore an integral component of the PDA–TPO dynamic. The knowledge required to be an effective probation officer cannot be limited to the academic and NVQ components of the Dip.PS, which is why we want to articulate a vision of knowledge as a multifaceted concept by introducing this four-fold epistemology typology. PDAs know that there is much more to probation practice than meeting the demands of the Dip.PS, than reducing practice to the objectively measurable.

Elements of a training strategy

When reflecting upon the elements of a training strategy for newly appointed PDAs, it should be acknowledged that this depends upon whether we are referring to full-time or part-time members of staff. Moreover, we wish to state clearly, and here we duplicate the point made when considering the PSR training strategy in Chapter 5, that it is not our intention to be prescriptive. Rather we simply want to provide a steer by exploring certain elements that could be considered for inclusion.

- The first element of this strategy is to undertake a knowledge audit of those appointed to the role, whether full or part time, to assess experience, knowledge, education and qualifications. This audit will contribute to clarifying the learning needs of each new PDA which, in turn, will inform the training strategy. (In fact a case can be made for undertaking a knowledge audit of the whole service that will help to identify those practitioners who could be suitable for the role.) The newly appointed assessor will have training needs in addition to those of trainees that must be met.

- PDAs will need access to background reading resources that are conducive to reading themselves into the job – see the end of this chapter for guidance in addition to consulting the many references scattered throughout this book on various subjects.

- Those responsible (established members of staff and managers within the training units of area services) must provide an overview of the Dip.PS for new staff, which includes: academic subjects that comprise the degree; how trainees organise their week; practice opportunities including reports and cases allocated to trainees; the NVQ process that initially focuses on planning the collection of evidence; the supervision process between PDA and TPO.

- Shadow an established PDA for a period of time, particularly where the NVQ process is concerned, to help to facilitate what is a steep learning curve.

- Attend relevant PDA meetings that focus on NVQ issues.

- Work towards the NVQ A1/A2 award, which helps to consolidate the assessor role.

- Link the PDA with an Internal Verifier who will provide support and undertake those other tasks referred to earlier in this chapter.

- Encourage the new PDA to consolidate a vision of what the Dip.PS process is trying to achieve – see Chapter 7, which looks at the role of the probation officer in some detail and in the rest of this book.

- Take responsibility for one's own learning and acquisition of diverse knowledge resources in relation to the PDA role, and be aware of the four-fold typology introduced above.

Conclusion: Further reflections on the NVQ

It should be reiterated that we have not set ourselves the task of producing an academic text that is intended to push back the frontiers of knowledge within the probation service, even though we refer to a range of academic resources throughout the book that will be helpful for trainees and PDAs. One of our central concerns is to provide trainees with a range of useful resources in relation to negotiating the Dip.PS, specifically NVQ underpinning knowledge, and to contribute to the TPO–PDA relationship. In doing so we want to be positive and constructive; our goal is not to undermine a training programme that, by this stage, should be well established, but to contribute to it. However, this does not mean that it is not permissible to raise questions about the efficacy of the Dip.PS, which is not only designed to produce competent probation officers (the minimum requirement) but should also inspire trainees to strive for quality. It should be clarified that we do not raise substantive objections to the academic component of the Dip.PS. To do the job effectively, trainees require the essential body of contextual knowledge provided by the universities and, as we have argued, the processes of HE have the potential to encourage essential critical and creative thinking skills. Nevertheless it is interesting to speculate on differences between university courses and the relative merits and differential experience and outcomes of face-to-face contact between trainees and university staff and distance-learning approaches.

If we do have concerns it is with the NVQ component and it is possible – particularly for those of us who have been involved with trainees for some time – to envisage a TPO programme that includes a somewhat modified NVQ. This is because we sometimes find ourselves pondering its efficacy in relation to developing performance. We are concerned about its capacity to create quality practitioners; we question whether the machinations of the NVQ process are an effective use of both TPO and PDA time and resources. It also needs to be acknowledged that it is possible to meet NVQ demands without being an adept practitioner, as we have already illustrated above, by working *to* rather than *from* the prescribed standards. In other words, we need to be aware of the possibility that being in possession of NVQ level 4 in Community Justice may not automatically guarantee that the candidate is a quality practitioner with the required level of knowledge, insight and understanding of offenders. If this tension emerges, then training arrangements must be able to rely upon the integrity of the PDA to deal with performance issues through supervisory and capability procedures, substantiated by supervision notes and periodic reviews. Meanwhile we impose a large responsibility on PDAs in the current arrangements to transcend the minimalism of the NVQ and to be transmitters of passion and encouragers of insight.

It is clear that trainees require academic knowledge (of underlying theory and explanatory frameworks) in addition to other forms of knowledge, and the know-how to blend the academic component when working with offenders in various practice situations. These knowledge requirements embrace, as we have already discussed: assessment; interviewing; engaging with offenders; communication; listening skills; diverse methods of working/effective interventions; strategies for protecting the public; effective use of partnership and other resources; writing reports; ethics and values that focus upon the 'how' of practice and building effective relationships; service policies and procedures. Our thesis is that knowledge and skill in these essential areas of practice can be achieved and assessed in a variety of ways that could include a truncated version of the current NVQ requirements. In fact a much more efficient and effective system can be envisaged that would enable the PDA to spend more quality time with the trainee when the latter is involved in the supervision of offenders and writing reports – the fundamentals of practice. This would provide greater opportunities for the PDA to teach, observe practice, coach, provide feedback on performance, make connections between theory and practice, ask relevant questions to stimulate knowledge building in relation to our four-fold typology, encourage reflection, resolve problems and be creative. It needs to be stated that all this can be achieved without the pressure to collect and then produce copious amounts of evidence in relation to performance criteria and range statements that take up an inordinate amount of time. This is what has happened in the past. However, it seems helpful to retain a proportion of items of underpinning knowledge as a mechanism that the PDA can use to test out the developing knowledge base of the trainee, while accepting its limitations. Therefore, a cogent argument can be developed for a much more limited NVQ with the aim of putting the emphasis on substance rather than process; this would in fact enhance, rather than detract from, the creation of quality probation officers. In other words, the right balance needs to be struck between engaging in probation practice and documenting aspects of performance. What we mean by this can be illustrated by turning our attention to process issues.

One of our main reasons for arriving at this potentially liberating conclusion is that there is too much emphasis on the process of the NVQ which, in our opinion, detracts from the substance of enabling trainees to engage with the realities of quality probation practice. A disproportionate amount of time and effort is devoted to the mechanics of collecting evidence and building a portfolio. Over recent years a bureaucratic leviathan has evolved. Consequently, there is too much emphasis on administration; there are too many forms to complete; an excessive adherence to rules and the minutiae of procedures that does not always meet the needs of TPOs. Furthermore, there are too many meetings that consider process rather than the substance and essential components of practice. At times the NVQ presents itself as a system for demonstrating competence in the mastery of a bureaucratic system, rather than the diverse knowledge resources and skill required by aspiring practitioners when working with offenders. Therefore a case can be made to liberate both trainees and PDAs from the burden of bureaucratic procedures and to refocus attention upon creating opportunities for trainees to acquire the knowledge and skill to work as effective probation officers, under the tutelage of a knowledgeable, imaginative and skilful PDA. This would be a much better use of PDA resources and would contribute towards effectiveness within the organisation and to the creation of quality staff, which should be the central aim of the Dip.PS. For these reasons we consider that the NVQ component needs to be reviewed and refined. In our view the fundamentals of probation practice can be primarily evidenced by PDA observations, supplemented by witness statements, and the testing-out of underpinning knowledge requirements by the PDA related to specific practice situations. Therefore, where the NVQ is concerned, within the context of the Dip.PS, we need to pose certain questions:

• What do we want to achieve and how best can we achieve it?

- Does the NVQ, in the way that it measures the production of evidence against standards, also demonstrate quality performance and effectiveness?

- Is the NVQ more concerned with outputs (simply meeting the standard) than outcomes (achieving clear performance objectives); quantity of evidence rather than quality?

- Is sufficient attention devoted to the holistic knowledge needs of trainees implied by our typology?

- Are we content with the notion of competence and minimum standards, rather than excellence; and is this good enough?

If it is decided in years to come that the NVQ must continue to maintain its current shape then it is important to find ways to accommodate the wider knowledge needs of trainees considered in this chapter.

Summary

In this chapter the particular role of the PDA is examined in detail. The broad context and range of the job is described as well as the specific roles of NVQ Assessor and Internal Verifier.

The relative advantages of specialism, semi-specialism and seniority in the PDA role are discussed. In a further reflection about the role we describe a range of qualities and knowledge required to be an effective PDA.

The chapter then considers the different types of knowledge with which a PDA must engage and describes a four-fold typology for probation knowledge: academic knowledge, knowledge for practice, ineffable knowledge and self-knowledge.

Some key elements to a training strategy are proposed and the chapter concludes with some further reflections about the limitations of the NVQ structure, the way these can be ameliorated by skilled, knowledgeable and motivated PDAs and the ways in which the current shape of probation qualifying training might be reviewed.

Further reading

Home Office (1999; April) *Diploma in Probation Studies*. London: HMSO.
Home Office (2001; 24 September) Probation Circular 136/2001: *Probation Staff, Recruitment and Training – Funding for Training Consortia*. London: HMSO.
QCA (1998) *Assessing NVQs*. London: Qualifications and Curriculum Authority.
QCA (2001) *The NVQ Code of Practice*. London: Qualifications and Curriculum Authority.

Chapter 7

Being a probation officer

Introduction

At the heart of work as a probation officer are relationships. Probation officers work with people and successful outcomes to that work depend upon constructive relationships. The key relationships are with:

• offenders

• other probation staff

• people from other agencies.

Arguably relationships with the public and with victims are also crucial but engagement with these groups is still largely a specialist role. Although these relationships take place within particular contexts and prescribed frameworks of policy, protocol, guidelines and best practice, they are complex and unique. These relationships exist and are expressed through communication. Successful relationships for the probation officer depend, therefore, upon a good understanding of these contexts and frameworks and on a range of well-developed communication skills. The development of this understanding, and in particular of those skills, requires a continuing reflective and reflexive approach after qualification. Without such an approach it becomes easy to conduct these central relationships in a kind of automatic mode, based on previous experience and knowledge and not tuned-in to the uniqueness of each encounter and your impact on it.

Even with reflective and reflexive approaches to personal/professional development, relationships cannot be distilled simply into expressions of sophisticated skills, knowledge, understanding and insight. Relationships inevitably also have an emotional component. Probation officers conduct their work in the context of relationships and have feelings about those relationships, which raises two important and perhaps connected issues. The first is about dealing with the emotional content of probation work and ensuring that some emotional growth and/or development will accompany other aspects of professional development. The second is about values: to what extent are personal values part of a probation officer's motivation and animation and what is the relationship between personal values and the values of the probation service and, indeed, other agencies with whom the probation service works?

In this chapter we explore these aspects of sustained work in the probation service, taking responsibility for continuing professional and emotional development, the development of professional/probation identity and personal and professional values in the probation service.

Continuing professional development

Some universities are offering post-graduate opportunities designed to be appropriate to probation officer development and some of these are built around principles of work-based learning and the notion of the reflective/researcher practitioner. Meanwhile the National Probation Service has not yet developed a post-qualifying training framework. Different models are being applied to support newly qualified officers in their first year; some areas offer little or no support (based on the assumption that the new qualification arrangements were designed to produce officers who could 'hit the ground running'), some offer reduced caseloads for a limited period and there are some very few examples of specifically designed support and supervision. Beyond this potentially challenging first year in practice the service will need to be clear about how it intends to support continuing development. There are a number of options, the most likely of which seems to be the continuing development of Occupational Standards at higher levels, and in specialist areas, which could be clustered into a framework of post-qualifying awards. However there is a strong argument for reflecting the evidence-based practice culture of the service with post-qualifying arrangements in which probation officers are supported to develop as reflective practitioners, practitioner researchers and action researchers.

Meanwhile the probation service continues to develop and change, priorities shift, Occupational Standards are reviewed and new offender programmes become available. This creates a full agenda for area training resources and for the training consortia. In this climate it is particularly important that newly qualified probation officers are confident and competent to take some responsibility for their own continuing development. This confidence can only develop if all concerned are clear that qualifying training is not about producing a finished article. Notwithstanding the goal of 'hitting the ground running', trainees in particular need to be clear that much of the knowledge they have acquired has a limited shelf-life, that how they use much of this knowledge will change and develop over time and that many of the skills learned and accredited can and should be developed beyond notions of competence. Perhaps the most important quality of trainees following qualifying training should be insight into their own strengths, weaknesses and processes of learning and the skills and motivation to use this insight to continue to develop.

Learning in practice

Despite the different ways in which individuals prefer to learn (see Honey & Mumford, 2001) and the well-established processes and cycles applied to learning (e.g. see Kolb, 1984), learning in practice is dependent on two factors. We get good at doing things, first, by practising them and, second, from feedback about our performance.[1]

Practice

The workplace provides unlimited opportunities for practice but development requires a frame of mind in which practice is not viewed exclusively as part of 'custom and practice', i.e. set behaviours to be mirrored as closely as possible. Practice needs largely to be viewed as a process requiring continual review. There is much in the role of the probation officer that is about getting things right, or not getting things wrong, but inevitably much of the job is about working in spheres of much less certainty and where high-level performance involve what Donald Schon calls 'professional artistry' (Schon, 1987). This view of practice as a process and this goal of developing professional artistry require trainees to adopt a very particular sense of their identity as probation officers. A competence-driven qualification programme built around notions of Occupational Standards might almost seem to contradict these ideas, and so the notion of qualifying training as just a start needs to be built into expectations and processes from the outset. Similarly, workplace cultures will vary a lot across the probation service but in the hurly-burly of heavy workloads and sustained pressure it seems unlikely that pursuit of professional artistry will be very visible on the surface of those cultures. Trainees need to be prepared for this and to take opportunities to explore the workplace and engage with colleagues and identify particular opportunities and support. Similarly, the probation service needs to look at ways in which strategies to be learning organisations impact and support continuing professional development.

Feedback

The NVQ assessment is built around a process of planning, feedback and review. There is a great strength here in developing habits of planning learning, identifying learning needs and insight into strengths and weaknesses. The problem is that the process is targeted at a prescribed range of competence and at a prescribed level of performance. Furthermore, in the time-limited Diploma programme there is limited opportunity for the process to bend naturally to particular individual need or respond to naturally occurring experiences in the workplace. Nevertheless the process is

[1] Educationalist Phil Race (see Race, 1999) conducts a powerful workshop exercise in which he asks large groups to think of something they are good at and then to write down on a Post-It how they became good at it. He then asks the group to write on another Post-It how they know they are good at it. The Post-Its are then stuck onto two whiteboards where the commonly understood truth can be seen vividly. People get good at things by practising (apart from the odd one or two 'I was a natural') and people know that they are good at things because they have been told.

strong and the habits healthy and conducive to continuing professional development. The NVQ process is also characterised by observation of practice and it is this process of observation, as part of assessment and planning for assessment, that provides a regular opportunity for feedback from PDA to trainee. The quality and context of this feedback are clearly very important and are a central part of creating an effective learning environment (see Chapter 6 for further discussion). Similarly, the best academic processes are characterised by informal/formative and formal/summative feedback and increasingly prescribe structures for ongoing Personal Development Planning.[2]

These kinds of feedback are much less certain once trainees move into practice. Instead of a PDA, new officers will generally be working directly to a team manager, and instead of regular review and planning of professional development, new officers will begin to engage with the annual appraisal cycle. Even when team managers are able to offer regular supervision they can only feed back in response to written work they have seen, perhaps occasional glimpses of practice and to case discussion and issues brought by the officer. More often in fact team manager supervision takes the shape of workload review and some level of quality inspection by reference to records. It would hardly be surprising that a more managed service in terms of National Standards alongside national, area and local targets in relation to assessment, report writing, referral to and completion of orders and accredited programmes and enforcement, has stretched the team managers and indeed made the role more managerial rather than senior professional.

In some areas and teams 'buddy' systems exist where new officers are paired with experienced staff for support and sometimes include regular meetings. Elsewhere, new officers meet regularly in the first period of their appointment to discuss with each other, or with a facilitator, the problems and issues they are experiencing. There have been experiments with action learning sets for new officers. However, there has not yet been a proper review of the experience of new probation officers (this despite concerns about retaining trained staff) and it is clear that there is inconsistency within and across areas and that limited learner support is a common experience of newly qualified officers.

The learning environment

The situation is of course no clearer or consistent for experienced officers, many of whom might be experiencing a tension between their own training

---

[2] Universities are required by the QAA to ensure that all students are provided opportunities to plan, reflect, review and evaluate their overall development. As a result, universities have applied a range of Personal Development Planning policies and strategies. See www.qaa.ac.uk for further information.

and experiences in the service, the radically reshaped training arrangements and the rapid changes and refocusing of the service in recent years. Unless these dynamics and the impact on them of the large new cohorts of newly qualified officers are addressed, healthy learning environments are unlikely to emerge. It is easy to imagine experienced officers feeling jaundiced about change, dominating the workplace culture and inducting new officers into that culture. The power of this kind of workplace culture is well documented, as is its resistance to the impact of training. (See, for example, Reiner, 1978, and Waddington, 1999, in relation to the power of work culture in the police force.) Even when these processes do not take place it is again easy to imagine uneasy relations or at least underlying uncertainty between the old and the new.

As line managers are stretched to deliver development support, and as training consortia and departments are taken up with centrally driven and specialist training events, and as no post-qualifying development framework is yet emerging nationally, and as there are also potential integration difficulties in the transition period between old and new training arrangements, people at all layers of the service need to consider ways in which a learning environment can be fostered in the workplace. If a culture of feedback is at the heart of such a learning environment then the informal or formal encouragement or participation in peer review processes might be a very good starting point. This would be a process that goes beyond traditional 'buddying', which is mostly one-way traffic with the inexperienced having special access to the experienced. Peer review would be based around mutual observation and feedback. Such a process is integral to accredited programme delivery and evaluation but could make a significant contribution to developing learning team culture.

Appraisal

Although strongly influenced by national and local priorities, appraisal provides an opportunity for officers to legitimise and give shape to their professional development. At its best appraisal should offer more than just an opportunity for the organisation to express its agenda and priorities. Appraisal in a learning environment is premised on the notion of a dialogue between the organisation and the individual in which there is an attempt to plan how to maximise the contribution an individual can make to the organisation and the contribution the organisation can make towards meeting the objectives of the individual. Such a culture of appraisal acknowledges the richness and diversity that individuals bring to the work and seeks to nurture and value it. Figure 7.1 represents this model of appraisal, with each party acknowledging from the outset that organisational and individual goals are not the same thing and that appraisal can offer a way of harmonising

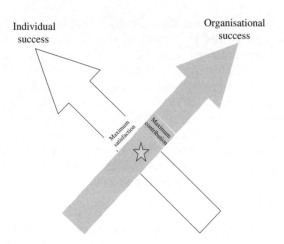

Figure 7.1 Harmonising values and goals in appraisal

goals. In this model of appraisal the language of real personal values is encouraged.

Perhaps one of the more problematic aspects of a competence-based approach to staff development is that it can be seen as emphasising the need for general skills. Certainly the qualifying award is built around standards for generalised probation work with no scope for options, personal preference or interest. Similarly, a competence-based approach sets standards of performance at 'good enough' that sometimes leaves little scope or incentive for the pursuit of excellence.

From a management perspective, and again in terms of seeking higher levels of consistency across a national service, a generalist and 'good enough' probation officer may be a useful model and a highly desirable bottom line target. However, such a model does not in fact reflect the real world of probation practice and the real working lives of probation officers. In reality probation officers have strengths, weaknesses, preferences and interests. Competence approaches can work well in identifying and targeting action in relation to weaknesses, and newly qualified officers are well advised to engage in areas with which they feel less confident, notwithstanding their completion of the NVQ. Beyond this baseline competence, however, the probation service depends on the careful nurturing of higher-level skills, enthusiasm, imagination and particular interests because it is these qualities in staff that generate new ideas, a learning climate, animation in the service and inspired practice. Harnessing these qualities is the art (rather than the science) of good management and is how the best middle managers in probation still lead and develop excellent practice.

Reflection

Newly qualified officers will of course take advantage of any support made available in the early stages of practice. They will engage with the appraisal process and try to use that process to address their particular learning needs in a way that will be effective for them. They will also engage with supervision and clarify the parameters of that supervision. For example, will it offer opportunities for reflection about practice? Beyond this, new officers should also look for other opportunities for dialogue about practice and ideally opportunities to observe others and be observed in practice. Dialogue is particularly important because it can provide a vehicle for learning through reflection. Written reflection alongside or as part of open records is impractical. It takes an exceptional individual to sustain a reflective journal alongside the pressures of practice. Dialogue is in fact a more effective vehicle for reflection.

To learn through dialogue, feedback, observation and reflection requires motivation, allies and encouragement. It also requires focus and purpose. There are three aspects of practice that can promote different aspects of professional development and can provide that focus:

- *Processes*. How do the processes of and changes in the probation service inform our understanding of criminal justice policy? How do those processes and changes affect practice? How does the probation service work? What are the connections between the national centre, regional networks and local operation? Where does the probation service fit into bigger pictures of criminal justice, community safety and crime reduction? How does the probation service measure success? Evaluate its work? Contribute to understanding about crime?

- *Personal performance*. What is good about your practice, what is less good and how would you like to improve?

- *Critical incidents*. It is often from the new, the complex, the difficult and the unexpected that we are able to learn much. Probation work is often characterised by such events. What happened? Why? How was it managed? Has it happened before? How should it be dealt with next time? What have you learned? What has the probation service learned? How do you feel about it?

Emotional development

Psychologists often discuss behaviour in terms of actions, thoughts and feelings. Professional or occupational behaviour in probation qualification is assured through the processes of the Dip.PS where the focus in both the NVQ and the degree element is on action and thoughts, observed competence underpinned by prescribed knowledge and understanding. It is not surprising that emotional competence is not addressed because assessment and measurement of this area is difficult and some would say controversial. Psychometric tools do exist to measure emotional intelligence but the connections between this quality and competent practice are not established and it is certainly not clear what processes develop or improve emotional intelligence.

Outside of the possibilities and prospects of selection processes to find candidates emotionally equipped for probation work and the application of processes to support emotional development, probation staff and newly qualified officers in particular will often need to take some responsibility for ensuring their emotional well-being. To do this it is helpful to consider two factors: emotional support and self-knowledge.

Emotional support

There is a model from the world of health professionals (Shaw et al., 1978; Machin & Stevenson, 1997) that describes occupational competence in terms of adequacy, legitimacy and support. In this model (see Figure 7.2) competence and confidence in a role can only develop when all three elements come together. Adequacy is the knowledge and skills needed to fulfil the role. Legitimacy is clarity about expectations and understanding about the legal, statutory and professional basis of the role. Support is one of the resources needed, but emotional support is also needed to do the job.

The model can be useful in identifying the source of lack of confidence, and particularly so, because it allows that the source of confidence and competence goes beyond knowledge and skills. The model raises the question for probation staff about what emotional support is available to do the job.

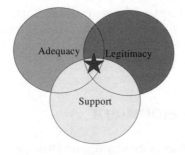

Figure 7.2 Confidence and competence

More specifically, in what environments, and with which people, is it possible to talk about how you feel on a daily basis in relation to difficult or challenging pieces of work, and in a general way about the experience of becoming and being a probation officer where you are? Traditionally the probation service has accommodated a strong team culture. Probation officers generally still work in teams and can enjoy a strong sense of shared experience, often working in the same geographical patch and often experiencing the same organisational pressures and professional challenges. There has been little, if any, research on the impact of change on this team culture in the probation service, or on the impact on the experience of shared identity of the radical shifts in probation qualifying training and the rapid growth in numbers of qualified staff in recent years.

For newly qualified officers the issue of emotional support is likely to be a particularly important feature of developing confidence. In particular, new officers need to be given the chance to find out that feelings such as uncertainty, anxiety, distress, hopelessness and fear are quite normal and form a healthy and engaged response to the experience of probation practice. They need to be able to discover that it is all right to have feelings about the work, that others often feel or have felt the same way and, in particular, that absence of or the suppression of feelings is not a feature of competent practice. Further, they also need to know that feelings do impact on practice and that discussion with colleagues is a central and important way of dealing with this issue professionally. Healthy teams will draw new staff into this mutual support by processes of disclosure and sensitive enquiry. Where that sort of culture does not exist, there is a danger of isolation and finding a 'buddy' or ally or supportive friend (perhaps even the team manager) is an important priority.

Personal values

Becoming a probation officer involves a process of transition. The probation service still recruits trainees from a wide variety of cultural backgrounds, work, personal experience and academic accomplishment. In the application process – on the form at the assessment centre – applicants have to address the question of why they want to become a probation officer and what they think becoming a probation officer will involve. Among other things the process of selection seeks to establish levels of motivation and the presence of a realistic if undeveloped sense of what probation officers are and what they do. There is a clear sense that probation is a job you do because you understand something of what the probation service seeks to achieve, and you want to be part of that project. Historically these qualities have been thought of in terms of vocation. Here the idea is that the job on offer goes beyond being, for example, simply a way of making a living. The job in some way resonates with a need in some people who do not so much apply as offer themselves to it. There are also undertones of altruism in this vocationalism. People give up better-paid and more prestigious jobs to train as probation officers, and these people often talk about wanting to do something more worthwhile with their lives. Many applicants talk in terms of probation being important work and wanting to be part of it. Sometimes this vocationalism is expressed in terms of particular qualities. Probation is said to require very particular qualities (e.g. patience, empathy, caring, being able to get on with anyone) and some people, feeling that they have these qualities, describe the desire to put them to constructive use through the probation service.

Meanwhile the applicant needs to tread carefully through the process, being careful not to describe a commitment to the wrong sort of vocation. One of the interesting consequences of the clearer and more consistent message about the mission, goals, aims and objectives of the probation service is that there is a lot of clarity, and at times emphasis, on what the probation service is not. For example, it is not about social work, does not draw its legitimacy from social policy or a structural understanding of crime. It is not anti-custodial. The well-prepared applicants know all this and present their vocation and motivation in the context of some knowledge about current probation *mores*. This business of presenting an on-line message is the beginning of the process of transition to becoming a probation officer.

There is an extent to which much of this framing of motivation and vocation, and the expectation of that framing, are rather disingenuous. People choose jobs and change jobs for a host of reasons that are much more related to the complex and unique unfolding of their lives than to any sense of an ideal fit between job and self. There is no reason to believe that the experience of probation applicants is hugely different. As well as some affinity to what is understood about the work of the probation service, other reasons for applying are likely to include:

- Don't like what I do currently

- It seems quite interesting

- I'm curious about why people offend

- It is quite well paid

- It provides a level of professional status

- It pays while training

- I'll get a degree

- It seems very secure

- It opens doors to other opportunities

- I fit the bill

- I'll be good at it

- I need a change

- It's a good job to do part time

- It fits quite well with what I've been doing

- It fits quite well with what I've been studying

- I know some probation officers and I liked them

- The holidays are good

However, there is an extent to which the process of applying for a job requires candidates to play the game, and the game is no different for probation applicants than in any other job. The basic rule of the game is to say and present the things that the employer wants to hear. To play the game well it is important to know something about how the probation service currently presents itself and, in particular, the values it professes and with which it wants its staff to identify and, in some cases, act. Before some discussion of these dynamic institutional values we should look more closely at the notion of personal values. Before playing the game it is important to look more closely at whether or not this is a job we want to do.

In the same way that we are inclined to be disingenuous about why we want to be probation officers, we are also inclined to describe our personal values in terms that rarely reflect what we actually value most highly at different stages of our lives. Personal values are relative, fluid and represent personal priorities. They are not beliefs. Rather they reflect those aspects of our lives that we enjoy. They change in relation to the changing context of our lives and are not necessarily consistent between different parts of our identity: employee, probation officer, friend, colleague, partner, son/daughter, parent, citizen, neighbour, etc. The language that describes these real personal values is very distinct from that which routinely describes, for example, professional values or institutional values. Real personal values might be described in terms of:

- happiness

- fun

- wealth

- security

- fame

- respect

- family

- friendship

- love

- spiritual enlightenment

- health

- integrity

- power.

Meanwhile professional values (see Chapter 4), or the values that we apply to our work, flow from sets of beliefs and convictions about the nature of the world, the nature of knowledge and human nature. Historically the probation service drew these sets of values from the religious and moral convictions of its early practitioners and later from a developing social work tradition of values, and this development is discussed in Chapter 1. These values are important because they bring with them expectations, particularly in terms of *how* probation officers practise. They are also important because they are a significant part of how the world views the probation service. Professional values are part of the public face of probation. This provides an important part of the context for the relationships between the probation service and other agencies. For the individual probation officer they are also experienced as public perceptions of probation identity. Probation officers will feel more or less comfortable with this sense of professional identity.

Underpinning beliefs

Before discussing these probation values in more detail, it is worth considering the notion of underpinning beliefs. Although they are not the same as values, there is a relationship between what we believe and how we see the world. Beliefs can be said to be analogous to a lens through which we make sense of and understand the world. This is self-evidently true. Is sport about physical endeavour, the development of skills and the testing of these in competition? Or is it about winning? Watching your favourite football team might be a very different experience depending on which of these beliefs we hold. The interesting thing about these beliefs is that they tend to be parameters rather than fixed positions. Individual belief will be somewhere between the extremes, perhaps tending to one side more than another and probably changing over time in the light of experience and circumstance. If your favourite football team is the one your child plays for, then your view may be different from a Premiership team fan. As a Premiership fan your view might change as your team consistently wins or fails to win.

There are three underpinning parameters of belief or assumption that are pertinent when considering our own position in relation to probation values. There is no right or wrong answer to the questions posed but where we stand in relation to them will tell us something about the relationship between our own underpinning beliefs and the values of the probation service.

The ontological question

What is the nature of the world? In particular for probation officers, what is the nature of the social world? What is objectively real and what is the result of individual cognition? At one end of the parameter is the realist position: the social world is definable, testable and measurable; there is an objective social reality. At the other end is the nominalist: the world outside of the individual is just made up of names, concepts and labels that are used to construct reality. The social world is a construct.

So, what is crime? To the realist crime is a definable, measurable reality. To the nominalist crime is the label given to a range of unique individual experiences.

The epistemological question

What can we know of the social world and how can we communicate it? What is true and what is false? Is knowledge fixed and hard or softer and less tangible? The positivist argues that there are underlying patterns and laws about the social world and that we can explain and predict regularities and irregularities with the help of these laws. The anti-positivist argues that all knowledge is relative and that our only real understanding of the social world is through individual experience of it.

So, what do we know about poverty? The positivist will argue that we can define poverty in measurable terms, account for it, describe where it exists and with the right data explain the relationships between poverty and other social experiences. The anti-positivist will describe poverty as a construct and a relative concept and will argue that the nearest we can come to understanding poverty is through being poor or by trying to understand the experience of someone who is poor.

The question about human nature

What makes us what we are? Can we control our destinies and to what extent? For the determinist, people are what they are because of their history, situation, circumstances and environment. Furthermore, we can explain and sometimes predict people's behaviour on the basis of such information. The voluntarist argues that there is such a thing as free will and that people can choose behaviour and indeed can be creative in and with their lives.

So, how can we change people? The determinist will argue that change will be possible if we can control and manipulate a person's experience of the world. For the voluntarist, change will be primarily to do with a person's decision to make a change.

The relevance of the questions

Those considering, or indeed committed to, a career in the probation service might find it useful to think on these three questions about underpinning belief, different lenses that can be used to look at the world, to explore their own feelings about them and then consider where the probation service seems to stand in relation to questions about the social world, knowledge and human nature.

Probation values

How, therefore, is the probation service presenting itself to the world and to what extent are values part of that presentation? It is important to remember that these presented values are the values of the National Probation Directorate, a centralised arm of the criminal justice system directly responsible to the Home Office. They are the values not of a professional or occupational body but in part an expression of political will and intent. Of course they are also an expression contained by political expedience. Like personal values they can in part be discerned in the identification of priorities and aspirations and, like professional values, they can in part be discerned in expressions of how the probation service should be delivered or managed.

Somewhere near the front of these values is a concern with and for victims. What is interesting about this is that this priority is less to do with the work that the probation service does with and for victims (which both statutorily and in practice is still a very small and largely specialist proportion of the service's work) than with the frame of mind of the service. In working with offenders the service seems to be saying, we will have in mind the experience of victims. This priority also serves to confirm the probation service as an agency concerned with reducing the number of victims, i.e. an agency primarily concerned with reducing crime. In terms of public perception and political acceptability this is clearly a comfortable priority to espouse.

Another set of priorities that could be interpreted as an expression of values comes in the mission statement of the probation service, where the thematic aims are described as 'enforcement, rehabilitation and public protection'. This again has a comfortable feel in terms of public presentation and addressing public concern and fear of crime. These three items have always been on the probation agenda but their presentation as a central mantra for probation sets the context of work with offenders. The probation service works with offenders (to rehabilitate them), drawing on the power of the courts and state to assure compliance, and the power of scientific assessment to assure appropriate disposal (and public protection). Work with offenders, to rehabilitate them, ceases without compliance and is a secondary consideration if risk to the public is assessed as too high. This presentation inevitably sets up a tension in probation work that relies heavily on motivating, engaging and working *with* offenders rather than *on* them.

Working with offenders

A New Choreography (Home Office, 2001) develops three other themes that define the ground on which the probation service aspires to stand.

What Works

Effective practice, evidence-based practice, research-led practice and 'What Works' are all expressions of a commitment by the probation service to empirical approaches to practice. This is not expressed as a drive to develop the workforce in practitioner research but rather as deference to a particular body of research and to a centrally driven programme accreditation process. Reduced reconviction rates are the target and we await detailed impact studies. 'What Works' presents a technical and scientific picture of the probation service. Beyond pragmatic, accredited programmes are an idealised process of scientific assessment and the consequent selection of the pliable – the application of approved programmes in which programme integrity and firm enforcement to complete are essential. The probation service is committed to challenging targets in terms of numbers of offenders to be processed in this way and 'What Works' presents not only science, pragmatism and 'common sense' but also managerial competence and efficiency as central parts of the service identity.

Partnership

Central to successful probation practice is a shared sense of purpose with offenders. Accredited programmes depend on offenders being committed to addressing the particular issues addressed. Shared and agreed objectives and processes are the central currency of constructive probation work. Partnership in *A New Choreography* is less about this than about relations with other agencies. Again, the values being represented here are about the part the probation service aspires to play in the formulation and implementation of national strategy and the place the probation service occupies in relation to national, regional and local networks of agencies. The nature of relationships between agencies depends on many factors: relative statutory and political legitimacy; relative resources; relative clarity of agency aims and purpose, etc. At senior levels partnership between the probation service and other agencies is expressed as involvement in centrally driven attempts to promote 'joined-up' thinking such as around Community Safety Partnerships and Drug Action Teams. These processes do not lead to changes in the actions of participating agencies or how these actions are performed. They can, however, lead to better understanding of the role of respective agencies and become more dynamic in relation to allocating funding. Partnerships that are then created between funders and fundees, like the partnerships forged through probation partnership funding, are not partnerships founded in the notion of working together to achieve commonly agreed aims but rather are essentially purchaser/provider relationships in which the key elements are the contract and contract compliance. For probation officers generally these strategic and contractual partnerships are distant phenomena. The issue for them is what the impact of partnerships is on day-to-day relations with people they seek to work with from a very wide range of agencies. This is a complex and challenging part of probation work. Much depends on being well informed, having clear communications and managing successful interpersonal relationships. However, it is difficult to work successfully with people from other agencies without a good sense of who you are as a probation officer, the range and limits of your statutory, legal and professional legitimacy, the general and specific objectives of the probation service, and the particular skills, knowledge and perspective that you bring to any particular situation or problem.

Working with difference (diversity)

In *A New Choreography* there are strong statements about the value of diversity and, in particular, the value of a diverse workforce that reflects the diversity of the communities that probation serves. Probation has enjoyed some relative success in recruiting widely and continues to target improvements. An interesting current problem is the difficulty in recruiting men as practitioners and a particularly significant problem in the context of what is still an overwhelmingly male offender workload. Diversity presents two problems in relation to service delivery that are not addressed by diverse recruitment. First, to what extent does the probation service accommodate diversity among offenders (and victims) in the range of services delivered and how they are delivered? Second, to what extent and how successfully does the probation service work with offending that is motivated by difference? These issues are not addressed in *A New Choreography*. Appropriateness of services, for example, to black offenders and women offenders and sensitivity of services to issues of race, gender, sexuality and disability would best be tested by research on the experience of offenders on probation, and without the knowledge of such research it is difficult to plan development, change and improvement. As yet accredited and approved programmes do not address offending motivated by difference. This seems surprising in the light of the work over some years to develop ways of working with, for example, racially motivated offenders and with perpetrators of domestic violence. In the sense that the probation service would put into practice the idea of meeting the needs of a diverse community rather than just reflecting that diversity in its workforce, these areas might provide highly appropriate diversity targets. A diversity strategy that limits itself to recruitment, retention and promotion issues may result in lots of different people doing exactly the same things.

Offenders as people

Some of the same flavour and themes can be seen in the probation service response to the arrival of Human Rights legislation but in addition it is here that perhaps the probation officer might find an indication of the values that are more directly applicable to practice. Alongside the notions of probation striving for openness about what it does, involvement in the local communities in which it works and partnership (again) with those communities, we also find the acknowledgement of offenders as citizens. However, it may be rather optimistic to hope that Human Rights will provide a more humanitarian position for the probation service being perhaps more likely to emphasise the rights of victims of crimes than the citizenship of offenders (Nellis & Gelsthorpe, 2003). Nellis and Gelsthorpe describe the current period in probation in terms of a 'hiatus in thinking about probation values'

(p. 237). The future of probation values will depend on a number of factors. The more entrenched the service becomes in the objective, positivist and scientific responses to underpinning questions about crime, offending and offenders, the more it will define its activity in functional terms and the work of its staff ever more exclusively in terms of competence. Such a probation service may well espouse public accountability, transparency, consistency and efficiency as central values but this managerialist sense of values has little to do with probation work based in relationships of respect, honesty and openness.

Being a probation officer

It is perhaps appropriate to hang on to these last notions of respect, honesty and openness. Values form a complex area and probation values, which have been contested for some time, are in a state of flux at the moment. As a probation officer you need to be clear what the service is telling you about probation values, but it will not always be obvious how institutional values relate to the realities of practice. Much of what are passed off as institutional values in the probation service are in fact statements about what the probation service does and where it fits into the criminal justice system, public service and government strategy. You need to know this as you decide to join and stay in the probation service. You also need to know what you want from your life and from your working life as your career develops. These kind of personal priorities are legitimate and an important part of planning your career and maximising the animation you bring to the job. On the whole, we want to be with people who think like us and, in particular, we want to work with kindred spirits. Values can be the crucial part of this kinship but are complicated and difficult concepts that are difficult to debate in the abstract with colleagues. However, feelings and emotions about work are often the currency of intimacy with colleagues. We learn with and from colleagues through this kind of intimacy and it is a central support when the job becomes problematic. It is here in the hearts of probation staff, and expressed in how they work and what they feel about their work, that probation values actually reside. Those values will be as strong as the dialogue and sharing that sustains them, strengthened by debate, developed in the light of experience and validated by understanding and sometimes agreement.

Being a probation officer is difficult. Workloads are often high, offenders often challenging and decision-making and problem-solving complex. However, you do not want it to be easy. It is the difficulty, the uncertainty, the unexpected and the unknown, the knowledge that the next day will be different again, that makes being a probation officer so rewarding for many people. To keep this quality of being a probation officer alive it is important to remain curious and interested. Every day is different and every offender is new, but your joy in that reality or even your understanding of that reality will fade and wither unless you continue to ask yourself 'What is going on here?', 'Why is this happening?' and 'What do I feel about this?' The work will continue to be fresh and new, and as long as you are asking those questions you will continue to learn. To sustain this kind of animation in your practice is probably about more than sustaining a spirit of curiosity, important though this is. Whether connected to probation service values, some sense of emergent professional values or (more likely) personal values and beliefs, you need to care. The core of the enterprise is people in the form of probation officers working with other people we call offenders. To forget this central tenet is to impoverish the probation service and the contribution it makes to the criminal justice system.

Summary

This chapter considers how probation officers sustain their professional development and animation after qualification. It begins with a review of how people learn in the workplace and looks in some detail at the notions of practice and feedback. The constituents of a learning environment are considered, together with a model for appraisal.

It is argued that the probation service depends on its staff going beyond competent performance and that well-focused reflective practice can facilitate this development. The importance of emotional development is stressed and a model is presented in which emotional support is seen as an integral part of professional confidence.

Personal values are described in contrast to personal beliefs and some questions about underpinning beliefs are posed. We suggest that personal/individual responses, and the probation service position in relation to these questions, is likely to be different and of interest. Current probation values are also discussed.

Probation practice values are described in terms of a workplace culture of dialogue and emotional support. We suggest that animated practice is sustained by curiosity, emotional involvement and compassion.

Further reading

A good place to begin an exploration of how people learn is Boud, D. (ed.) (1985) *Reflection: Turning Experience into Learning.* London: Kogan Page.

Nellis, M. & Gelsthorpe, L. (2003) Human rights and the probation values debate. In W.H. Chui & M. Nellis (eds), *Moving Probation Forward.* Harlow: Pearson Longman, provide a good discussion of probation values.

Schon, D. (1987) *Educating the Reflective Practitioner.* San Francisco: Jossey-Bass, is an important influence about thinking about reflection and its role in learning and practice.

For a flavour of the values being promoted centrally it is important to be familiar with the probation strategy documents, e.g. the recent NPS Annual Plan for 2004/5 (National Probation Directorate, 2004) and the recent Home Office response (Home Office, 2004) to the Carter report (Carter, 2003). Partnership is a complex process and working in partnerships presents many different challenges. An excellent introduction to the subject is provided by Loxley, A. (1997) *Collaboration in Health and Welfare: Working with Difference.* London: Jessica Kingsley.

Chapter 8

From competence to excellence: Going beyond the codification of knowledge

Summary of Chapters 1–7

Chapter 1, in broad terms, sets the scene for the whole book, which is concerned to explore the twin themes of training and knowledge within the probation service and, by doing so, primarily benefit TPOs as they progress through the Dip.PS. Despite the fact that the probation system began towards the end of the Victorian era in 1876 with the work of the Police Court Missionaries, we had to wait until 1930 for the first Home Office Training Scheme that attempted to equip aspiring probation officers to work with offenders within a specific theoretical, ideological and political context. But even at this stage the training being provided, because of the realities of probation practice, was a blend of academic and practical topics that drew attention to the fact that probation officers required more than purely theoretical- and academic-oriented knowledge provided by the universities. It was thought, as we have already explored, that probation officers during the 1930s needed to know about economics, poverty, psychology, criminology, law and administration, in addition to writing reports for courts, supervising offenders on probation, custodial facilities and other institutions (Le Mesurier, 1935). Since the 1930s and until the present day the training of probation officers has taken different forms, from Police Court Missionary and Home Office to CQSW courses; from specialist to generic, back to specialist courses again with the introduction of the Dip.PS in 1998. Moreover, during this period the knowledge base of the service has progressed through a series of changes, a consequence of disparate influences and pressures, and changing political, social, ideological and economic contexts, including the introduction of the NVQ (Garland, 1985, 2001; also see Appendix 1 for additional information).

Chapter 2 initially continues with this broad historical overview of training and knowledge before proceeding to introduce the important theme of knowledge in vocational education. As the chapter progresses it is made clear that the knowledge requirements of trainees within the context of probation vocational education go beyond the demands and limitations of NVQ codification and also beyond the confines of the academic and theoretical component of the Dip.PS provided by the universities. Therefore an expanded concept of knowledge is inchoately introduced that is developed as the book unfolds.

Chapter 3 explores the development of the Dip.PS, Occupational Standards and, of course, the NVQ. Our analysis of each item of NVQ UKU (over 200 separate items) reveals a number of recurring key themes of which trainees need to be aware. These themes, clarified in Table 3.1, are: victim issues, explaining offending behaviour, legislation, local area policies and guidelines, professional values, risk assessment, effective methods of working with offenders, communication, enforcement and compliance, self-reflection, and confidentiality. Consequently, trainees need an understanding of these areas of knowledge to complete the NVQ and also to function as knowledgeable and effective probation officers. Moreover, these knowledge themes find a resonance with the academic component of the training course that, after 2003, will be delivered by distance learning in four consortia (and perhaps all consortia from 2008).

If Chapter 3 analyses all the items of underpinning knowledge to produce Table 3.1, Chapter 4 is a logical extension of its immediate predecessor because it provides TPOs with some of the essential resources on these major themes, in addition to pointing in the right direction of other useful sources of knowledge. Again all the knowledge resources contained in the book complement the academic component of the Dip.PS.

Chapter 5 continues to provide trainees with essential knowledge resources, but this time to engage confidently with the practice of writing PSRs. It can be strongly argued that court reports strike to the heart of the probation task because these documents encapsulate key probation skills that the trainee must begin to acquire – for example, assessment and intervention strategies. These documents also help to define the unique role occupied by the probation service within the sentencing process and wider criminal justice system. Consequently trainees need to know how to write reports; they need to acquire knowledge of sentencing practice and sentencing options at the magistrates' and crown courts. Furthermore, reports can be used as evidence for the NVQ, which means that they are important for trainees at different levels.

We think Chapter 6 is important because it explores the crucial dynamic between the PDA and the trainee that is at the heart of the Dip.PS, increasingly so within the context of the expansion of distance learning. It picks up some of the themes alluded to in Chapter 2 that began to explore the nature of knowledge within vocational education that takes us beyond the limitations established by NVQ codification, and the academic component, towards the creation of a multifaceted typology. It must be asserted, lest there is any confusion, that TPOs need the knowledge provided by the universities, and the knowledge to complete the NVQ derived from practice and academic sources. However, because of the complex, diverse, surprising and sometimes unexpected nature of probation practice, a much broader understanding of knowledge should be entertained, in fact must be entertained within probation vocational education. Within this context the PDA has a crucial role to play in modelling the knowledge that trainees require in order to be effective practitioners within the organisation and to achieve standards of excellence that take the trainee beyond codification and associated notions of competence and minimum standards. At the end of this chapter we speculate upon the NVQ with a view to suggesting certain refinements because we think that critical questions need to be posed to make this feature of the Dip.PS more beneficial to TPOs and PDAs.

Chapter 7, on 'Being a Probation Officer', considers probation work outside the context of qualifying arrangements and proposes that excellence in practice depends on continual learning and development. Furthermore, it is argued that this development needs to encompass the emotional demands of the job and consideration of the relationship between personal beliefs and values and the implicit and explicit values of the probation service. Learning processes for the workplace (practice, feedback, appraisal and reflection) are examined and models offered to help identify personal and organisational need. The notion of underpinning beliefs is explored and the relationship between these beliefs and values. We suggest that motivation or professional animation as a probation officer is strongly related to recognising and dealing with dissonance between personal and organisational values. The chapter begins and ends with the assertion that the currency of the probation task is relationships and, for the probation officer, largely individual relationships.

Therefore we hope that this book, at various levels, makes a contribution to the training of TPOs as they proceed through the Dip.PS; that the substantive chapters provide some of the essential knowledge resources for the NVQ which in turn complements the academic component, and stimulates the critical relationship between the TPO and the PDA. In our view it is this dynamic that is the difference between producing competent and quality probation officers. Let us try to bring this book to a close by returning to a number of historical and contextual issues, which is where we began in the first two chapters. The tenor is somewhat discursive and at times speculative and our intention is to raise issues for discussion.

Going beyond minimum knowledge requirements

The amateur and religiously oriented probation system that began in 1876 – subsequently established on a statutory basis in 1907 and continues into the twenty-first century – has always required knowledge to discharge its diverse responsibilities, just like any other profession. Beginning with a knowledge base (perhaps it is more accurate to say belief system) rooted in evangelical theology – and invoking metaphysical assistance in a process of change and normalisation to modern preoccupations with risk assessment, dangerousness, public protection, research-based interventions, and the renaissance of rehabilitation after 1997 – the service continues to draw upon diverse knowledge resources in pursuit of its objectives and cash-linked targets. However, with the advent of the first Home Office Training Scheme in 1930, at a time when an ideology rooted in saving inebriates' souls was slowly shifting towards secular diagnosis and rehabilitation, the knowledge base was increasingly formalised, systematised and professionalised – a development given impetus by evolving academic disciplines within the universities, particularly the criminological science of positivism that influenced the social enquiry report. Furthermore, probation officers have always required forms of practice knowledge to respond to the vagaries of workplace situations beyond the orbit of pure academic knowledge. Importantly, both academic and practice knowledge strands have complemented and enriched each other, a process that continues in the contemporary service. Within probation it is extremely difficult to sustain the position that one form of knowledge is more important than another, as though we have to choose between theory and practice. This is a false choice because it is not a case of either-or, but rather both-and, when the subject of knowledge is under discussion in a people-oriented organisation.

At this point in this final chapter it is possible to argue the position that, over recent years (since the 1970s), a paradox has emerged where our twin themes of training and knowledge are concerned within the probation service that can be expanded upon as follows. There is little doubt that probation work has become more complex, challenging, demanding and diverse within a rapidly moving political, social and economic situation. A culture of change and inexorable development has evolved in pursuit of effectiveness, and there is a greater clarity in terms of (stretch) objectives and targets delineated within the Choreography document when working with offenders. Furthermore, since 1997 we have witnessed the rebirth of rehabilitation (Garland, 2001, p. 176) in addition to the introduction of the OASys instrument, for example, referred to in Chapter 4, which is premised upon the collection of different sources of information that assists practitioners to make careful judgements about offenders in relation to risk of re-offending, harm and need. This instrument also draws attention to the important themes of domestic violence, public protection, child protection and Schedule 1 offenders, in a way that expects practitioners to know what they are thinking and doing. Consequently, the expectations upon the service are greater than they have ever been. However, the paradox that can be discerned within this process is that as the service has become more complex and the work more demanding, so the knowledge base for new staff could be potentially attenuated by the emergence of a culture influenced by NVQ knowledge codification in addition to, for example, National Standards. It may be argued that these twin developments have, inadvertently and unwittingly, encouraged an organisational culture more attuned to competence and minimum Occupational Standards rather than quality that, of course, requires less rather than more knowledge. In other words features initially introduced in a positive manner and with the best of intentions to establish minimum standards of performance, perhaps even to raise standards, contain within them the seeds of unintended consequences associated with limiting the professional knowledge horizons required to do the job effectively. We say again incontrovertibly that the NVQ in all its dimensions (evidence required to meet performance criteria, range, UKU) is an integral component of the Dip.PS and trainees must, of course, meet the demands of National Standards. Our point is that formalised and codified knowledge structures that are particularly associated with the NVQ only establish minimum standards of professional knowledge and performance rather than the inspiration to achieve excellence, as we started to articulate in Chapters 2 and 6, and which is one of the main discussion points in this book. The achievement of excellence and correspondingly effectiveness relies upon the acquisition and application of knowledge that goes beyond codification because of the complexity, illimitable, surprising and contingent nature of probation practice, and the fact that all the offenders we work with are different.

Within an industrial setting, if we are permitted to use this term, one can appreciate the relevance of an NVQ that assesses, for example, the competence of an apprentice joiner to screw two pieces of wood together, a fireman to ascend and descend a ladder safely, or a plumber to fix a water leak. In other words, the same task can be repeated and therefore competence unambiguously assessed. But within a probation context the salient difference is that while it may be possible to acquire the knowledge to perform certain tasks in the same way over a period of time to meet evidence requirements, practice situations emerge that will require forms of knowledge, understanding and insight that lead the TPO beyond NVQ demands because of the different backgrounds, experiences, needs, problems and circumstances of offenders. In this sense probation practice is dissimilar to joinery, the work of the fire service, and plumbing. There is a critical human dynamic to probation practice that defies attempts to squeeze offenders into prescriptive, measurable and therefore codified systems of knowledge; this is not the real world inhabited by the service's clients.

Let us try to broaden this discussion by analysing some of the possible features that account for the emergence of this apparent paradox. The analysis we provide undoubtedly caricatures the point we are exploring, but like all caricatures a vestige of truth can be extrapolated. It may be suggested that there is sometimes a tendency within contemporary practice to concentrate too much on the presenting problem when working with offenders – drugs, alcohol and unemployment, for example – without sufficient analytical detail being given to what lies beneath that necessitates asking the 'why' question sufficiently. Even though the casework-psychosocial approach has been discredited (Coulshed, 1988), at its best it drew attention to the importance of understanding the whole person; of exploring presenting and underlying problems; it encouraged the practitioner to think about the causes of offending beyond and below surface issues; and it facilitated an understanding of the individual. It may be argued that practice at its best continues to take cognisance of all these factors, which is predicated upon a comprehensive knowledge base, specifically when undertaking an assessment of an offender. But when contemporary practice does not conform to these best practice principles the historical reasons for this may be enumerated as follows. While the NVQ has the capacity to impose limits upon knowledge as we have already seen, similarly it may be speculated that there are other pressures that can be identified that threaten the scope of knowledge within the probation service.

Threats to knowledge

First, the decline of the rehabilitative ideal (see Chapter 1 and Appendix 1 for contextual information) is a significant factor when undertaking this analysis. During the halcyon days of rehabilitation, between the 1930s and the 1970s, the probation service was involved in the assessment, diagnosis and treatment of offenders within a social democratic welfare state environment, particularly after 1945. The professional task of the probation officer was to assess and then address those myriad personal and social factors associated with crime with a view to correcting and normalising the offender through a casework relationship that focused upon underlying causes, unconscious conflicts, childhood experiences and other significant events. Furthermore, this approach was inspired by a correctionalist criminology that understood crime as a product of adverse social conditions and psychological conflicts; the offender was not in full control of his actions; the emphasis was upon aetiology and individual need. Moreover, crime and offenders were deep subjects that had to be understood and explained, an approach that emphasised positive help rather than negative punishment, probation rather than prison. Even though we have witnessed the renaissance of rehabilitation since 1997 after a period of penal pessimism (particularly between 1993 and 1997), it is now but one objective among many that include risk assessment, public protection, concern for victims, enforcement, the benefit sanction and punishment in the community, rather than being the unifying ideology of penal welfare as it once was. Nevertheless it may be suggested that within a broader historical perspective that encompasses the period from the mid-1970s to 1997, but perhaps to a lesser degree since 1997, the displacement of the rehabilitative ideal as it was once understood has culminated in the knowledge base of the service being attenuated, which has had implications for our approach to individual offenders.

The next overlapping point to consider is the rise of the Justice Model during the 1980s (a return to neo-classicism after the decline of the rehabilitative ideal) that placed much greater emphasis upon the offence rather than understanding the offender. Therefore, what is the point, it may be asked, of spending time searching for underlying causes of crime and dipping below the surface of presenting problems if the offender is largely responsible for his behaviour and the main aim of sentencing is to proportionately punish rather than treat? Moreover, the rise of Justice Model thinking has been accompanied by shifts in criminological discourse that can be illustrated by saying that trainees continue to be introduced to anomie, relative deprivation, neo-positivism, sub-cultural theory and labelling during their training (see Appendix 2). However, it is equally true to say that the competing discourses of rational choice, routine activity, and crime as opportunity, have challenged the view that crime is a consequence of individual pathology, abnormality, deprivation, faulty socialisation and wider social factors. Rather it is the notion of crime as a consequence of rational decisions made by normal people that helps to justify a more punitive rather than welfare-oriented approach. Therefore within this neo-classical paradigm there is much less need to understand and explain which has obvious implications for knowledge requirements. It should be stated that even though this is not the only discourse in circulation (if it were there would be little point continuing to write PSRs), nevertheless it is a development that supports the view that you need less knowledge because there is not much that needs to be understood and little to explain. Before moving on from exploring the implications of the decline of rehabilitation and rise of Justice Model thinking on knowledge, it is instructive to refer to David Garland who looks at these two paradigms from the standpoint of changing conceptions of justice. He says that:

> At the turn of the twentieth century, the strict classicism and formal justice of the Enlightenment began to be challenged by new conceptions which placed less stress upon formal equality, proportionality, and strictly applied general rules and which emphasised instead the importance of substantive results, the need for individual consideration, and the value of professional flexibility. This new, more substantive conception of justice . . . has existed ever since as an important strand in our cultural fabric, a strand which runs alongside the still resilient liberal tradition in a continuous process of dialogue and interplay.
>
> GARLAND, 1990, p. 206

Therefore, different approaches to offenders have implications for the scope of knowledge and conceptions of justice.

The third point that has resonance for our analysis is the threat to the knowledge base of probation that comes from fluctuating political imperatives and economic pressures. Economic constraints have always pervaded the public sector and there has always been a sense that one can never do as much as one would like because there is always a shortage of money within social services, education, health, including probation, despite expanding budgets over recent years. It we take a longer-term view then it should be acknowledged that the 1962 Departmental Committee Report (Home Office, 1962) was concerned, among other things, to ensure that the probation service is efficient and the interests of the Exchequer safeguarded. By 1984 the Statement of National Objectives and Priorities (SNOP) was primarily concerned with the management of financial resources more economically, efficiently and effectively, as this was the Home Office document through which the Financial Management Initiative was applied to the probation service (Whitehead, 1990; see Chapter 3 for a more detailed analysis of this period). It may be observed that one of the significant implications of the SNOP document was a shift of emphasis from providing tax-payers' money in pursuit of offender need, to finite resources determining the policy (you can only do a specified amount of probation work with a fixed amount of money). Therefore, against this background we have witnessed the introduction of a new language within the probation service in the form of cost-benefits; value for money; cash limits; public–private partnerships (the mixed economy); objectives and cash-linked targets. The point is that the probation service is conscious that the work undertaken with offenders, from risk assessment and public protection to the provision of appropriate help, comes at a price and that the resources allocated in pursuit of objectives can be reduced if targets are not met. The probation service, in addition to the public sector as a whole, is at the mercy of fluctuating economic conditions that have implications for political priorities, social and penal policy (Brownlee, 1998, ch. 4; Garland, 2001). The adequate provision of offender services, detailed assessments linked to understanding, and the preparation of quality PSRs for magistrates and judges are all premised upon a comprehensive knowledge base that must be paid for. Therefore, we simply raise the point that in years to come (and this is a process that has gathered momentum since 1984) knowledge in probation will be affected by the prevailing economic and political context, the ongoing pressures for public sector reform, the tax and spend balance, and the development of a mixed economy within the public sector. These are some of the tensions we live with and need to be aware of, and it is the 'knowing the price of everything and value of nothing' syndrome (the reader is also referred to Chapter 2 and the reference to the knowledge economy and the pressure to reduce the scope of knowledge to its economic utility).

Another factor we think complements our analysis is to consider legislative developments since 1993 particularly (see the relevant sub-section in Chapter 4 for details of specific items of legislation). It can be discerned that a harsher, less understanding, more punitive criminal justice system emerged during the previous decade, manifested by certain legislative developments. Therefore this change of attitude and culture in relation to sentencing policy, it could be argued, has adversely affected the knowledge base of probation, albeit in a subtle yet insidious manner at times, with the result that there is less emphasis upon the need to understand offenders because they are considered to be less deserving of help. In fact the message that was articulated strongly by the Conservative administration during the mid-1990s was that we should condemn more and understand less, in addition to emphasising the needs and rights of victims over those of offenders. What will be the effects of subsequent legislation on and for probation knowledge?

The final analytical strand we wish to consider as we ponder some of the possible pressures for the attenuation of knowledge within probation is the prevailing attitude towards enforcement. The proper enforcement of community sentences and licences must be taken seriously by the probation service because it is one of six cash-linked targets at the time of writing this book (the other five are accredited programmes completions, Drug Treatment and Testing Orders, PSR proposals on ethnic minority offenders, victims, and basic skills). Current policy, enshrined within National Standards, is to return offenders who are the subject of community sentences to court after two unacceptable absences (see relevant sub-section in Chapter 4 for further details). Even though it is right and proper to expect offenders to adhere to the requirements of a community sentence after being provided with an opportunity (courts and communities demand it), it is equally proper to understand that offenders are often in the grip of numerous problems that can adversely affect their ability to attend every appointment at the required time (Mair & May, 1997, p. 30). It should also be recalled that it was because of these criminogenic factors that they were made the subject of a community sentence in the first place. Therefore, assessing and subsequently acknowledging those personal and social problems associated with offending and the accompanying struggle to comply with reporting instructions produces knowledge; and this knowledge should facilitate empathy and understanding. Also, understanding the circumstances of individual offenders should produce discretion, which is an important ingredient in the pursuit of formulating judgements and making decisions regarding enforcement in relation to acceptable and unacceptable absences. All these factors, within this decision-making framework, are the prerequisites of justice and fairness within the criminal justice system, because unless there is discretion there can be no justice. Therefore, informed enforcement practice that begins with intelligent decisions on acceptable and unacceptable absences depends upon deep knowledge and understanding. We do not want to collude with, condone, or excuse inappropriate behaviour, but there is a professional duty to understand the circumstances of individual offenders, which depends upon being in possession of a comprehensive knowledge base that can be compromised, to some degree, by enforcement procedures that are too stringent and unforgiving, combined with the additional threat of the benefit sanction that is not conducive to rehabilitative objectives (one needs to be present in court to witness some of the problems created by this measure).

Therefore, the lurking dangers within these overlapping developments that have emerged over recent years – that is, if there is a vestige of truth in our analysis which has drawn attention to the decline of the rehabilitative ideal; the rise of the Justice Model; a new, more punitive, and therefore less than helpful criminological discourse; political and economic constraints; legislative developments during the 1990s; enforcement practice in conjunction with the benefit sanction that can produce extremely harsh consequences for offenders – are that conditions have been created within which the professional knowledge base within probation can be adversely affected. Furthermore, it may be argued that the NVQ has emerged as part of a process that has drawn attention to competence, minimum standards and rational efficiency, but this process carries within itself the possibility of unintended consequences that impose limits on knowledge and understanding of those offenders who are to be found at the heart of the probation enterprise. What should be reiterated against the background of our analytical framework is that responding to the demands of NVQ knowledge codification will not, on its own, prepare the TPO to respond insightfully and effectively to all the contingencies of probation practice that, in turn, is not conducive to the achievement of vocational excellence and organisational effectiveness. This is primarily because NVQ knowledge codification is premised upon the attitude that 'this is all you need to know to do the job'. Such an approach to practice can have the unintended effect of lowering standards and narrowing the field of vision for practitioners, which is not the result we want to achieve within the context of probation training. In fact a probation culture that only strives to meet codified knowledge standards could result in the trainee, in addition to level 3 candidates, acquiring only a limited understanding of the unique person with whom the practitioner is working (McWilliams, 1992) which, in turn, will have serious consequences for the critical functions of assessment, intervention strategies, writing PSRs and public protection procedures. The principle of more rather than less knowledge is a good thing per se within the probation service.

Consequently, the point we must return to again, because we think it lies at the heart of TPO training in future years, is that knowledge delivered by and derived from the universities as an integral component of the Dip.PS is indubitably important, and the universities will continue to have a central role to play in probation training. Moreover, knowledge gleaned from various practice opportunities (simply doing the job) under the watchful eye of the PDA when undertaking face-to-face work with clients, and meeting the evidence requirements of the NVQ, is equally important. Trainees need to acquire knowledge to achieve the degree and the NVQ, which are the indisputable components of current training arrangements. Nevertheless both trainees and PDAs must grasp the equally important fact, as well as all those with an interest in developing staff, that the NVQ is designed to establish competent performance only. This is why it is so important within vocational education – and probation is a good example – to understand the illimitable nature of knowledge requirements in order to move towards the notion of quality that should be our uncompromising goal. As such, knowledge should be approached as a multifaceted concept within probation training, which is radically different to knowledge codification which inadvertently supports a culture that imposes limits upon what practitioners need to know. This is why the discussion in Chapter 2, developed in Chapter 6, suggested a four-fold typology of knowledge, the first two elements of which we have just reiterated. However, as soon as trainees begin to receive practice opportunities they will begin to appreciate that to work with different offenders, formulate careful judgements and make decisions, they will be taken on a journey beyond the first two types (experienced and thoughtful practitioners and PDAs know this).

First, it is important to aim beyond the codified elements of types one and two (refer again to Chapter 6) and, in particular, to exploit the processes of reflection and planning implicit in both, in order to develop the good thinking and tacit knowledge needed for the complexities and surprises of practice. For example, when thinking through the most appropriate proposal to offer the crown court judge in a complex PSR it will not be enough to identify the seriousness of the offence, the aggravating and mitigating factors, previous convictions, response to previous sentences and the offender's personal circumstances. Connections will need to be made during and after the process of assessing this knowledge to previous knowledge and experience, critical issues, learning needs and plans for future work. One of the 12 NVQ units – D102: *Process Information Relating Individuals' Offending Behaviour* – lends itself to the PDA observing the trainee undertaking a PSR interview. Underpinning knowledge item 4 within D102 refers to current definitions of risk that the trainee needs to know something about. However, this item of underpinning knowledge, in addition to other items scattered throughout the NVQ, does not refer to or demand knowledge of those more subtle and insightful thought processes that need to be demonstrated by the practitioner when making a judgement about risk. In other words, it is possible to be able to recite definitions of risk without possessing the knowledge and understanding to make a careful judgement about risk, which requires good thinking and an ability to ask pertinent questions that takes the trainee beyond codified knowledge expectations. This knowledge as good thinking is also required, for example, when the trainee has to make a judgement about risk of re-offending and harm that could necessitate initiating a Multi-Agency Risk Management or Multi-Agency Public Protection Meeting. This further illustrates what we mean by a body of knowledge that lies beyond the codified in academic and NVQ knowledge that has an illimitable, ineffable, immeasurable and subtle quality; it is knowledge that emerges from and is found within the chance happenings of practice situations and is associated with good thinking, artistry and the ability to reflect in and on action.

Knowledge types three and four complement these enhanced interpretations of academic knowledge and knowledge for practice. Ineffable knowledge and self-knowledge are the sources of motivation to learn and to strive for excellence, and they are connected to a desire and passion to be part of a community of practice and to a dynamic associated with personal and professional values. Ineffable knowledge and self-knowledge can only thrive in environments that encourage learning and involve relationships in which the traditions, stories and passion of practice are communicated.

The PDA–TPO dynamic

In our view the relationship between the PDA and the TPO is a pivotal dynamic when discussing training and knowledge within the context of the Dip.PS and the wider needs of the organisation. Therefore, it is instructive to refer to Bandura's *Social Learning Theory* (1977), which emphasised the process of learning that occurs by observation and modelling (thus complementing learning derived from classical/respondent conditioning; operant conditioning; and cognitive learning – see relevant sub-section in Chapter 4). In other words, a person copies the behaviour being modelled by someone else. It may be suggested that this process of learning finds a resonance within the professional relationship that should exist between the PDA and the TPO and is a critical feature in the acquisition of vocational knowledge in all its complex and illimitable dimensions. For example, the PDA has a responsibility to model relevant and appropriate behaviours and knowledge features in relation to quality probation practice; and to model knowledge in relation to the 'what' and 'how' of practice to facilitate effectiveness (Appendix 6). Therefore, the approach to the TPO should be this: I am, as your PDA, going to model the knowledge that you require to prepare a PSR, to interview an offender, to communicate effectively, to think things through and solve problems, to formulate careful judgements, to select effective intervention strategies, to undertake a risk assessment that takes cognisance of all relevant items of information and, of course, to relate theory to practice. This is why the selection, appointment and training of assessors are of fundamental importance when considering the success of the Dip.PS training programme. The PDA should be located at the centre of the four-fold typology of vocational knowledge when working with the trainee.

A further illustration can be provided at this point that is drawn from a typical PDA–TPO encounter. A trainee is experiencing problems with a PSR that specifically concerns the most appropriate proposal to offer the court. The offender is already subject to two community sentences for theft offences that are not overly serious, and the second CRO was made for an offence committed prior to the imposition of the first CRO. The client has committed yet another theft offence of moderate seriousness while subject to these two orders and the TPO is considering the imposition of a third community sentence, but this time a CPRO. Is this appropriate? Can this proposal be justified having regard to all the circumstances? Is it commensurate with the level of seriousness involved and associated aggravating factors? Is it credible to consider a third community sentence in these circumstances? Or should the trainee consider the merits of a Deferred Sentence because the two existing community sentences are due to terminate during the next three months and could coincide with a three-month period of deferment? Would this be a more appropriate sentencing strategy at this point, which could eventually result in another community sentence? The knowledge issues being explored here within the context of this scenario being played out between the PDA and the TPO illustrates that neither the academic component of the Dip.PS, nor the codified knowledge elements within the NVQ, has equipped the TPO with the knowledge to resolve this sentencing dilemma. Therefore, additional knowledge resources are required in this practice situation which are associated with formulating judgements, artistry and good thinking that exemplifies the importance of the PDA–TPO dynamic. The PDA has a responsibility to model the thought processes involved and diverse knowledge resources required that takes both the PDA and the TPO beyond codified systems when working with individual offenders.

Suggestions for further improvements

In this penultimate section we briefly want to point towards those areas of probation practice in which developmental work is required in future that will facilitate quality performance. In our view there are three main areas of interest that should be pursued.

The NVQ

Attention should be given to the component parts of the Dip.PS, particularly the rationale of the NVQ. A case can be made for refining the NVQ along the lines suggested towards the end of Chapter 6 that would necessitate initiating a discussion with area services, consortia directors, Home Office, National Probation Directorate, Criminal Justice National Training Organisation, City and Guilds, and the universities sector. In our view there needs to be a shift away from the bureaucracy of the NVQ towards the substance of probation practice in a way that would be conducive to vocational excellence and organisational effectiveness and from a preoccupation with forms to face-to-face contact between trainees and clients that are observed by the PDA. We must be clear about the result we want the NVQ to achieve, and what it is able to achieve, by analysing its efficacy through the lens of our four-fold typology and Bloom's taxonomy. It should be acknowledged that the NVQ has its limitations in pursuit of excellence and that there are critical features of probation work that are not easy to measure because of its ineffable nature.

The PDA

Attention should also be given to the role of the PDA because of its importance for the future of the probation service. At certain points in this book, particularly Chapter 6 and again in this conclusion, it has been made clear that the relationship between the PDA and the TPO is at the heart of the Dip.PS. Moreover, we have invited both the PDA and the TPO to dip below the two substantive component parts of the Dip.PS to appreciate that the notion of quality embraces aspects of practice that include good thinking and artistry and even passion, which are not easily measured. Perhaps the time has come to introduce a specific PDA award that embraces more than the NVQ Assessor qualification (A1/2). Some of the discussions contained in this book could make a contribution to the shape of such as award.

Ongoing professional development

The year following the completion of the Dip.PS is a neglected area of practice. This is a critical time not only for consolidating what has been learned, but also for developing the knowledge and skill conducive to excellence. The newly qualified probation officer should be encouraged to continue academic learning; reflect on some of the issues raised in this book; and acquire a deeper knowledge and understanding of offenders, in addition to assessment and intervention skills, writing reports, learning about artistry through reflection. In this process there should be a close link between training units and managers within teams in which the new probation officer is located.

Observation of practice and critical feedback must continue (by training unit staff and team managers) beyond the scrutiny of case records as this will facilitate insight, awareness and understanding of offenders' lives. We invite the probation service to perceive initial training as a process of three years' duration that comprises two years undertaking the Dip.PS followed by the first critical year located in a team as a probation officer. We consider that this will contribute to vocational excellence.

Final comments

This book functions at different levels and tries to appeal to different audiences in the way it provides historical material that

- contextualises the twin themes of training and knowledge;

- provides resources that will help both NVQ level 4 and 3 candidates;

- elucidates the notion of knowledge within probation by introducing a four-fold typology that takes the discussion beyond codification;

- challenges the concept of competence and minimum standards in favour of vocational excellence that depends upon a comprehensive knowledge base underpinning practice;

- advocates more rather than less knowledge.

Importantly the book acknowledges the critical importance of the relationship between the trainee and the PDA.

As we make our final comments we want to clarify that the subject of knowledge within probation training, the knowledge required to achieve quality performance, vocational excellence, and organisational objectives, is a complex field of enquiry. To reduce knowledge to a prescriptive and measurable formula would certainly help to simplify matters for both trainees and assessors, but this is not possible or desirable because of the surprising, contingent and sometimes abstruse nature of the job that fundamentally engages with people, not inanimate and predictable objects. Even though it is possible to establish baseline knowledge by way of academic subjects and the NVQ, it should be made clear that this will not be sufficient for practitioners; hence the need to reflect on our typology that attempts to capture the fact that multifaceted and surprising practice situations demands a multifaceted approach to knowledge. If knowledge could be reduced to something that is prescribed and static, and if we could produce a neat, tidy and clearly definable package that could be applied in the same way to all offenders (a body of knowledge that 'fits-all' circumstances), then the training of TPOs and other practitioners would be a relatively simple task, and performance would be easy to measure. But this description does not fit the complex, dynamic, surprising and illimitable nature of practice. Therefore we say again for the last time that knowledge within the vocation of probation – its shape, scope and diversity – is a complex field of enquiry, but we hope that this book brings to the surface some of this complexity in addition to providing resources for trainees and raising issues that require further exploration.

There can be little doubt that knowledge is power in the sense that it can be utilised to dominate and control within the criminal justice system. Alternatively, it can be perceived as a force for good when working with offenders because of its association with the language of deep understanding, discretion, professional judgement and, of course, justice (Garland, 1990, and his discussion in Chapter 9). It is a force for good in the way that it can humanise the process of justice by considering individual offenders and enabling professional flexibility. This is knowledge being used to promote decency and humane values. Moreover, knowledge can facilitate the formulation of balanced judgements and defensible decisions in relation to individual offenders and their victims. Knowledge in the probation service, like punishment and other big subjects, can be analysed from different perspectives and there is little doubt that knowledge as power and knowledge as a force for good exist side by side. Finally, it is our contention that an approach to knowledge within probation that understands its illimitable and multifaceted nature, plus its dimensions beyond the parameters imposed by codification, can help to raise standards for trainees, assessors and all other practitioners.

Summary

This chapter begins with an overview of the preceding seven chapters. It then discusses the need to ensure that qualifying training is not constrained by notions of minimum standards and allows for and encourages the pursuit of excellence and the acknowledgement of the individuality of offenders and officers. The constraining threats of notions of knowledge for the very identity of probation officers are identified, as is the central importance of the dynamic between the PDA and the trainee to produce a creative learning environment.

Proposals are made for developing and improving aspects of current probation qualifying training arrangements, updating the role of the NVQ, and structuring support for PDA development and a clear framework for continuing professional development post-qualifying. The chapter concludes with final comments about the layers of knowledge addressed by this book and the need for continued exploration of the tension between the knowledge that defines probation and the multifaceted knowledge that a probation officer requires.

APPENDICES

Appendix 1

Influences that have shaped five key phases of probation history

This appendix identifies some of the influences that have shaped the different phases of probation history. It is intended to contribute to the discussion contained in Chapter 1 that trainees may find helpful.

From 1876 to the 1930s: Saving souls (metaphysics)

The work of Police Court Missionaries began in 1876 during the second half of the Victorian era (1837–1901). It should be acknowledged that, initially, their work was located within a political, social, economic, cultural, ideological and religious context characterised by classical economics, laissez-faire individualism, evangelical religion and a self-help philosophy of hard work. Moreover there was a fit between this context and the tenets of penal practice characterised by the responsibility of the legal subject, classical criminology, prison labour, absence of state aid for offenders, punishment and deterrence. This indicates that, to some degree, penality is shaped by its social context (Garland, 1985). Police Court Missionaries, from 1876, understood their work as saving offenders' souls by divine grace. This is the period of the amateur Christian missionary motivated by faith and evangelical theology. In fact this was the sustaining ideology from 1876 to the 1930s despite the fact that during the closing years of Victorian society an important transition occurred from the Victorian penal system to a new penal welfare system that dominated most of the twentieth century. A changing mode of production (economic change) brought about political and ideological developments that had consequences for social and penal policy. The probation system was established upon a statutory footing in 1907 which should be understood against a background of a crisis in British society that focused on (a) the role of the state in relation to economic and social issues and (b) the condition and regulation of the working class. Some of the features to consider during this period are:

- the first stirrings of positivism as opposed to classical criminology;

- the search for alternatives to prison for recidivist inebriate offenders;

- the Summary Jurisdiction Act 1879 and Probation of First Offenders Act 1887;

- a reforming Liberal Government from 1905 to 1915 that introduced changes in relation to unemployment, insurance, social security, pensions, education and, of course, the creation of the probation service;

- the Probation of Offenders Act 1907, and the focus on reform, rehabilitation and welfare as an alternative to punishment;

- the establishment of the principle of advise, assist and befriend.

The 1930s–1970s: Diagnosis, curing by casework and the rehabilitative ideal (science)

Over a period of time a different sustaining ideology emerged that may be described as the rehabilitative ideal. This is the era of assessment, diagnosis and treatment (the medical model), leading to rehabilitation that was the unifying symbol at the heart of the criminal justice system. By this stage the probation officer addressed the personal and social factors associated with crime, with a view to correcting and normalising the offender through a casework relationship. This is the era of correctional criminology that understood crime as a product of psychological conflicts and social influences: crime and offenders are deep subjects that must be understood and explained; the offender is not in complete control of his behaviour; the focus is therefore on root causes, social problems and individual need. Therefore, from saving souls to the period of the rehabilitative ideal we witness an ontological shift (this means the way the probation officer understood the offender) that may be described as follows: from saving souls to curing by casework; from sinner to patient; from metaphysics to science; from evangelical religion and classical criminology to positivism; from salvation via God's grace to the professional and secular intervention of the probation officer. This is the period of the expert within the penal system and the goal was the perfectibility of man within the new social democratic welfare state, particularly after 1945. Importantly the first Home Office Training Scheme was introduced in 1930 and the developing Social Enquiry Report supported the claim to professional status and emerging professionalism within the service.

The 1970s and 1980s: The decline of the rehabilitative ideal (penal pessimism)

The penal system, like other social institutions, is shaped by its historical context, which includes political, social, economic and ideological conditions, and the state and class relations. The period of the rehabilitative ideal fitted with social democratic politics, the welfare state and consensus between the political parties. However, this was fractured after 1973 because of the oil crisis. Therefore the system witnessed:

• economic, political, social and cultural change;

• the break up of post-war consensus, economic decline, rising crime, the disenchantment with treatment, the drift into law and order accompanied by the rise of the New Right in British politics (Conservative Government from 1979);

• academic critiques of treatment as theoretically faulty, systematically discriminatory, and inconsistent with principles of justice;

• empirical research in Britain and the USA (Martinson; Brody; IMPACT) that questioned the efficacy of the rehabilitative approach.

As change at different levels had profound implications for the penal welfare system, where does the service go from here and how does it understand its mission in this new situation? What about its underpinning and sustaining ideology?

The 1980s: Alternatives to custody (penal pragmatism)

If the probation service no longer understood itself as saving souls or curing by casework, the response to the collapse of the rehabilitative ideal produced

a new rationale: alternatives to custody. This was articulated in the Statement of National Objectives and Priorities in 1984 that was published by
the Home Office (also J. Pointing (1986) *Alternatives to Custody*, Blackwell).
Moreover, we see the development of Radical/Marxist, Personalist, and
Managerial perspectives in probation (McWilliams, 1987) that were an
attempt to fill the void left by the decline of the rehabilitative ideal. At the
same time we see the rise of the Justice Model reflected in the Criminal
Justice Act 1991 that emphasised the offence rather than the offender, proportionality and just deserts.

The 1990s: Punishment in the community and public protection (renaissance of rehabilitation after 1997)

The first point to make is that from 1993 the new optimism following the
CJA 1991 that put probation centre stage was largely abandoned for a
tougher and more populist approach under the banner of 'prison works'.
From 1993 to 1997 was a difficult period for probation, and attitudes hard-
ened within the criminal justice system against the offender, reflected in legislation. However, after 1997 we see the renaissance of rehabilitation in the
form of the 'What Works' initiative and the current framework is characterised by: risk assessment and OASys; public protection; victims; MARMM
and MAPPP procedures; research-based interventions; managerialism and
accountability (the 3 E's – economy, efficiency, effectiveness); cash-linked
targets; enforcement and the benefit sanction. The creation of the Dip.PS in
1998 was detached from social work training.

There was also the CJA 2003, incorporating the Halliday report, that will
have far-reaching implications for the probation service and the wider criminal justice system.

Appendix 2

Criminological perspectives: Help for practitioners

This book is not an academic textbook on criminology. However, we acknowledge that probation practitioners make use of criminological perspectives to explain offending behaviour. Practitioners should be curious about human behaviour in general but particularly the reasons why people offend, and criminology provides a few clues. One of the functions of criminology is to analyse the causes (aetiology) of crime, and it is said that the Italian Raffaele Garofalo in 1885 was the first to use the word 'criminology'. Criminology has subsequently been described as a multidisciplinary social science that draws on economics, philosophy, biology, genetics, psychiatry, psychology, anthropology, geography, and sociology, in its attempt to explain crime. We could not improve on the books that have already been referred to in the relevant sections of Chapter 4. However, it may be helpful to provide a brief overview of some of the main perspectives that trainees will encounter during the two years of the Dip.PS.

Classical Criminology (C. Beccaria, 1735–95; J. Bentham, 1748–1832). This asserts that people freely choose to commit crime because they are rational beings and are therefore responsible for what they do. The punishment must fit the crime (proportionate to and commensurate with the level of seriousness) and the costs of crime should outweigh the benefits. Therefore, it does not seek to reform the offender but looks back to the offence with a view to imposing the most appropriate punishment that will deter future indiscretions. (See rational choice, routine activity, and crime as opportunity theories in the twentieth century.)

Positivism (C. Lombroso, 1835–1909; R. Garofalo, 1852–1934). If classical criminology says that people freely choose to offend, positivism is concerned to discover those positive features that are associated with and determine crime. Therefore, if people are not responsible for the crimes they commit then the aim is not to punish but to treat, reform and rehabilitate, after assessment, diagnosis and classification. Classical criminology looks back but positivism looks forward with a view to intervening and correcting those features that cause crime. It should be acknowledged that positivism has manifested three main dimensions: the biological/genetic make-up of offenders; psychological positivism locates the causes of crime within the individual – for example, faulty personality; sociological positivism turns its attention to social factors.

The Chicago School and Ecology Theory. This theory turns away from the individual and biological/genetic explanations of positivism, towards those locations and neighbourhoods (in Chicago, for example) that revealed consistency in patterns of crime. So why did some localities have higher rates of crime than others even when the population changed? Could it be that certain localities are criminogenic?

Anomie/Strain Theory (E. Durkheim; R. Merton; A. Cohen; R. Cloward; L. Ohlin). The phenomenon of crime is more than a consequence of free choice (classical paradigm) and more than positive factors located within the individual (positivism). In other words, crime is a consequence of wider social, cultural, socio-economic structures. Strain theory postulates the disjuncture between the legitimate aspiration to be successful in terms of material success, but without the legitimate means and opportunities of achieving these goals because of one's place within the social structure. Strain theory makes us look beyond the so-called faulty individual to wider socio-economic factors.

Cultural Deviancy Theory. Offenders belong to a subculture whose values are at odds with the dominant, mainstream culture.

Differential Association (E. Sutherland) and *Social Learning Theory* (A. Bandura). The former perspective says that criminal behaviour is learned, just like any other form of behaviour, from others who ascribe to antisocial values. In addition to the role of the environment in learning, Social Learning Theory postulates that behaviour can also be learned at a cognitive level by observing and then copying the antisocial behaviour that has been modelled.

Control Theory (T. Hirschi). Here the focus is placed upon why people do *not* offend, rather than why they do. Therefore, people do not offend because of bonds and attachments to family, school, community, the workplace and friends. This perspective draws attention to the importance of involvement in pro-social and conventional activities.

David Matza. If Hirschi said that most people would behave in an anti-social manner without protective socialisation in the form of social control, Matza believed that offenders are not too different from law-abiding people because, for most of the time, they live in a conventional manner. Occasionally, however, bonds and attachments to conventional forms of behaviour are weakened and certain individuals drift into offending episodes, using techniques of neutralisation to justify what they do and avoid guilt: condemn the condemners (police and judges are corrupt); deny injury (no real harm was done); deny the victim (he had it coming).

Labelling Theory. This perspective diverts attention away from the individual offender towards the operation of the criminal justice system itself. In other words, it is the reaction of those who comprise the criminal justice system (police, social workers, probation officers) that can make matters worse by negatively labelling the offender. This process may bestow upon individuals a deviant identity that could help to maintain deviance rather than reduce it. This perspective forces us to reflect on how we interact with offenders and the impact of our language, judgements and decisions. At times professionals within the criminal justice system could be doing more harm than good, albeit inadvertently and unwittingly.

Radical/Marxist Theory. In this perspective, which began to take hold during the 1970s with Taylor, Walton and Young, it is said that the entire capitalist system is criminogenic. Therefore attention should not be focused on faulty individuals (as in positivism), but upon the whole political, social and economic system in order to produce a fully social theory of deviance. Instead of treating and correcting the individual the wider social structure needs to be changed to make it less criminogenic.

The criminology texts referred to throughout this book, particularly in Chapter 4, will take trainees deeper into the subject. However, the two books that are of inestimable value, particularly at the beginning of probation training, are:

David Smith's *Criminology for Social Work* (1995)

The Oxford Handbook of Criminology (2002)

Appendix 3

Client or offender: The labelling perspective

One of the consequences of the transition from a social work-oriented service within the criminal justice system, encapsulated in the adage to advise, assist and befriend, to a more law and order perspective defined by the language of punishment in the community, is the shift from the noun *client* to the noun *offender*. It may be suggested that, at first sight, this linguistic shift is of little consequence; therefore, it does not need to precipitate disquiet. By contrast it could be asserted that the change from client to offender is deeply symbolic of wider changes within the criminal justice system, particularly since 1993. Therefore, if this change of noun is more than a semantic squabble between those with an eye for language, then it may be suggested that we need to be careful about our terms and labels within the probation service, primarily because the noun *offender* could be misleading. What we mean by this is that even persistent offenders do not dedicate every waking minute to engaging in offending episodes (even though it may sometimes appear to be so to probation officers). In other words, the noun *offender* does not accurately capture what offenders do; they do offend, obviously, but their lives consist of something more than offending episodes. Probation practitioners use the word *offender* and so will trainees. However, our simple point is that we must be careful with our use of language because of the insights of the labelling perspective.

The labelling perspective shifts the focus of attention from the individual offender and offences to the operation of those who constitute the criminal justice system. If practitioners within the criminal justice system label a person as an offender, then this is tantamount to giving a dog a bad name; the person could learn to behave in a way that is consistent with the ascribed negative label; the label could confirm and then sustain a deviant identity that has important implications for the person's future behaviour and the wider community.

Even though practitioners resort to the noun *offender*, which has been encouraged over recent years, let us be careful with the labels we use – offender, smack head, alcoholic – because we may inadvertently be doing more harm than good. This is why we prefer the word *client* because it more accurately captures the reality we have to deal with and respond to. The noun *client* is more neutral and less emotive; it encompasses both offending episodes and law-abiding behaviour without overtly negatively labelling the person. By contrast the word *offender* draws attention to one negative aspect of a person's life in a way that *client* does not. Therefore is it client or offender? We often use these two words interchangeably but we prefer *client* to *offender* because of the insights drawn from the labelling perspective. As practitioners we need to be careful with language when working with offenders and communicating with staff.

Appendix 4

Joining loose wires to make connections: Developing practice awareness

Effective probation practice that protects the public and strives to reduce re-offending makes connections between various strands of information, particularly at the PSR stage. For example, you are interviewing a client who has pleaded guilty to Excess Alcohol and Assault Police. Previous convictions disclose other motoring and violent offences and a discernible pattern emerges. You know what the offender has done, both recently and historically, but you also want to understand why, which leads you to excavate biographical details. By posing appropriate questions, beginning with childhood years, you discover that he recalls that his father drank to excess and there were frequent arguments between father and mother over drinking habits. Therefore:

> You are exploring connections between the current offences, previous convictions, and a childhood that witnessed alcohol-fuelled arguments between the offender's parents. When trying to explain the offender's behaviour (answer the 'why' question) could you begin to theorise that this is a consequence of learned behaviour (copying the behaviour of his father), or are there other explanations that you need to consider? If, to some degree, it appears that there is a connection between childhood experiences and current alcohol-related offending, what can you do about it? What are the implications for effective methods of working with this offender? Three simple questions can be posed when working with clients: What have you done? Why have you done it? What can be done about it by the probation service?

There is another possible connection about which you are beginning to theorise that leaves you feeling concerned and must be explored. Your client recalls frequent arguments between his parents when he was a child. Therefore:

> Did these arguments spill over into domestic violence? We know that children caught up in domestic violence episodes may become perpetrators themselves, and this is beginning to concern you because your client currently lives with his partner and young child. This needs to be verified. Consequently, what began as a report on Excess Alcohol and Assault Police has led you to consider the possible connections between offending behaviour and wider areas of concern: domestic violence; public protection dimension; child protection concerns; could your client be a Schedule 1 offender?

The practice lessons that can be extrapolated from this case example are as follows:

- Trainees and other practitioners need a knowledge of offending behaviour and its possible causes in order to make connections, and this book makes a contribution to this objective by the resources and references provided. Knowledge of criminology and psychology, for example, will help you to pose the right questions to explore why someone has offended.

- Armed with a knowledge of human development and relevant academic disciplines, you need to ask the right questions during interview to check out your hypothesis that there could be possible connections that are generating concerns.

- In addition to background knowledge and asking the right questions, you need to cultivate insight, awareness and understanding that will enable you to make important connections with implications for risk assessment, public protection and effective methods of intervention. Moreover, any concerns about domestic violence, public protection, child protection, sex offenders and Schedule 1 status has important implications for multi-agency risk-management procedures, triggered by OASys.

Once again it is important to draw attention to the item of UKU that underpins the probation practice that we are exploring: 'The ways in which the physical, social, psychological and emotional development and functioning of individuals affects their behaviour and its associated patterns'.

Appendix 5

Methods of working with offenders

The National Probation Service is committed to working with offenders by using the research-based cognitive-behavioural approach (see relevant section in Chapter 4) that is designed to address deficits in relation to thinking, social, and problem-solving skills. Furthermore, practitioners need to be aware of an additional repertoire of complementary skills that can be selected to facilitate the process of change (the multi-modal approach). While the academic component of the Dip.PS should introduce TPOs to the theory that underpins all aspects of practice, one of the implications of distance learning could be that PDAs within Training Units will have to facilitate practice workshops that focus on effective interventions that complement the assessment process. It should be acknowledged that an increasing number of offenders will be directed towards accredited programmes (mainly group work), which is a cash-linked target. Nevertheless, practitioners will continue to work on a one-to-one basis with offenders both prior to and after the completion of a programme. Consequently, all practitioners need to be aware of the following complementary methods of working. Our task at this point is simply to raise awareness of these methods, in addition to directing the trainee and PDA to those resources that provide more information about theory and practice particularly within the context of organising probation skills workshops.

The cycle of change

This model (Prochaska & DiClemente, 1983, 1984) acknowledges that change is a process, not a one-off event, and that personal motivation to engage with the change process is something that ebbs and flows from smoking to offending. Moreover, the location of the person on this cycle (pre-contemplation, i.e. offenders perceive they do not have a problem; contemplation, i.e. weighing up gains and losses and thinking about offending; decision, i.e. choices are being made to do something about the problem; action, i.e. steps are being taken to change; maintenance, i.e. strategies to maintain change; lapse, i.e. a return to offending) determines the intervention strategies to employ. This can be a useful exercise to do with offenders at the beginning of their orders, and it should be emphasised that motivation to change can be influenced by the practitioner.

Motivational interviewing

This is a method for helping people to identify and then address their problems, and is particularly helpful for those who are ambivalent about the change process. Miller and Rollnick (2002) have defined this approach by saying that 'Motivational Interviewing is a particular way to help people recognise and do something about their present or potential problems. It is particularly useful with people who are reluctant to change and ambivalent about changing. It is intended to help resolve ambivalence and to get a person moving along the path to change.' In addition to the reading material about this approach, a collection of videos that demonstrate the methods being applied are extremely helpful for trainees and PDAs.

Crisis intervention and task-centred methods

Both of these methods attempt to improve a person's capacity to deal with those problems generated by living. They can help to remove those obstacles that get in the way of change and are worth considering. It should be acknowledged that probation clients often manifest a range of personal and social problems that intrude upon the process of change we would like the offender to actively pursue. In an ideal world they would attend the accredited programme, never miss a session, and learn to avoid offending episodes. The reality of probation practice is often very different to this ideal type scenario, which means that practitioners may have to resort to various techniques to deal with the problems being presented.

Solution-focused approach

This approach deals with those personal problems that can affect the goals of supervision. It focuses upon the person rather than providing an in-depth analysis of problems and the concern is to determine what would constitute an achievable solution for the person concerned.

Pro-social modelling

This approach should underpin all aspects of practice. Quite simply it is about the practitioner being aware of behaving in an appropriate manner and setting a good example to clients. Additionally this approach reminds us of the importance of giving clients praise and rewards for relevant and appropriate behaviour. It is a statement of the obvious.

Therefore, the simple point we are making is that the cognitive-behavioural approach should be understood and practised in conjunction with additional complementary methods of intervention when working with, and trying to respond to, the diverse needs of offenders after careful assessment. Moreover, the PDA has a role to play in facilitating workshops that develop the skills required by trainees when working with offenders. Nevertheless it is important to state that because offending is associated with social and economic factors (as opposed to personal inadequacies) then practitioners will find themselves having to address the employment, training, educational, accommodation and basic skills needs of offenders. Therefore a balance needs to be struck between appropriate methods of working with individual offenders and providing opportunities to facilitate a stake in society. TPOs should reflect upon the comment made by David Garland in 1985 when he said: 'Today's penal complex does not prevent or stop crime in the main – the normal forms of socialisation and integration do that' (p. 260). Therefore, in addition to employing diverse methods of working with offenders, an important probation task is to link, as far as possible, offenders with these normal forms of socialisation and integration.

Further reading

Chui, W.H. & Nellis, M. (2003) *Moving Probation Forward: Evidence, Arguments and Practice*. Harlow: Pearson Longman. Chapters 8, 9 and 10 are extremely helpful for both trainees and PDAs.

Coulshed, V. (1988) *Social Work Practice: An Introduction*. London: Macmillan.

Garland, D. (1985) *Punishment and Welfare: A History of Penal Strategies*. Aldershot: Gower.

Miller, R. & Rollnick, S. (2002) *Motivational Interviewing: Preparing People for Change* (2nd edn). London: Guilford Press.

Payne, M. (1997) *Modern Social Work Theory* (2nd edn). Basingstoke: Macmillan.

Prochaska, J.O. & DiClemente, C. (1983) Stages and processes of self-change of smoking: Toward an integrative model of change. *Journal of Consulting and Clinical Psychology*, **51**, 390–395.

Prochaska, J.O. & DiClemente, C. (1984) *The Transtheoretical Approach: Crossing the Traditional Boundaries of Therapy*. Malabar, FL: Kreiger.

Targets for Effective Change is material that is extremely helpful for practitioners because it provides worksheets that can be used with offenders to facilitate change within the context of a cognitive-behavioural approach.

Appendix 6

Differentiating the 'what' from the 'how' of practice

At first sight this may appear to be a strange distinction to make but we would like the reader to consider the following. The *what* of probation practice, in the sense of clarifying what the service does, is clearly articulated in the Choreography document: risk assessment, protecting victims, providing evidence-based programmes, intervening early in the lives of young offenders, enforcement, writing reports, valuing diversity, building an excellent organisation and effective performance management framework. However, if the service wants to be effective it also needs to consider the dimension of the *how* as well as the *what*. Therefore, what we mean by the *how* of practice can be explored in the following way.

Carl Rogers (1961) said that human beings have two basic needs which are for self-actualisation (a striving for personal development) and positive regard (the need for affection, love, respect). Traux and Carkhuff (1967) drew attention to the importance of empathy, genuineness and warmth in successful therapeutic relationships, later reinforced by Joyce Lishman (1994) when she confirmed that the essential components of building a social work/probation relationship are genuineness, warmth, acceptance, encouragement and approval, empathy, responsivity and sensitivity. Martin Davies (1985) said that the social worker needs to get two things right, which are the quality of the relationship and the achievement of results. Therefore it seems clear that there is a distinctive motif within probation and social work literature that draws attention to the quality of the relationship between practitioner and client which indicates that how the work is undertaken is as significant as what is done. In other words, we should undertake the 'what' of practice within a framework that takes cognisance of warmth, understanding and acceptance, which are dimensions of the 'how'. Moreover, we are asking practitioners to be aware of an ethical value framework that is sensitive to tone and manner when working with offenders.

Importantly the effective practice agenda draws attention to the notions of reasonableness, fairness, encouragement and being consistent as important ingredients of 'What Works', because this set of attitudes can facilitate legitimacy and credibility within the working relationship between practitioner and client. What we extrapolate from this is that if practitioners promote the 'how' of practice in the way being explored here, then it is likely that clients will give their assent to the authority contained within the probation officer role because it is being exercised in the right way; this will also encourage the client to return to the office on a weekly basis, comply with the court order, and engage with the supervision process. This raises the issue of the importance of the nature and quality of the professional relationship.

During the last ten years it may be suggested that, to some degree, the emphasis has been placed upon punishment in the community; a return to just deserts; challenging and confronting offending behaviour; the need to be economic, efficient, effective; focus on policy, aims, objectives and targets; systems and administrative procedures; at the expense of the quality of the relationship between the probation officer and needs of the individual client. Therefore the purpose of this practice vignette is to redress the balance by drawing attention to a constellation of ideas that facilitate the creation of an ethical framework within which we should locate the effective practice agenda. In other words we should strive to balance the 'what' with the 'how' and to see them as complementary facets of practice, rather than having to choose between competing alternatives. Quite simply it appears that unless the practitioner can relate with offenders in a manner that expresses warmth, empathy, courtesy and encouragement, effectiveness will be compromised.

Further reading

Armstrong, I. (2003) *Ethics and Values in Probation Practice: How Probation Staff Engage With Offenders*. Dissertation produced by a TPO in Teesside for the academic component of the Dip.PS.

Bottoms, A., Gelsthorpe, L. & Rex, S. (2001) *Community Penalties: Change and Challenges*. Devon, UK: Willan.

Chapman, T. & Haugh, M. for HMIP (1998) *Evidence Based Practice: A Guide to Effective Practice*. London: HMIP.

Davies, M. (1985) *The Essential Social Worker: A Guide to Positive Practice* (2nd edn). Aldershot: Gower.

Halmos, P. (1965) *The Faith of the Counsellors*. London: Constable.

Lishman, J. (1994) *Communication in Social Work*. Basingstoke: Macmillan.

Rogers, C. (1961) *On Becoming A Person: A Therapeutic View of Psychotherapy*. London: Constable.

Traux, C.B. & Carkhuff, R.R. (1967) *Towards Effective Counselling and Psychotherapy*. Chicago: Aldine.

Glossary

Aetiology

Medically, the study of the causes or origin of disease. More generally a narrative account of first causes or giving an explanation of the origin of something. The cause of a situation or problem.

Androgogical

Adults learn differently from young people. More importantly, their reasons for learning are very different. Andragogy, the theory of adult learning, attempts to explain why adults learn differently from other types of learners.

Codification

The act of codifying; arranging in a systematic order. Determining the parameters of a subject and composing definitive lists on that basis.

Criminogenic

Producing or tending to produce crime. In probation the notion of criminogenic needs is especially important. These are the factors or needs to be addressed that will reduce the likelihood of crime. This is in contrast to the needs that, if addressed, will not reduce the likelihood of crime and so are not to be prioritised.

Epistemology

Epistemology (Greek episteme = knowledge; logos = word, so literally words about knowledge) is the theory of knowledge. What is knowledge, how is knowledge gained, how much can we know, what is truth and what is certain? What is the relation between the one who knows and the object known?

Leitmotif

'Leading Motive' (German). Literally the use of a musical phrase to identify a certain person, character, idea, place, situation, allusion or thing in a dramatic work, especially an opera, usually repeated every time the person appears in the work. Used here to mean a dominant and recurring theme.

Meta-cognition

Understanding one's thought processes from an outside perspective. Self-awareness of how you learn, leading to the ability to apply strategies to improve learning. Being able to do something well and also being able to explain that skill.

Metaphysics

The philosophical study of being and knowing. What exists? What makes up the world, the universe? Metaphysics is a branch of philosophy that investigates the nature of reality, existence, time, space and being. Originally a title for those books of Aristotle which came after the Physics, metaphysics responds to questions about reality that lie outside of those that can be addressed by measurement and science.

Ontology

Another word derived from the Greek that means the study of the nature of being and existence. Ontology is the study of what there is and is often contrasted with epistemology, the study of what we know.

Taxonomy

In biology this is the science of naming and classifying organisms. More generally it is a scheme that maps out a body of knowledge and defines the relationships among the pieces. It is used for classifying and understanding a body of knowledge.

References

Ashworth, A. (2000) *Sentencing and Criminal Justice* (3rd edn). London, Dublin and Edinburgh: Butterworths.

Avis, J., Bloomer, M., Gleeson, D. & Hodgkinson, P. (1996) *Knowledge and Nationhood.* London: Cassell.

Bandura, A. (1977) *Social Learning Theory.* Englewood cliffs, NJ: Prentice-Hall.

Barr, H. (1966) *Probation Research. A Survey of Group Work in the Probation Service.* HMSO.

Bloom, B.S. (1964) *Taxonomy of Educational Objectives: The Classification of Educational Goals.* London: Longman.

Bochel, D. (1976) *Probation and After-Care: Its Development in England and Wales.* Edinburgh and London: Scottish Academic Press.

Bottoms, A.E., Gelsthorpe, L. & Rex, S. (eds) (2001) *Community Penalties: Change and Challenges.* Devon, UK: Willan.

Bottoms, A.E. & Preston, R.H. (1980) *The Coming Penal Crisis.* Edinburgh: Scottish Academic Press.

Boud, D. (ed.) (1985) *Reflection: Turning Experience into Learning.* London: Kogan Page.

Brody, S.R. (1976) *The Effectiveness of Sentencing.* HMSO.

Brownlee, I. (1998) *Community Punishment: A Critical Introduction.* London: Longman.

Carter, P. (2003) *Managing Offenders, Reducing Crime.* Home Office.

Chui, W.H. & Nellis, M. (eds) (2003) *Moving Probation Forward: Evidence, Arguments and Practice.* Harlow: Pearson Longman.

CJNTO (2003) *Skills Foresight Analysis.* Community Justice National Training Organisation.

Coffield, F. (2000) Lifelong learning as a lever on structural change? *Journal of Educational Policy,* **15**.

Coulshed, V. (1988) *Social Work Practice: An Introduction.* London: Macmillan.

Crow, I. (2001) *The Treatment and Rehabilitation of Offenders.* London: Sage.

Davies, M. (1969) *Probationers in their Social Environment.* HMSO.

Davies, M. (1985) *The Essential Social Worker: A Guide to Positive Practice* (2nd edn). Aldershot: Gower.

Dawtry, F. (1958) Whither probation. *British Journal of Delinquency,* **8**(3).

de Shazer, S. (1985) *Keys to Solution in Brief Therapy.* New York and London: W.W. Norton.

Downes, D. & Morgan, R. (2002) The skeletons in the cupboard: The politics of law and order at the turn of the millennium. In M. Maguire, R. Morgan & R. Reiner (eds), *The Oxford Handbook of Criminology* (3rd edn). Oxford and New York: Oxford University Press.

Farrington, D.P. (2002) Developmental criminology and risk-focused prevention. In M. Maguire, R. Morgan & R. Reiner (eds), *The Oxford Handbook of Criminology* (3rd edn). Oxford and New York: Oxford University Press.

Folkard, S., Fowles, A.J., McWilliams, B.C., McWilliams, W., Smith, D.D., Smith, D.E. & Walmsley, G.R. (1974) *IMPACT Volume 1. The Design of the Probation Experiment and the Interim Evaluation*. HMSO.

Folkard, S., Smith, D.E. & Smith, D.D. (1976) *IMPACT Volume 2. The Results of the Experiment*. HMSO.

Garland, D. (1985) *Punishment and Welfare: A History of Penal Strategies*. Aldershot: Gower.

Garland, D. (1990) *Punishment and Modern Society: A Study in Social Theory*. Oxford: Oxford University Press.

Garland, D. (2001) *The Culture of Control: Crime and Social Order in Contemporary Society*. Chicago: University of Chicago Press.

Garland, D. (2002) Of crimes and criminals: the development of criminology in Britain. In M. Maguire, R. Morgan & R. Reiner (eds), *The Oxford Handbook of Criminology* (3rd edn). Oxford and New York: Oxford University Press.

Gherardi, S. (2003) Knowing as desiring. Mythic knowledge and the knowledge journey in communities of practitioners. *Journal of Workplace Learning*, **15**(8), 352–358.

Giddens, A. (1989) *Sociology*. Cambridge: Polity Press.

Gillen, T. (1998) *Assertiveness*. London: Institute of Personnel and Development.

Hammond, W.H. (1969) The results of evaluative research. In *The Sentence of the Court*. HMSO.

Haxby, D. (1978) *Probation: A Changing Service*. London: Constable.

Hayes, N. (1998) *Foundations of Psychology: An Introductory Text* (2nd edn). Surrey: Nelson.

Heasman, K. (1962) *Evangelicals in Action: An Appraisal of their Social Work in the Victorian Era*. London: Geoffrey Bless.

Herbert, L. & Mathieson, D. (1975) *Reports for Courts*. London: National Association of Probation Officers.

Hollin, C.R. (1989) *Psychology and Crime: An Introduction to Criminological Psychology*. London and New York: Routledge.

Hollin, C.R. (2002) Criminological psychology. In M. Maguire, R. Morgan & R. Reiner (eds), *The Oxford Handbook of Criminology* (3rd edn). Oxford and New York: Oxford University Press.

Hollis, F. (1972) *Casework: A Psychosocial Therapy* (2nd edn). New York: Random House.

Home Office (1909) *Report of the Departmental Committee on the Probation of Offenders Act 1907*. Cmnd 5001, HMSO.

Home Office (1922) *Report of the Departmental Committee on the Training, Appointment and Payment of Probation Officers*. Cmnd 1601, HMSO.

Home Office (1936) *Report of the Departmental Committee on the Social Services in Courts of Summary Jurisdiction*. Cmnd 5122, HMSO.

Home Office (1961) *Report of the Inter-Departmental Committee on the Business of the Criminal Courts*. Cnd 1289, HMSO.

Home Office (1962) *Report of the Departmental Committee on the Probation Service*. Cmnd 1650, HMSO.

Home Office (1984) *Probation Service in England and Wales. The Statement of National Objectives and Priorities.* HMSO.

Home Office (1999) *Diploma in Probation Studies.* Home Office.

Home Office (2001) *A New Choreography: An Integrated Strategy for the National Probation Service for England and Wales, Strategic Framework 2001–2004.* Home Office.

Home Office (2004) *Reducing Crime – Changing Lives.* Home Office.

Home Office & HM Prison Service (2002) *Offender Assessmen System (OASys) User Manual.* Home Office.

Honey, P. & Mumford, A. (2001) *The Learning Styles Helper's Guide.* Maidenhead: Peter Honey Learning.

Howe, D. (1987) *An Introduction to Social Work Theory.* Aldershot: Wildwood House.

Hudson, B. (1987) *Justice Through Punishment: A Critique of the 'Justice' Model of Corrections.* Hampshire and London: Macmillan.

Hudson, B. (2002) Punishment and control. In M. Maguire, R. Morgan & R. Reiner (eds), *The Oxford Handbook of Criminology* (3rd edn). Oxford and New York: Oxford University Press.

Jarvis, F.V. (1974) *Probation Officers' Manual.* London: Butterworths.

King, J.F.S. (1964) *The Probation Service* (2nd edn). London: Butterworths.

Kolb, D. (1984) *Experiential Learning: Experience as the Source of Learning and Development.* London: Prentice-Hall.

Lea, M. & Street, B. (2000) Staff feedback: An academic literacies approach. In M. Lea & B. Stierer (eds), *Student Writing in Higher Education: New Contexts.* Buckingham: Open University Press.

Leadbetter, D. & Trewar, R. (1996) *Handling Aggression and Violence at Work.* Lyme Regis: RHP.

Leathard, A. (ed.) (1994) *Going Interprofessional: Working Together in Health and Welfare.* London: Routledge.

Leeson, C. (1914) *The Probation System.* London: P. and S. King & Son.

Le Mesurier, L. (1935) *A Handbook of Probation.* London: National Assocation of Probation Officers.

Lishman, J. (1994) *Communication in Social Work.* Basingstoke: Macmillan.

Loxley, A. (1997) *Collaboration in Health and Welfare: Working with Difference.* London: Jessica Kingsley.

Machin, T. & Stevenson, C. (1997) Towards a framework for clarifying psychiatric nursing roles. *Journal of Psychiatric and Mental Health Nursing,* **4**, 81–87.

Mair, G. & May, T. (1997) *Offenders on Probation.* HORS 167, HMSO.

Martinson, R. (1974) What Works? Questions and answers about prison reform. *The Public Interest,* Spring, 25–54.

McGuire, J. (2000) *Cognitive-Behavioural Approaches: An Introduction to Theory and Research.* London: HMIP.

McWilliams, W. (1983) The mission to the English police courts 1876–1936. *The Howard Journal of Criminal Justice,* **22**, 129–147.

McWilliams, W. (1985) The mission transformed: Professionalisation of probation between the wars. *The Howard Journal of Criminal Justice,* **24**(4).

McWilliams, W. (1986) The English probation system and the diagnostic ideal. *The Howard Journal of Criminal Justice,* **25**(4).

McWilliams, W. (1987) Probation, pragmatism and policy. *The Howard Journal of Criminal Justice*, **26**(2).

McWilliams, W. (1992) The rise and development of management thought in the English probation system. In R. Statham & P. Whitehead (eds), *Managing the Probation Service: Issues for the 1990s*. Harlow: Pearson Longman.

Miller, W. & Rollnick, S. (1991) *Motivational Interviewing: Preparing People to Change Addictive Behaviour*. New York and London: Guilford.

Morrison, B. (1997) *As If*. London: Granta Books.

National Probation Directorate (2004) *Annual Plan. Bold Steps: Objectives and Targets 2004/5*. National Probation Directorate.

National Standards (2000; revised 2002) *National Standards for the Supervision of Offenders in the Community*. Home Office.

Nellis, M. (1995) Probation values for the 1990s. *The Howard Journal of Criminal Justice*, **34**, 19–44.

Nellis, M. (2001) The new probation training in England and Wales: Realising the potential. *Social Work Education*, **20**(4), 415.

Nellis, M. & Gelsthorpe, L. (2003) Human rights and the probation values debate. In W.H. Chui & M. Nellis (eds), *Moving Probation Forward*. Harlow: Pearson Longman.

O'Connell, W. (1998) *Solution Focused Therapy*. London: Sage.

Parsloe, P. (1967) *The Work of the Probation and After-Care Officer*. London, Henley and Boston: Routledge & Kegan Paul.

Payne, M. (1997) *Modern Social Work Theory* (2nd edn). Basingstoke: Macmillan.

Prochaska, J. & DiClemente, C. (1983) Stages and processes of self-change of smoking: Towards an integrative model of change. *Journal of Consulting and Clinical Psychology*, **51**, 390–395.

Prochaska, J.O. & Diclemente, C. (1984) *The Transtheoretical Approach: Crossing the Traditional Boundarics of Therapy*. Malabar, FL: Kreiger.

QCA (1998) *Assessing NVQs*. London: Qualifications and Curriculum Authority.

Race, P. (1999) *Enhancing Students' Learning*. Birmingham: SEDA.

Raynor, P. (2002) Community penalties: Probation, punishment, and 'what works'. In M. Maguire, R. Morgan & R. Reiner (eds), *The Oxford Handbook of Criminology* (3rd edn). Oxford and New York: Oxford University Press.

Reiner, R. (1978) *The Blue Coated Worker*. Cambridge: Cambridge University Press.

Revans, R.W. (1998) *The ABC of Action Learning*. London: Lemos & Crane.

Richmond, M.E. (1922) *What is Social Case Work?* New York: Sage.

Rogers, C. (1961) *On Becoming A Person: A Therapeutic View of Psychotherapy*. London: Constable.

Sainsbury, E. (1977) *The Personal Social Services*. London: Pitman.

Schon, D. (1987) *Educating the Reflective Practitioner*. San Francisco: Jossey-Bass.

Shaw, S., Cartwright, A., Spratley, T. & Harwin, J. (1978) *Responding to Drinking Problems*. Baltimore, MD: University Park Press.

Sieminski, S. (1993) The 'flexible' solution to economic decline. *Journal of Further and Higher Education*, **17**(1).

Simon, F.H. (1971) *Prediction Methods in Criminology*. HORS 7, HMSO.

Sinclair, I. (1971) *Hostels for Probationers*. HORS 6, HMSO.

Soden, R. & Pithers, R.T. (2001) Knowledge matters in vocational problem solving: A cognitive view. *Journal of Vocational Education and Training*, **53**(2), 205.

Stevenson, J. (2001) Vocational knowledge and its specification. *Journal of Vocational Education and Training*, **53**(4), 647.

St John, J. (1961) *Probation, the Second Chance*. London: Vista Books.

Stone, N. (1999) *A Companion Guide to Enforcement* (3rd edn). Kent: Shaw & Sons.

Symes, C. & McIntyre, J. (eds) (2000) *Working Knowledge: The New Vocationalism and Higher Education*. Buckingham: SRHE/Open University Press.

Taylor, I., Walton, P. & Young, J. (1973) *The New Criminology: For a Social Theory of Deviance*. London, Boston and Henley: Routledge & Kegan Paul.

Thompson, J. (2000) Community Justice NVQ and Probation Qualifying Training: A case study. In A. Morgan (ed.), *The Utilization of National Vocational Qualifications in Higher Education Institutions*. UVAC/ University of Glamorgan.

Traux, C.B. & Carkhuff, R.R. (1967) *Towards Effective Counselling and Psychotherapy*. Chicago: Aldine.

Waddington, P.A.J. (1999) Police (Canteen) sub-culture. *British Journal of Criminology*, **39**(2), 287–309.

Walker, H. & Beaumont, B. (1981) *Probation Work: Critical Theory and Socialist Practice*. Oxford: Blackwell.

Whitehead, P. (1990) *Community Supervision for Offenders*. Aldershot: Avebury.

Wilkins, L.T. (1958) A small comparative study of the Results of Probation. *British Journal of Delinquency*, **8**, 201–209.

Index